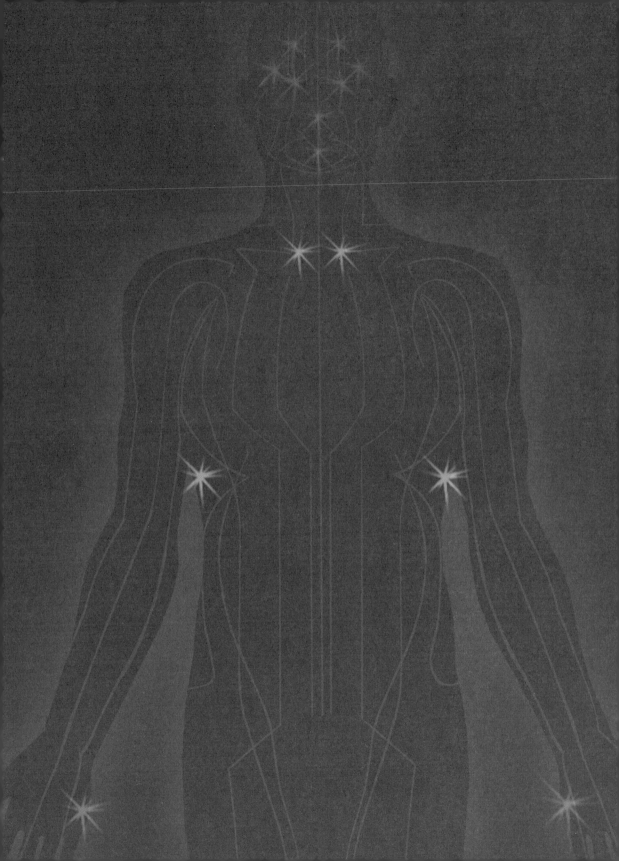

Praise for *The Tapping Solution*

*"I believe Nick Ortner's teachings are easy to use and practical but work like magic. He certainly has taught me to magically release or dissolve problems of all sorts through the process of tapping. You will love this book, **The Tapping Solution**—I certainly do."*

— **Louise L. Hay,** author of *You Can Heal Your Life*

"Put away your skepticism; this really works. I have worked with Nick and had great results with tapping in my own life."

— **Dr. Wayne W. Dyer,** author of *Wishes Fulfilled*

*"I heartily recommend **The Tapping Solution!** Read this book and start tapping your way to better health and a better life. "*

— **Christiane Northrup, M.D.,** author of *Women's Bodies, Women's Wisdom* and *The Wisdom of Menopause*

*"**The Tapping Solution** shares the transformative properties of Emotional Freedom Techniques (EFT) and details, through real-life stories of healing, the brilliance and effectiveness of tapping. Great strategies that help you to release your fears. Nick does an amazing job of laying down the framework of this groundbreaking new healing movement."*

— **Debbie Ford,** author of *Courage, The Right Questions,* and *The Best Year of Your Life*

*"Wow! **The Tapping Solution** reveals how to address both the emotional and physical problems that tend to hamper your life. Nick Ortner is a genius at this amazing method. Read this one now and break free forever!"*

— **Dr. Joe Vitale,** author of *The Attractor Factor*

"Nick Ortner gives his readers a wealth of information on the history of tapping, the proper way to tap, and personal accounts of the ways tapping has successfully enriched lives. What a delightful resource."

— **Gay Hendricks,** author of *The Big Leap* and co-author of *Conscious Loving*

"EFT has vastly improved the quality of my life and my work, and I can't think of a better person to bring this profound practice to you than Nick Ortner. He's my personal coach and now, through this groundbreaking book, he can be yours. Don't miss this healing opportunity. It could not only transform your life, it could also save it."

— **Kris Carr,** *New York Times* best-selling author of *Crazy Sexy Kitchen*

"Nick Ortner is a master at EFT who offers a practical and easy-to-learn process that will easily guide you toward a life of healing from negative emotions, physical pain, anxiety, and so much more. A wonderful way to rewire your brain for an amazing life."

— **Arielle Ford**, author of *The Soulmate Secret*

"In my darkest year, I discovered tapping, and, miraculously, this unorthodox approach to making sense of my life moved me out of the fog and into the sunshine. Nick Ortner's thoughtful and informative book will help you to understand the what, why, and how of this revolutionary healing technique."

— **Chip Conley**, founder of Joie de Vivre Hotels and author of *PEAK* and *Emotional Equations*

"If you want to improve your life exponentially, listen to Nick Ortner. As one of the foremost teachers and leaders in the method of meridian tapping, Nick empowers people worldwide to expand their minds and lives. **The Tapping Solution** is one of the most practical and useful tools to learn the methods of meridian tapping and how to apply them successfully to everything you do. Follow the guidance and methods that Nick shares in this wonderful book and expect your life to change in miraculous and beautiful ways."

— **Carol Tuttle**, author of *The Child Whisperer*

"Nothing comes closer to 'magic' than the positive results I have personally witnessed using EFT on thousands of my patients who suffered from physical and emotional pain and illness. EFT can lead you to incredible breakthroughs on your healing journey, and it can help you in your daily life. Nick Ortner is one of the leaders in teaching this valuable resource in a practical way, and this book will help you utilize this enormously beneficial tool effectively."

— **Dr. Mercola**, founder of Mercola.com, most visited natural-health site in the world

"Not only does Nick Ortner have an enormous amount of integrity as a person, his book is filled with that same integrity with his true desire to make people aware of the healing impact of tapping. His message needs to get out to the world so we can be empowered to initiate our own healing process through the Emotional Freedom Techniques. I love the scripts; they break down tapping into an easy-to-do practical way. I feel like I can put the techniques Nick offers in his book to use right away. Simply following the scripts in the book will enable you to let go of major issues immediately."

— **Lisa Garr**, host of *The Aware Show*

"Nick Ortner has arguably done more to promote the art and science of EFT tapping than anyone else on the planet—and his new book seals the deal. Nick's innovative approaches make the remarkable gifts of tapping accessible to everyone. This book can serve as the perfect guide for an interested newcomer, the lay practitioner, or the clinical therapist. You will benefit immediately from tapping as it is shown here, and as you playfully explore its uses with others, tapping will astound you for years to come."

— **Paul R. Scheele, Ph.D.**, author of *Natural Brilliance, Drop into Genius,* and *PhotoReading,* and developer of Paraliminal Technology

"Nick Ortner has opened more than half a million people to the power of tapping on acupuncture points to enhance their happiness and well-being. With **The Tapping Solution,** *he personally guides you, providing crystal-clear instruction on how to change the patterns of thought and behavior that hold you back, how to improve your relationships and your success in the endeavors that matter to you, and how to live a healthier, happier, more prosperous life."*

— **Donna Eden and David Feinstein, Ph.D.**, co-authors of *The Promise of Energy Psychology*

"I believe EFT to be the one of the biggest breakthroughs in psychology and medicine in a century. Nick Ortner's powerful presentation of EFT makes this the book you need in order to understand and learn EFT fast. Warm, funny, and compassionate, it's founded on deep personal experience. It contains many detailed case histories, fascinating sidebars, dozens of practical exercises, and targeted tapping scripts to unlock the magic of EFT in your life. Nick shows how EFT is grounded in the latest discoveries in neuroscience, yet he never loses sight of making EFT useful and relevant to the real-life problems we all face. If you want to break the patterns that have held you back in your life, this book is the key."

— **Dawson Church, Ph.D.**, author of *The Genie in Your Genes*

"Desperate for a life change, but afraid to do something different? Then you won't want to miss **The Tapping Solution.** *This book can help you examine what's holding you back—personally, physically, mentally—and finally, once and for all, work through it using tapping. Nick Ortner demystifies the technique and shows you how you can apply it in just about any area to achieve the positive changes you desire for your life."*

— **Ruth Buczynski, Ph.D.**, licensed psychologist, president of The National Institute for the Clinical Application of Behavioral Medicine

"Tapping has totally changed my life. At first I thought it was just another gimmick or stunt. But it's not. It's a game-changing technique that will take you deeply into yourself and assist you to feel the emotional freedom that is your birthright. And I am forever grateful to Nick Ortner for introducing me to tapping. This book is a must!"

— **Mastin Kipp**, CEO/founder of TheDailyLove.com

*"Deepest gratitude to Nick Ortner for being so instrumental in delivering EFT (tapping) into enough hands to finally usher in the well-deserved tipping point in energy medicine. **The Tapping Solution** is a hopeful compilation of the past successes and future possibilities of EFT. With this thoughtful guide through EFT's history and its everyday applications, Nick demonstrates how profound healing is possible for millions of people who need and deserve it. Thank you, Nick, for combining the hope and science behind this practice. Tapping is bound to shape our future for the better!"*

— **Carol Look**, author of *Attracting Abundance with EFT*

"Nick Ortner has taken a unique system of transformation and made it available to everyone. He is a miracle of action, and lives by and through the powerful mode of healing that is 'tapping.' If you are ready to quickly move those huge life challenges, stories, and traumatic events to be a thing of the past, then you have the right book in your hands in this moment. Seize the opportunity to fundamentally shift into new possibilities—read this book right now."

— **Jennifer McLean**, author, healer, and host of *Healing with the Masters*

"Nick Ortner is a man on a mission to change the world, person by person, in a direct and very personal way. He reveals how much power we really do have to change our lives if we just decide to try his elegant method. Life opens up, possibility abounds, and we rediscover our greatness when we truly release the past, heal from trauma, and shift ingrained habits—and he shows you how fast and easy that can happen. A dazzling approach that will change you . . . if you are ready."

— **Margaret M. Lynch**, creator of
"The 7 Levels of Wealth Manifestation" and CEO of NESC, Inc.

*"EFT is the most powerful new transformational technology to come along in years, and the inspiring stories in **The Tapping Solution** give readers a first-hand account of its effectiveness. Nick Ortner's thorough exploration of tapping and its benefits will leave you with the quickest way I know to tackle your problems, whether physical or emotional. I highly recommend it."*

— **Jack Canfield**, co-author of *Chicken Soup for the Soul* and
Tapping into Ultimate Success

"The Tapping Solution not only provides cutting-edge treatments for many of the problems that ail us, but real-life, unbelievable stories that will inspire you to jump right in and add this profound method to your healing arsenal."

— **Marcia Wieder**, CEO/founder of Dream University

"Having this book in your hand is like holding the map to any personal treasure you wish to uncover. The results for those who use tapping, believers and skeptics alike, are nothing short of amazing and always seem to bring perspective, clarity, and calm to whatever the issue is at hand—physical, emotional, or spiritual. On top of that, having Nick as your guide is like having a trusted, caring friend at your side every step of the way. Keep this book close . . . it's your personal development preparedness tool kit for our ever-changing modern times."

— **Kevin Gianni**, health author, www.RenegadeHealth.com

"Tapping your way to health is not only fun, it is healing. I highly recommend you begin today!"

— **C. Norman Shealy**, M.D., Ph.D., president of Holos Institutes of Health

The Tapping Solution

A REVOLUTIONARY SYSTEM
FOR *STRESS-FREE LIVING*

NICK ORTNER

HAY HOUSE, INC.

Carlsbad, California • New York City

London • Sydney • Johannesburg

Vancouver • Hong Kong • New Delhi

Published and distributed in the United States by: Hay House, Inc.: www.hayhouse.com® • *Published and distributed in Australia by:* Hay House Australia Pty. Ltd.: www.hayhouse.com.au • *Published and distributed in the United Kingdom by:* Hay House UK, Ltd.: www.hayhouse.co.uk • *Published and distributed in the Republic of South Africa by:* Hay House SA (Pty), Ltd.: www.hayhouse.co.za • *Distributed in Canada by:* Raincoast: www.raincoast.com • *Published in India by:* Hay House Publishers India: www.hayhouse.co.in

Indexer: Jay Kreider/Index It Now
Cover design: Michelle Polizzi
Interior design: Riann Bender
Interior photos/illustrations: © 2011 Lindsay Kenny

Library of Congress Cataloging-in-Publication Data

Ortner, Nick
  The tapping solution : a revolutionary system for stress-free living / Nick Ortner. -- 1st ed.
    p. cm.
  Includes bibliographical references and index.
  ISBN 978-1-4019-3941-0 (hbk. : alk. paper) 1. Emotional Freedom Techniques. 2. Stress management. 3. Stress (Psychology) 4. Mind and body therapies. 5. Change (Psychology) I. Title.
  RC489.E45O78 2013
  155.9'042--dc23
                        2012041418

Hardcover ISBN: 978-1-4019-3941-0
Digital ISBN: 978-1-4019-3944-1

16 15 14 13   4 3 2 1
1st edition, April 2013

Printed in the United States of America

CONTENTS

FOREWORD

Paula was having terrible, debilitating headaches and migraines on a near-daily basis. She had endured them for the last decade; she was in constant pain. Even with the migraine and sleep medication I prescribed to her, she found herself at the emergency room as often as four times a month because her pain and resulting insomnia were so persistent. In addition to her medication, she made lifestyle modifications that have been shown to help people in similar situations—cutting out gluten, meat, and dairy; creating a sleep routine; taking supplements—all to no avail. Her headaches never seemed to subside, and they were ruining her life.

As a doctor, there's nothing more disheartening than watching your patients suffer. I decided to refer Paula to my friend Nick Ortner, whose work with EFT, or "tapping," I'd heard was seeing incredible results. I'd met Nick the previous year through a mutual friend. During our conversation, he'd explained the science behind tapping and why it works so well on such a diverse range of health and wellness issues—everything from managing physical and emotional pain to erasing phobias to maintaining better relationships. While I was hopeful that the technique would resolve Paula's condition, I still had my doubts. I shared this uncertainty with Paula, but at that point she was willing to try anything. It was clear to both of us that she needed a new way to heal, a new way to break her dependence on medications that were likely to undermine her health if used as a long-term solution.

Several months passed before I got a full report on Paula's progress, though I heard tidbits of good news along the way, such as hearing that her pain was decreasing and she was taking less medication. When I did hear from Paula, I was profoundly amazed. Paula was not only 100 percent pain free but also completely off all her medications. In working with Nick, using tapping to successfully navigate what she described as an "emotional journey," she had been liberated from her pain and her medications. Finally, she'd been given the chance to resume a normal, active, fulfilling life. What a difference!

Having seen firsthand the powerful effects of tapping, I, of course, wanted to learn even more. I began to research it on my own and became convinced of the benefits of tapping in conjunction with the functional medicine I had been using to heal thousands of people for more than two decades. To this day, I refer challenging cases to Nick, whose results with tapping continue to be consistent and long lasting.

As a practicing functional medicine doctor and passionate proponent of advancing our understanding of health care, I'm very excited about the possibilities held by tapping. In medicine, as in all science, we need to push the boundaries of what we know and evaluate how we approach and pursue healing. It is both our job and our responsibility to continually search for the most effective ways not only to treat the symptoms of disease but also to adopt an approach that targets the imbalance or blockage that is causing ill health. Rather than watering the leaves of a withering tree, so to speak, we must tend to the tree's roots so it can thrive on its own.

Tapping targets the root cause of health and wellness challenges by interrupting the body's stress response quickly and effectively. As you will discover in this book, tapping is a powerful tool for enabling health on multiple levels: mental, emotional, and physical. From depression, anxiety, and stress-related disorders like PTSD and fibromyalgia to physical pain and a lot, lot more, tapping is producing consistent and compelling results. When combined with a healthy lifestyle, including a wholesome, plant-rich diet, regular physical exercise, and natural supplements to support health at a systematic level, tapping is a fast-acting, non-invasive way to proactively manage the stress that so often leaves our bodies vulnerable to disease.

Taking a moment to peer into the future of medicine, speculating briefly on how we, as a culture, will understand and manage our lives and our wellness in the years and decades to come, I can easily envision a world in which tapping helps to liberate us from unnecessary medications, promote wellness, and create bigger, better, and more loving and abundant lives. I am both honored and excited to contribute to creating this new world and hope that you, too, will use this book to reap the endless rewards tapping has to offer.

Mark Hyman, M.D.

INTRODUCTION

I looked pretty silly. At least, *I* thought I did.

It was the spring of 2004. I was sitting alone, staring at a computer screen, talking to myself, and tapping different parts of my body. If you'd glanced through my window and seen me, you might have thought I'd lost it.

In truth, I *was* going a little crazy. The neck pain I'd woken up with that morning was so bad that I wasn't sure how I'd get through the day. You know the kind of pain I'm talking about. You sleep in the wrong position and wake up with a crick in your neck. You spend a day, sometimes two, sometimes three, moving your head slowly and looking like a robot to the rest of the world.

I was willing to do just about anything to make it go away.

Including something as seemingly strange as tapping.

I had been hearing a lot about "tapping," or EFT (Emotional Freedom Techniques). Said to be a combination of ancient Chinese acupressure and modern psychology, tapping is said to remedy a vast number of issues. I'd been reading one miraculous story after another, so I thought, *Why not? Might as well try it and see what happens.*

To my astonishment, the pain—which would normally have taken days to go away—vanished within ten minutes. Ah, relief! To be able to turn my head again like a normal person and not feel uncomfortable all day! This tapping thing actually *worked*.

I was ready to go on with my day, satisfied to be pain free. But suddenly, it hit me: this was about a lot more than neck pain. If tapping worked on my neck, what else could it help me change? Like many of us, I had one particular worldview—one that did not include instantaneous pain relief. This little experiment opened my mind to an ocean of possibilities that I had never before contemplated.

Let's face it: many of us have been taught to think that it takes a certain amount of time to "fix" or change a problem—if we believe it can be fixed at all. But what if pain, health concerns, addictions, weight issues, relationship challenges, and financial problems really *could* be resolved—quickly and easily? What if the impossible was actually possible?

These are the thoughts that started percolating after my first tapping experience. Heck, maybe the neck pain had been inhibiting blood flow to my brain—and only now was I able to think more clearly! I started to see—to imagine—what else I might be able to change in my life and how I might be able to help those I loved.

At first, it was no more than a hobby. I used tapping extensively on myself and then began working with friends and family. Soon, I was taking on private clients. Those around me quickly learned that if they shared any issue that was going on in their lives—from a physical challenge to a debilitating emotion—they'd better get ready to tap! No one was spared from my insistence that they try this incredible process.

And again and again, I was blown away by what I saw. Back then, I just threw all these results in the "don't really know how this works, but it does, and that's all I care about!" category. But now the latest science and research is shedding light on the principles underlying the tapping process and why it offers such radical, positive change.

At the time I found it, EFT was already being used by tens, if not hundreds, of thousands of people around the world. A thriving community existed, its members exploring these principles together and sharing the results. But there was still a tremendous amount of skepticism about the process. I felt a compelling desire to play a part in helping to spread this tool even further.

So, without any filmmaking experience—and with a limited budget that consisted of maxed-out credit cards and a few short lines of credit—I decided to make a documentary film that would capture the incredible results EFT was facilitating. Enlisting the help of my younger sister, Jessica, and my best friend, Nick Polizzi (yes, there are two Nicks here!), I set out to document the effects of this technique in a tangible way. One that not only was compelling to watch but also taught people how to use the technique and demonstrated its amazing results.

We spent the first six months of the process on a cross-country trip interviewing a slew of experts, doctors, psychologists, psychiatrists, personal-development speakers, and best-selling authors who were using EFT themselves. Again and again, they shared their personal passion, enthusiasm, and positive experiences with us. But while that footage was compelling and educational, it didn't tell the whole story. We also had to capture the stories of real people using the technique. And not just describing their past experiences; we wanted to show EFT's actual results, in real time.

That's what brought me and Nick Polizzi, in the fall of 2007, to the home of Jodi McDonald. Jodi was suffering from fibromyalgia, a painful and often misunderstood condition. We were visiting her home in Austin, Texas, to gather some preliminary footage in advance of an event scheduled to take place a few weeks later: ten people with a variety of serious issues—chronic back pain, fibromyalgia, grief, insomnia, and more—were being brought together to see how EFT could help with their challenges.

We were there to document Jodi's condition and the challenges she was facing prior to beginning the tapping work. I was excited to meet Jodi, find out exactly what was going on in her life, and see how EFT might help.

Looking at Jodi's vibrant smile and energetic eyes, you wouldn't have guessed the severity of her pain. She was frequently reduced to crawling on the floor, and during the course of a typical night, her pain would wake her as many as 15 or 20 times. And you also wouldn't have suspected that her chronic knee pain had forced her to give up the long nature walks she'd enjoyed for many years.

But the truth was, Jodi's pain was so acute that she could barely make it up a short flight of stairs. Eight years after her diagnosis, her fibromyalgia was running—and slowly ruining—her life.

A teacher, healer, aspiring writer, wife, and mother of four, Jodi was determined to keep living fully. However intrusive the pain, she could not accept that her disease was, as the doctors told her, "incurable." A firm believer in positive psychology and the Law of Attraction, she was determined to keep smiling. She simply refused to give up on her own life.

After a few minutes talking to Jodi, two things were obvious. First, she'd lived through several traumatic experiences as a young girl, including watching her mother being beaten by her father. Second, in spite of it all, Jodi had dedicated herself to being a positive, productive person who spent most ot her time helping others.

She did her best to be happy, went to all the right doctors, and tried alternative approaches. She'd done everything she could to overcome the pain and heal, but it just wasn't working. So what was going on? And could this strange-looking technique help?

My heart went out to Jodi, and I wanted to start EFT with her right then and there. But I had to wait; we'd agreed that she would not be introduced to the work until the four-day event a few weeks later.

Once Jodi shared her story with us (and some amazing food, definitely the best stop of the trip foodwise!), Nick and I hit the road again. We traveled to visit the rest of the beautiful people who would be attending the event, people desperate for an answer, desperate for change.

Donna, diagnosed with breast cancer, suffering physically and emotionally from the disease—and from debilitating insomnia.

John, a Vietnam veteran with 30 years of intense chronic back pain. Pain that doctors, surgeries, and pain medication had not helped.

Rene, suffering from debilitating grief after losing his wife in a car accident just 90 days earlier.

Jackie, terrified to speak in public and too shy to pursue many of the things she wanted.

And more. To say my heart was open after meeting these amazing people is an understatement. If these ten people were suffering so, if they were searching for answers for their life challenges and just not finding them, how many millions or billions more were in the same place? The ultimate question for me was, could tapping really help?

I'll share more about what happened throughout this book. But just to give you a little taste, let me tell you what happened for Jodi. Jodi, diagnosed with an "incurable" condition that nobody had been able to help her with, was pain free by the *second day* of the four-day event! Years later, she remains pain free, and her life has been transformed in many other ways. (I'll cover more of her inspiring story in Chapter 6.)

If Jodi had such an extraordinary result with such a difficult condition, what's possible for you?

It's your turn. Are you ready for that kind of change?

Do you have issues or circumstances in your life that you'd like to change? Childhood trauma, anxiety, physical conditions, weight problems, financial difficulties, relationship challenges? Whatever your situation, EFT has proven to be dramatically effective. In this book, we'll go in depth—exploring each of these issues (and more), as well as how you can use tapping to work with them, to change the *basic patterns* that underlie these challenges in your life.

I don't have to be psychic to know that you have been running the same patterns, sometimes with little change, for your whole life. I don't have to even meet you to guess that you are frustrated with doing the same things over and over again—and, as can be expected, getting the same results.

You've probably said to yourself countless times, "Oh, I can't believe I did that again!"

"Why did I say that to him . . . again?"

"Why did I eat that food . . . again?"

"Why did I skip exercising . . . again?"

"Why am I short on money . . . again?"

"Why am I frustrated [or angry, lost, overwhelmed, anxious, tired, or whatever your 'thing' is] . . . again?"

And I'm being easy on the language here. It's likely you're not as kind to yourself. Most of us add in a $*@%# or two!

On top of your negative thinking and behavior, there's the fact that you *are* trying to improve. And yet . . . you're still not getting the results you want. It adds insult to injury! It would be one thing if you were unaware of your patterns and behaviors. But you are! And yet they keep running. As we'll explore, much of your current behavior actually started before you were seven years old! And it was learned from parents, teachers, society, and friends.

In the past, the challenge was that we could identify these patterns—but not a way to move them, to actually *do* something about them. We could go to a psychologist or psychiatrist and discuss the issue week after week, but we often got minimal results. At the very least, the results were slower than we wanted. We could meditate on the issue, which could lighten the load, but we found it coming back days or even hours later. We could "will" ourselves to change, an often-painful procedure that rarely lasts. Sometimes we succeeded, sometimes we didn't. But overall, the methods available did not give us an unshakeable sense of being in control of our own lives.

Until now.

EFT works unlike anything I've ever experienced. It's set to revolutionize our world. In fact, it's already revolutionizing parts of the world, as you'll learn in Chapter 13, where we explore some of the amazing work being done with trauma relief around the globe. But before we get to what it can do for the world, let's figure out how it can change just one life: yours.

Remember those patterns we talked about? Finally, there's a way to interrupt, disengage, dissolve, and vanquish them. Tapping gets to the root of what's going on, balancing the mind and body and changing what we do, how we feel, and how we experience the world. Tapping can be used for *everything*, and I'll explain why in the next chapter. But we'll first focus on using it in key areas of your life—the ones that are likely to be affecting you the most. Later, you'll learn how to apply it to whatever is going on, how to teach it to others, and how to share it with the world.

About This Book

The first two chapters of this book are vitally important, because they set the framework for everything that follows. Chapter 1 covers the discovery and history of tapping and the most recent scientific findings that are validating this process.

In Chapter 2, I break down the EFT process so you can see how it works and have a direct experience of tapping yourself. One of the most exciting things about tapping is that you can *immediately* feel the difference it is making on your body and mind. No need to study a process for hours or give it 30 days before you see results.

Once you've learned the basics of the process and experienced its power to help you, we'll take a look at some of the reasons why you might not be ready to change. Underlying the desire to change are often unconscious or semiconscious ideas and beliefs—patterns that are stopping the desired change from happening. In Chapter 3, we'll apply EFT to these patterns in order for you to get the best results with the rest of the book.

Chapter 4 explores how to use EFT to immediately reduce stress levels in your life and relieve the general state of anxiety and feeling of being overwhelmed that many of us face.

Chapter 5 is perhaps the most powerful, in that we examine the correlation between negative childhood events and experiences, and our current circumstances. Some of the most dramatic results I've seen with EFT come from this exploration.

From there, the next two chapters take a closer look at EFT and the physical body. Chapter 6 is a general view of how stress affects the body and how we can use EFT to aid healing, while Chapter 7 focuses directly on using EFT to relieve physical pain.

In Chapter 8, we address using EFT to eliminate cravings, improve body image, and lose weight. While I know this is a concern for many readers—and that many of you are going to want to skip straight to this—I suggest that you don't. You need the information from the preceding chapters to make using EFT for weight loss more effective.

In Chapters 9 and 10, I will reveal some of my most powerful personal experiences with EFT—including attracting the love of my life and changing my beliefs and subsequent experiences around money and finances. I'll show you how you can do the same, at speeds that will startle you!

Chapter 11, which starts off with a story that will make you laugh, gives you the tools to face some serious issues: your deepest fears and phobias. In Chapter 12, we cover an extensive list of other applications for EFT, each of which could easily have had its own chapter: insomnia and deepening sleep, working with children, improving athletic performance, healing addictions, and more.

Chapter 13 is perhaps the most inspirational, as we learn of the groundbreaking and beautiful EFT work that individuals and organizations are conducting around the globe.

In the final chapter, Chapter 14, I present a new vision for you and your life, using EFT. Within that chapter you will find hope, possibility, and new ideas that will spring you forward into the life you've always dreamed of.

And throughout the book, you'll find tapping scripts to help you bring the benefits of this process into your life. I'll also highlight some of the doctors, psychologists, and psychiatrists who are using EFT in their practice in Professional Profiles. This will open your eyes to some of the ways in which tapping is being used in traditional medical environments.

I am honored to be your guide on this journey. My deepest desire is that you find within the pages of this book the hope, magic, miracles, and possibility that I have experienced using EFT. My life has been transformed by this process and continues to be transformed on a daily basis. I know the same thing can happen for you and your loved ones.

It's time to change those patterns . . .

It's time to have a healthy, fit, vibrant body . . .

It's time to manifest abundance, prosperity, and happiness . . .

It's time to have fulfilling, nurturing, positive relationships . . .

It's time for *The Tapping Solution!*

CHAPTER 1

A MONUMENTAL DISCOVERY

All truth passes through three stages. First, it is ridiculed. Second, it is violently opposed. Third, it is accepted as being self-evident.

ARTHUR SCHOPENHAUER

Dr. Roger Callahan was in a bind.

He had been in this position before, but that didn't make it any less frustrating.

A traditionally trained psychologist, he was working with his client Mary, who had struggled with a severe water phobia since she was a child. Mary wasn't just afraid of swimming; she was afraid of water in all forms—from bathtubs to rain to oceans to swimming pools. Her level of fear was so extreme that she couldn't even bathe her two children, and she was plagued by nightmares about water. This had been going on for as long as she could remember. Now in her 40s, she had sought Dr. Callahan's help.

Dr. Callahan was doing his best, but it just wasn't working. He had been treating Mary for the past year, using all the traditional psychotherapy techniques in his tool belt: cognitive therapy, hypnosis, relaxation therapy, rational-emotive therapy, systematic desensitization, biofeedback, and more. They were all he knew, and they were the techniques that were accepted by psychologists, psychiatrists, and the public at large.

This wasn't the first time those techniques had failed. Dr. Callahan had been disappointed with the lack of concrete results and the length of time it took for change to happen for many clients. He and Mary had made only minimal progress in the year they had worked together. She was able to sit on the edge of Dr. Callahan's swimming pool and put her feet in the water, but she was full of anxiety when she did. After sessions near the pool, she left with a pounding headache from the stress of the treatment!

Dr. Callahan, ever curious about the functioning of the body and mind, had around that time been studying the body's meridian points. Meridians, the basis of the ancient Chinese medical system of acupuncture, are defined as energy channels that carry the vital life force, or *qi,* to the organs and other systems of the body. Running up and down either side of the body, each meridian is associated with a different organ—stomach, gallbladder, kidney, and so on. Each meridian also has what's called an "endpoint," a specific location on the surface of the body where you can access the energy channel. This point can be manipulated using acupuncture needles or simple touch (acupressure) to balance or unblock the energy flow through that particular meridian.

In one therapy session, Mary revealed that thinking about water caused a terrible feeling in the pit of her stomach. In a flash of insight, it came to Dr. Callahan that tapping on the stomach meridian endpoint—just below the eye—might alleviate Mary's pit-of-the-stomach sensation. So he asked her to tap that spot with her fingertips.

Mary did as she was asked. To their mutual surprise, after just a few minutes of tapping, she soon exclaimed, "It's gone! That horrible feeling I get in the pit of my stomach when I think about water is completely gone!" She went to the edge of the swimming pool to see if her fear had changed as well and discovered that she felt no anxiety at being close to the water.

From that day forward, her water phobia and her nightmares about water were gone. That was more than 30 years ago, and Mary is still free of her fear today.

Imagine Dr. Callahan's astonishment at this turn of events. After working so hard with Mary, trying the range of conventional psychotherapy techniques and even some alternative techniques, he happened on the solution—tapping below the eye! And, perhaps more important, the phobia remains cured for 30 years, never to affect Mary again. How did this happen?

Tapping Evolves

As a result of the experience with Mary, Dr. Callahan deepened his study of meridian endpoints, exploring the combination of traditional psychotherapy with tapping on different parts of the body. He developed a set of "algorithms," or sequences of tapping, to address different issues. If you had a phobia, such as a fear of heights, you would use one sequence of tapping points (under the eye, under the arm, and at the collarbone, for example). If you were angry about something— i.e., if your boss said something that just set you off—you'd use a different sequence (eyebrow, under the eye, under the arm, and at the collarbone).

After learning and using Callahan's algorithms, one of Dr. Callahan's students— a man named Gary Craig—determined that the sequence of the tapping isn't as important as simply doing the tapping. To make tapping easier, he created a single sequence, which is the basis of what he later termed EFT, short for "Emotional Freedom Techniques." The EFT sequence was designed to hit all the major meridian endpoints, regardless of the issue. We will go into this sequence in great detail in Chapter 2, but as an overview, the tapping sequence starts with the hand, then moves to the inner eyebrow, the outer eyebrow, underneath the eye, under the nose, the chin, the collarbone, and the side of the rib cage, then ends at the top of the head.

Gary's genius lay not only in simplifying the process and adding some refinements but also in creating a community around the technique. He documented case after case of people using it for themselves and then shared their incredible results with the world. Thousands of people around the globe are now aware of tapping and use it in their daily lives.

Dr. Callahan had his breakthrough with Mary in 1979. In the three decades that followed, no Western scientific explanation for tapping could be found. How was it that Mary and so many others lost their phobias, anxiety, and other problems simply by tapping certain acupoints? In just the past few years, however, much has been learned about the science behind tapping.

When you're experiencing a negative emotional state—angry or upset or fearful—your brain goes on alert. It prepares your body to enter a full-blown, fight-or-flight response. This response evolved to mobilize the body to face an external threat—think of a tiger coming after your ancient ancestor. All the body's defense systems are turned on to support either fighting or fleeing from the danger. Your adrenaline pumps, your muscles tense, and your blood pressure, heart rate, and blood sugar all rise to give you extra energy to meet the challenge.

The stressors in ancient days were very real threats to survival. Today, however, the fight-or-flight response is rarely activated by a physical threat. Most of our fight-or-flight responses today are triggered *internally*, as in the case of Mary's fear of water: her body went into a threat response when she even *thought* of water.

For many of us, the internally generated stress response is triggered by a negative memory or thought that has its roots in past trauma or conditioned learning from childhood. The stress response in the body takes the same form, whether the trigger is the tiger (external) or a negative memory (internal). The adrenaline flows, the heart races, and so on.

Beyond prior experience or negative memories, daily life is filled with small fight-or-flight experiences. Your boss sends you an e-mail that upsets you; as you sit down to eat lunch, you stress about your weight; you go home to a messy house and a ton of chores. In all these scenarios, your body is preparing you to fight or flee.

You might be saying, "My body doesn't go into fight or flight over all these little events," but in fact it does! It's not the adrenaline and cortisol rush you'd get if you were chased by a tiger; it's a lower-grade response. But when you add up hundreds or thousands of these responses in a given week or month, the cumulative effect on the body and mind is massive. The ongoing fight-or-flight response leaves us worn down, sick, upset, overweight, stressed out, and just generally unhappy with our life situations.

What tapping does, with amazing efficiency, is halt the fight-or-flight response and reprogram the brain and body to act—and react—differently. Let's look at how that happens.

The Almond in Your Brain

Science has established that the stress response begins in the amygdala. The almond-shaped amygdala (the word comes from the Greek for "almond") is one of the components of the limbic system, or midbrain. The midbrain is located between the frontal lobes (the cortex) and the hindbrain (also called the reptilian brain—the earliest, most primitive part of the brain). The limbic system is the source of emotions and long-term memory, and it's where negative experiences are encoded.

The amygdala has been called the body's smoke detector. "Uh-oh, here comes trouble," says the amygdala. "Something is threatening our safety." It signals the brain to mobilize the body in the fight-or-flight response. An early negative experience can program the amygdala to raise the alarm when something similar triggers it in the future. If you spoke in front of the class in fourth grade and someone laughed at you because of a mispronunciation or a stumble, your embarrassment may have caused the mind and body to connect "danger" with speaking in front of people. After that, similar experiences—or even the *expectation* of similar experiences—can set off the amygdala. Remember, the body does not distinguish between an actual threat and what the amygdala perceives as a threat. As a result of this early training, the daily stressors of life can signal the amygdala to raise the alarm.

Though we're not yet sure why, tapping seems to turn off the amygdala's alarm—deactivating the brain's arousal pathways. Tapping on the meridian endpoints sends a calming response to the body, and the amygdala recognizes that it's safe. What's more, tapping while experiencing—or even discussing—a stressful event counteracts that stress and reprograms the hippocampus, which compares past threats with present signals and tells the amygdala whether or not the present signal is an actual threat.

The Proof

Research at Harvard Medical School over the past decade has shown that stimulation of selected meridian acupoints decreases activity in the amygdala, hippocampus (another part of the limbic system), and other parts of the brain associated with fear. In fMRI and PET brain scans, you can clearly see the amygdala's red alert being called off when acupoints are stimulated.[1] This is exciting and cutting-edge research!

While the Harvard studies focused on needles, a double-blind study comparing the penetration by acupuncture needles with pressure (without needles) on the meridian points (as in tapping) found similar improvements with either method. Informal studies have shown that tapping may in fact work *better* than needles in the treatment of anxiety disorders.

Another study confirms the Harvard findings. In this case, researcher Dawson Church, Ph.D., looked at a different component of the fight-or-flight reaction: cortisol levels. Like adrenaline, cortisol is a stress hormone released during the stress response.

In a randomized controlled trial—the gold standard of scientific research—Dr. Church and his colleagues studied changes in cortisol levels and psychological symptoms in 83 subjects after they received an hour-long EFT tapping session, an hour of conventional talk therapy, or no treatment (the control group). Cortisol levels in the tapping group dropped significantly, down by an average of 24 percent—with some showing results as high as 50 percent. Meanwhile, for those in talk therapy and the control group, there was no significant change in cortisol levels beyond the normal lowering that happens during the day as time passes. The reduced cortisol levels in the EFT group correlated with decreased severity in anxiety, depression, and overall psychological symptoms.

Dr. Church shared with me the behind-the-scenes story on this study, further demonstrating how powerful these results truly are. When he sent the samples to the lab to test for cortisol levels, he expected to get the results back in a few days, in time to present the findings at a medical conference where he was scheduled to speak.

He was dismayed when the results were delayed and he wasn't able to present them at the conference. In fact, they were delayed for several weeks. Upon following up with the lab, he learned that they believed that there was either something wrong with the samples or with their equipment and that they were recalibrating everything and running the tests again and again.

Why? Because the results were so far beyond the normal levels of cortisol reduction that they were convinced there must have been a mistake! Eventually they confirmed what Dr. Church knew all along, that there had in fact been a dramatic and unprecedented reduction in cortisol levels.

Working with psychological issues by tapping on the meridian acupoints is part of an emerging field known as "energy psychology," which has been called "acupuncture without needles." Numerous studies have demonstrated the effectiveness of acupuncture, a sophisticated healing system that has been in use for 5,000 years. Now there is mounting evidence supporting the efficacy of energy psychology as well.

In fact, the research on energy psychology compares favorably to standards set by the Society of Clinical Psychology (Division 12 of the American Psychological Association [APA]) as an "evidence-based approach." According to David Feinstein, Ph.D., a clinical psychologist who has served on the faculty of the department of psychiatry at the Johns Hopkins School of Medicine, "the research evidence for energy psychology, coming from more than a dozen countries, suggests that it produces outcomes for a range of conditions that are unusually rapid, effective, and lasting."

In a research review published in a flagship APA journal, Feinstein reported that existing studies of acupoint stimulation appear to meet the Division 12 criteria for designation as "well-established treatments" for phobias and test-taking anxiety and as "probably efficacious treatments" for PTSD, public speaking anxiety, and depression. Three-fourths of the existing research had been published in the four years prior to his 2012 review, suggesting that research on energy psychology is quickly accelerating and that more conditions for which it is effective will be added to the list.

Dozens of studies have now demonstrated the effectiveness of tapping for a variety of disorders and issues. You can find a detailed account of these studies at www.thetappingsolution.com/research.

These studies clearly show EFT's efficacy regarding some of the most challenging issues we face as humans: PTSD, trauma, phobias, and more. If tapping works so well on the hardest issues, then it stands to reason—and I'll demonstrate in the rest of this book—that it should be just as effective, if not more so, on the "smaller" issues we face, such as problems in relationships, weight loss, limiting beliefs, and trouble with finances.

Beyond the Science and Research: Observable Evidence

While I'm delighted by the recent progress in research backing up what many of us have known for a long time—i.e., that tapping works—I think it's important to note that we need to look beyond specific research studies, which are expensive and laborious to conduct, to another powerful element of truth: observable evidence. This is where EFT shines. Thousands of case studies, both individual and those written by practitioners, clearly document the results. The remainder of this book, where I share personal experiences and those of other practitioners, joins this growing body of evidence.

You *Can* Change Your Brain

To look deeper into why tapping is so successful in stopping phobias, anxiety, PTSD, and other problems, let's go back to the limbic system. Not only does tapping halt the stress response, but the combination of stimulating acupoints while thinking of an upsetting event or problem also retrains what's called the *limbic response*.

Retraining the limbic response is the basis of the psychological technique called exposure therapy, which is what Dr. Callahan was doing with Mary. Over time, he had Mary approach the swimming pool and later dangle her feet in the water—gradually exposing her to the source of her phobia.

In exposure therapy, the person is exposed either *in vivo* (e.g., in a real situation, like Mary at the pool) or by *imagining* a scene or event that creates limbic arousal, or "triggers" the response. But this kind of conventional exposure therapy often works very slowly. In Mary's case, after a year and a half, her anxiety level during her *in vivo* treatment was still high and caused her painful headaches.

When you tap while recalling an upsetting scene from your childhood, you are doing a modified version of exposure therapy. The exposure happens when you think about the upsetting scene. Tapping often retrains the limbic system rapidly. Here's how it works. When you think of something that causes you anxiety or other uncomfortable feelings, the thought sets off the amygdala fire alarm. Tapping as you trigger your fight-or-flight response sends the message that the amygdala can deactivate, even though the threatening thought is still present. With repetition, the hippocampus gets the message: this thing that was previously filed as "dangerous" is not, in reality, a threat.

Why Focus on the Negative?

One of the questions I often get when I first share the tapping process with people is, "Why are we tapping on negative thoughts? I don't want to think about negative things! What about the law that 'what you think about increases . . .'?"

It's a great question. I absolutely understand where people are coming from. But the reality is that these so-called negative thoughts are present, whether you think about them consciously or not. Like the pile of bills that you stick in a drawer because you don't want to look at them right now, they're still there—and they're still due! Our unprocessed emotions, beliefs, and traumas are still operating and controlling our lives. We need to address them—to look at them, admit they are there, and work through them—in order to clear them.

We're not harping on the negative; we're focusing on it for a short period of time. Tapping addresses the issue and clears it. Then we can move on to positive ideas, inspirations, and affirmations.

Instead of calling the emotions we're tapping "the negative," we can call them "the truth." They are the truth about how you feel right now; they are the truth about what happened; they are the truth about what you believe. You explore that truth to see how you can change it to a more *empowering* truth.

The amygdala learns not to set off the alarm. You remain calm, and the hippocampus now categorizes the experience as nonthreatening. The hippocampus is the structure in the limbic system that controls contextual associations. The formerly upsetting event or thing is now filed as "no big deal." So the next time you think about or encounter the trigger, the amygdala will not set off the alarm—and you will not be plunged into a stress response.

After doing tapping on a particular issue, I often hear clients say that they "just can't connect with it anymore." They still have the memory, but there's no strong emotion attached to it. That's because the limbic system has refiled the memory in a neutral, and sometimes even positive, way.

Scientists speculate that retraining the limbic system in this way permanently alters the neural pathways in your brain; that the conditioned fear pathways in the amygdala are eliminated. This fits with recent scientific discoveries regarding the *neuroplasticity* of the brain—i.e., that the brain's pathways are not permanent; they can be altered. To put it simply, you can develop new ways of thinking and perceiving the world. You don't have to stay with your old fixed viewpoints. Like Mary, you, too, can release debilitating fears, thoughts, and memories.

Through tapping, painful memories—and your focus on a specific part of them—can change. I've tapped with people on negative childhood experiences and then had them remark, "When I visualize my family as I was growing up, I'm actually seeing them smiling now and remembering all the good times we had." Did we alter the past or change their memories? Of course not. But we did clear the emotional trauma and the subsequent focus on negative experiences. When that happens, the positive experiences, which were always there, can rise to the surface.

. . . .

Tapping Tip: Why Tap?

If altering the limiting pathways in your brain or changing your biology isn't enough of a motivation to get you to tap, consider the negative effects of frequent stress responses on your health. If not cleared through tapping or another technique, the emotions connected to disturbing events, experiences, or thoughts will continue to trigger the stress response in you, perhaps many times a day. Numerous studies have demonstrated the injurious effects of such stress on the body.

"One of the most important epigenetic influences is stress," states Dawson

Church. "The emotional trauma of stress is now known to affect the expression of over one thousand genes, including many that influence aging and cell regeneration."

In Chapter 6, which explores using EFT to heal physical issues, we'll take a closer look at how stress affects the body—and how tapping can alleviate this stress and thus assist in the healing process.

. . . .

East Meets West: Ancient Chinese Acupressure and Modern Psychology

Acupuncture has been used for thousands of years in the East, primarily in China, to heal the body and block pain. In fact, acupuncture has been used to perform invasive surgeries with no anesthesia! How could this be? Well, the latest research is showing that acupuncture—and acupressure, of which tapping is a form—increases the body's endorphin levels, the "feel-good" neurotransmitters we hear so much about.

This increase in neurotransmitters is likely why most people feel good just doing the basic tapping, even if they're not focused on an issue. In fact, you can tap anytime you want, just on the points that feel good to you, and you'll often experience an increase in calm and contentment. The collarbone point (see page 21) is a favorite for most people; a couple of thumps on it can be relaxing and can elevate your mood.

While acupuncture is becoming more accepted in the West and is even recommended by traditional doctors and hospitals, until recently we didn't have any "Western proof" for how it works. But in recent years, researchers have discovered what are called the "Bonghan channels."

Named after Kim Bonghan, a North Korean researcher who published papers describing them in the 1960s, these tiny, threadlike, microscopic anatomical structures correspond with the traditional acupuncture meridians or channels. Stereo-microscope and electron-microscope images show the tubular structures are 30 to 100 micrometers wide and run up and down the body, like the ancient meridian channels. As a reference point, one red blood cell is 6 to 8 micrometers wide, so these structures are tiny!

You can think of the Bonghan channels as a fiber-optic network in the body. They carry a large amount of information, often beyond what the nervous system or chemical systems of the body can carry.

In other words, tapping lies at the intersection of the Eastern lineage of acupressure/acupuncture and the Western lineage of psychology and other mind-body processes. As I suspect you'll agree by the end of this book, that intersection is where true magic can happen.

Not Just for the Professionals

While EFT has been establishing its scientific and psychological underpinnings, I was attracted to it because it is so safe and easy to apply to oneself and others. In fact, many of the most successful EFT practitioners have been trained primarily in the tapping methodology, with no formal study in psychology or medicine. Certainly, each kind of training brings its own benefits; a doctor brings an understanding of the body to the practice of EFT and might have certain advantages or insights that others don't. But, as my friend and EFT expert Dr. Patricia Carrington likes to say, "It's truly the people's method."

Gary Craig, the founder of EFT, was in fact a Stanford engineer who had a natural understanding for people and their problems. He was able to apply the tapping method that he learned from Dr. Callahan—and improve upon it. My personal background is similar. My primary desire is to help people, to spread this important tool, and to educate people in how they can use it to change their lives.

For that reason, this book is about *you* and *your journey.* It's about you experiencing change and getting the results you most desire. We'll cover when you might want to contact an EFT professional for specific help or advice, but you can do incredible things for yourself, simply by applying the ideas and concepts presented here.

So, now that you've seen the accumulating evidence showing that EFT works, I'm sure you're chomping at the bit to have an experience yourself! And that's just what we'll do in Chapter 2.

QUICK START: EXPERIENCE TAPPING NOW

If someone can be traumatized in 30 seconds,
why can't they be healed in a day, an hour, a minute?

RICK WILKES, EFT EXPERT

Jackie, a successful real-estate agent from Canada, had a terrible fear of public speaking. Many of us are afraid to speak to large audiences, but Jackie's fear was with all audiences, large or small. Even being on a conference call with colleagues, people she knew and trusted, made her nervous and anxious.

This obviously affected her work. It limited her ability to get out in the world to grow her business, and, perhaps most important, it affected her experience of life. You can imagine the burden of constantly feeling worried that you will be judged for not saying the "right" thing. A smart woman like Jackie was shutting herself down from contributing her ideas due to an overwhelming fear of judgment from others.

Jackie went through the tapping protocol, focused on clearing childhood beliefs around not having a voice, not being heard, and not being able to speak up. She specifically focused on her experiences of seeing her brothers punished by her father and not being able to intervene and protect them. These experiences during her formative years had conditioned her mind and body to have a negative reaction when sharing herself with others. Tapping while focusing on such events retrained her brain and body's responses, and her fears vanished.

She's grown her business dramatically since then. More important, she finally feels comfortable and at ease in her interactions with others.

Pain Free in Minutes?

Mandy, a single mom, came to me with complaints of sporadic pain throughout her body. A variety of doctors could find no physical explanation and told her it was "all in her head." While part of her agreed, she was frustrated that the only solution they offered was ongoing pain medication that interfered with her life. We started tapping together, and in just a few minutes, the pain in her jaw, which had been hovering at around an 8 on a scale of 1 to 10, was reduced to a 5.

"What's the emotion behind this pain?" I asked her. She was quick to respond.

"Anger," she said. Specifically, anger related to a difficult work situation. After spending a few minutes discussing and tapping on the anger, the pain in her jaw released completely, a result that felt nothing short of miraculous for her.

What was physically wrong with her jaw? Likely nothing. The pain was just her body's way of expressing anger that she couldn't voice in other ways. (Mechanically, the pain might have come from decreased blood flow to the area due to chronic tension that we released through tapping.) Today Mandy knows that if she feels pain in her body, the question to ask is not "What's wrong with my body?" but rather "What is my body trying to tell me?" And she knows she can use the tapping process to clear the emotion—and the pain.

Letting Go of the Past

Lori found herself single and lonely at the age of 45. Having recently gone through a difficult divorce and several negative dating experiences, she felt hopeless. Not only had she lost faith in her ability to attract the right man, she was unwilling to open herself up to any more pain. In her mind, relationships equaled pain. The safest thing was not even to try.

We tapped through the experience of her divorce, her beliefs about herself, and her beliefs about men. In essence, we cleared all the "baggage" she was carrying about relationships. Step by step, she opened her heart to the possibility of new love—and created a vision for what that relationship could look like.

Experience Tapping Now

These are just a few examples out of the tens of thousands of amazing stories that result from the use of EFT. I'm sure by now you're curious to experience the powerful and dramatic effects tapping can have in your own life.

Of everything I've seen in the ten years I've been exploring tapping, my favorite part of the process remains its simplicity, how easy it is for anyone to learn, put into practice, and benefit from.

The reality is, we're all extremely busy. We don't have time to study a complicated process, hoping that somewhere down the line, we might see results. Unfortunately, much of the material in the self-help/personal-development world focuses on concepts and ideas—and as much as some of us enjoy the intellectual pursuit of studying, learning, and exploring different concepts, what we're looking for is real change.

We want to actually lose the weight, heal our bodies, improve our finances, find the relationship we most desire or improve our existing one, and so forth. Tapping can do all of this and more.

Getting started is easy, as I've said. I will go over each of the eight simple steps in detail later on, but I will list them for now:

1. Choose your "Most Pressing Issue" (MPI) and devise a reminder phrase (see pages 16 and 20).

2. Rate the intensity of your MPI on the 0-to-10 Subjective Units of Distress Scale (SUDS; see page 18).

3. Craft a setup statement (see page 18).

4. Tap on the karate chop point (see page 21) while repeating your setup statement three times.

5. Tap through the eight points in the EFT sequence (see page 21) while saying your reminder phrase out loud. Tap five to seven times at each point.

6. Once you have finished tapping the eight points in the sequence, take a deep breath.

7. Again rate the intensity of your issue using the 0-to-10 scale to check your progress.

8. Repeat as necessary to get the relief you desire.

Now that you have a sense of what you're diving into, there's only one more question to ask yourself: are you ready for some real change, right now? If so, keep reading!

What's Bothering You Most?

I find that the easiest way to start tapping is to focus on what I call the MPI, or Most Pressing Issue. We all have one; it's the issue, problem, or challenge that dominates our mental and emotional space in the present. If I asked you, "What's bothering you most right now?" what would your answer be? What are you most stressed or worried about?

Some common MPIs include:

Work. My boss is driving me crazy!
My body. I've had a terrible backache for days.
My husband. We got in a fight last night, and I can't stop thinking about how upset I am.

Take a moment right now and answer these questions for yourself: *What is bothering me the most right now? What is the most pressing issue in my life?* Many people find it helpful to write down the MPI. That said, you can certainly do it in your head as well.

Got it? If several come up, as they well might, pick one to start with. No right or wrong here, just go with your gut. (Using your intuition is a theme you'll hear a lot about with this process.)

Once you have your MPI, I'd like you to define it a little further. Maybe the issue you came up with is *I'm mad at my husband.* This is a rather broad statement, so think about the specifics behind the situation. For example, rather than saying, "I'm mad at my husband," you might say, "I'm mad at my husband because of what he said to me last night."

. . . .

Tapping Tip: Getting Specific

One of the things I hear most from people learning to tap is that they "never know what to say." Throughout the book, I'll provide you with sample statements you can use for MPIs, but the circumstances you're facing are unique; there's no way for me to guess exactly what's going on for you. I'll point out general themes, but you'll need to take it from there—tailoring your language to your specific experiences. You can trust your instincts; as long as you follow the process as it is laid out, it's nearly impossible to get tapping wrong.

It is equally important to be as specific as you can. Tapping on a more general issue can certainly improve your mood and make you feel better. But adding details that create specificity—particulars that pinpoint an experience, such as when it happened, who was involved, what you felt in your body, and so on—draws the focus more clearly to that particular issue. As a result, you'll have a better ability to rewire the brain's response to it.

If you ever get stuck on the exact language, just focus on the feeling. Or visualize a picture of what happened (or is happening) and then describe it. Do whatever it takes to get a clear memory or feeling, and that will do the job.

Here's an example. A broad, or global, MPI statement might be *I have this pain in my shoulder.*

A more specific MPI statement would be *I have this pain in my left shoulder when I lift my arm.*

And an even *more* specific statement would be *I have this shooting, burning pain in my left shoulder when I lift my arm.*

Here's one for an emotional event:

Global: *I'm angry.*

More specific: *I'm angry at my boss for what he said to me.*

Even more specific: *I feel this anger in my chest at my boss for telling me I'm not doing my job well enough.*

You can get specific in many different ways. Sometimes asking yourself deeper questions again and again can help narrow down your specific feelings. For example:

"I'm angry at him." Why?

"Because he was a jerk." What did he do?

"Because he didn't call me back." And how does that make me feel?

"Angry." How angry?

"Really angry!" What would that be on a 0-to-10 scale?

"Seven!" Where do I feel the anger in my body?

"My chest, it's about to explode!"

Now you have more specific details on what you're angry about, how angry you are, where you feel it in your body, and so forth. Always try to be as specific as possible!

. . . .

Using SUDS, the 0-to-10 Scale

Now that you know your MPI, I want you to give it a number on a 0-to-10 scale. This is called the SUDS, or Subjective Units of Distress Scale. Think about your MPI, and notice what it brings up in your body. What level of distress does it bring up for you? A 10 would be the most distress you can imagine; a 0 rating would mean you don't feel any distress at all. Don't worry about getting the SUDS level exact or "right"—just follow your gut instinct. Think about the anger you feel toward your husband. If you're really boiling, you might rate it an 8 or a 9. If you're still feeling angry but have cooled off a bit from last night, you might rate it a 5. To see a significant shift in an issue, start with something you can rate at 5 or higher.

Crafting Your Setup Statement

Now that you know your SUDS level, the next step is to craft what's called the "setup statement." This brings forward the energy of the MPI that you're going to be working on. Once you know your setup statement, you can start tapping.

The basic setup statement goes like this:

Even though _____ [fill in the blank with your MPI], *I deeply and completely accept myself.*

So you might say, "Even though I'm angry at my husband for what he said to me last night, I deeply and completely accept myself."

Or "Even though my back hurts, I deeply and completely accept myself."

Or "Even though I'm stressed out about the upcoming work deadline, I deeply and completely accept myself."

Go ahead and try to create a setup statement for your current most pressing issue. Don't worry about getting the language perfect. Whatever your MPI is, simply fill in the blank.

Once you have your setup statement, the tapping can begin. You'll start by saying it three times, all the while tapping on the karate chop point (see page 21). You can tap with whichever hand feels most comfortable to you. Tap at a pace and force that feels right; you can't get it wrong!

After you've said the setup statement three times, you'll move on to tapping through the eight points in the EFT sequence, while saying the reminder phrase.

Accepting Ourselves with the Problem

Along with the concern about focusing on the "negative," some people don't feel comfortable with saying they accept themselves in light of the problem they're tapping on. The problem simply seems too big, important, or intolerable to allow for self-acceptance.

If you find that you really, truly can't make that statement—it's rare, but it happens—that's okay. You can skip it and just keep tapping on the issue without the setup statement and then try again later. But for most of us, it's very important to say it, even if it feels hard.

When we accept ourselves as we are, we aren't "settling" or "keeping the problem in place." We're showing love and compassion for ourselves—for our feelings, our situation, and our history.

That self-acceptance often goes a long way toward actually clearing the issue. As the old saying goes, "what you resist persists." Oftentimes, it's when we accept ourselves as we are that the most dramatic change happens!

. . . .

Tapping Tip: Stick with Me . . .

If you're anything like me, tapping will seem strange at first. It takes a little effort to memorize the points and understand the process.

But stick with me through these next couple of pages—go over them a few times if you need to—and take the time to really learn the basic steps. The investment you put in now will make all the difference, and once you know the basics, things will move very quickly.

. . . .

Choosing a Reminder Phrase

The reminder phrase is short—just a couple of words that bring to mind your MPI. You will speak this phrase out loud at each of the eight points in the EFT sequence (see page 21). For example, if your MPI has to do with the anger you feel at your husband, you might tap through each point in the sequence saying, "This anger . . . this anger . . . this anger . . ." Other examples of reminder phrases might be:

This fear I'm feeling . . .
This sadness . . .
This frustration . . .
This back pain . . .
This headache . . .

And so forth.

You're repeating the reminder phrase out loud to remind yourself of the issue at each point. This reminder phrase serves to keep your focus on the MPI so you don't get distracted. It also acts as a barometer, helping you determine along the way how true the MPI feels to you.

Once you get used to tapping, you can change your reminder phrase as you tap through each point. For example, you might say, "This anger . . . this red-hot anger . . . it's burning in my chest . . . am so angry . . ." I will offer this kind of evolving reminder phrase in the tapping scripts throughout the book. But to start with, keep it simple and say the same statement at each point.

Tapping Through the Points

Once you have your reminder phrase, you are ready to start tapping through the eight points of the EFT sequence. These points are

1. Eyebrow
2. Side of eye
3. Under eye
4. Under nose

5. Chin
6. Collarbone
7. Under arm
8. Top of head

Tapping Points

eyebrow — top of head

side of eye — under nose

under eye — chin

collarbone

under arm

www.TheTappingSolution.com

karate chop

The same meridians run down both sides of the body, meaning you can tap with either hand, on whichever side of the body feels best to you. You can even tap both sides of the body at once if you'd like (it's not necessary, however, as you'll hit the same meridian lines, regardless of which side you tap). Tap five to seven times at each stop as you work through the sequence. This doesn't have to be an exact count. If it feels right to tap 20 times—or 100—on one point, then do it! The idea is simply to spend enough time at that point to speak your reminder phrase and let it sink in.

Ready to give it a try? Start by saying your setup statement three times while tapping on the karate chop point. Then move on to tap your reminder phrase at each of the eight points in the sequence—eyebrow, side of eye, under eye, under nose, chin, collarbone, under arm, and top of head. Don't worry about getting it perfect the first time around; just do your best and have the experience!

Check In

You've now completed a round of tapping! First things first: Take a deep breath. Feel your body and notice what's happening for you. Ask yourself, *Did the issue shift? What thoughts came up for me while tapping? How do I feel on the 0-to-10 scale now?*

Go back and think about the thing your husband said last night and see how it feels to you now. You might find that the anger, which was seething before, is now merely simmering. In that case, you can tap a few more rounds using the same language and clear the issue altogether.

Or you might find that, as you were tapping on the anger about what your husband said last night, you thought of something else he said three weeks ago that made you even madder. That's great! Not that you're mad at your husband, but that you're identifying for yourself what's *really* going on. In that case, you can move on from the anger you felt last night to tap on the issue from three weeks ago. In this way we "peel the onion," revealing layer after layer of an issue in order to find resolution, freedom, hope, and understanding.

My advice is to keep tapping until your Most Pressing Issue finds enough relief that you feel really good about it. This may mean getting the SUDS level down to a 2 or 3, which may feel manageable to you, or it may mean clearing it altogether so it's at 0. Tap long enough to release your pain, be it physical, emotional, or spiritual. Stick with it. Do five rounds; do ten rounds. Commit yourself to getting the relief you need. Then, once you've cleared your MPI, move on to the next issue you want to release.

Tapping Quick Reference Guide

Once again, here are the eight steps of EFT tapping. It may be helpful to bookmark this page so you can come back to it as you move on to the chapters that follow. That said, most people learn these steps rather quickly, so you may not need this reference for long!

1. Choose your Most Pressing Issue (MPI).

2. Rate your MPI using the 0-to-10 SUDS.

3. Craft a setup statement, using your MPI to fill in the blank: *Even though _____, I deeply and completely accept myself.*

4. Speak your setup statement three times while tapping on the karate chop point.

5. Tap through the eight points in the EFT sequence while saying your reminder phrase out loud. Tap five to seven times at each point, starting with the eyebrow and finishing at the top of the head.

6. Take a deep breath.

7. Rate the intensity of your MPI using the 0-to-10 scale.

8. Repeat, or move on to a different MPI.

You can also watch me demonstrating the process on video here:
www.thetappingsolution.com/tappingvideo.

Tapping Targets

In the previous section, we tapped on an emotion—anger. Throughout this book, we will cover a variety of issues that benefit from tapping, from distressing emotions like anger to weight problems, relationships, and even money issues. Whatever issue is being tapped on in any given round is called the "target." As you tap, different layers or aspects of that target will arise. Often you start with one target and then find something else underneath it—a layer! For example, your target might be the anger you feel at a friend for a comment she made. As you tap on that anger, it may clear away—leaving a different layer, such as sadness. Then, as you tap through the sadness, you may realize that you are actually frustrated at yourself for not standing up to this friend when she makes rude comments. And so it continues, until you fully clear an issue. Working through these layers might seem tedious at first; but the reality is, emotional, physical, and spiritual experiences are often multilayered. Unless we address every layer or aspect of an issue, we can't hope to fully clear it.

So how do you know which target to choose to start your exploration with tapping? The four most common types of targets to work with are **symptoms/side effects, emotions, events,** and **limiting beliefs.** In the sections that follow, we'll cover each of them in turn.

In order to help you identify these targets in your mind, I'd like to introduce you to a great visual created by my friend—and EFT expert—Lindsay Kenny, called the tapping tree. This creative visual shows each target category and how it affects particular MPIs.

The Tapping Tree: Identify Your Targets

Symptoms/Side Effects (The Leaves): Addictions, PTSD, heart ailments, hypertension, weight issues, asthma, self-sabotage, pain and illness, clutter and procrastination, etc.

Emotions (The Branches): Shame, guilt, remorse, rejection, anger, resentment, sadness, depression, powerlessness, fear, anxiety, stress, etc.

Events (The Trunk): Detached parents, bullied growing up, abandoned/betrayed, abused in any way, over disciplined/criticized, physically punished, family fighting/shouting, unsupported or unloved, alcoholic parent, etc.

Limiting Beliefs (The Roots): "I can't do anything right," "I'm not safe, I'm not okay," "I'm not lovable," "I'm different," "I'm not worthy," "I'm not good enough," etc.

In this illustration, the roots of the tree are our limiting beliefs—what we believe to be true or not true about ourselves and the world. The trunk of the tree represents past events, often traumatic, that still affect us today. The branches are the emotions that come up, including things like anger, sadness, frustration, and hopelessness. Finally, the leaves bear the side effects or external symptoms that manifest and create distress in our lives.

Throughout the rest of the book we'll skip around to various points in the tapping tree—tapping on symptoms, emotions, traumatic events, and underlying beliefs alike. The majority of MPIs are multilayered. For example, you may have an outward physical symptom, as well as a distressing emotion, both stemming from one childhood event. You may discover that when you tap on one part of the tree, another part gets handled. For example, tapping on a "root" limiting belief may also have profound effects on a "leaf" symptom or side effect.

Symptoms and Side Effects

Symptoms and side effects you might choose as tapping targets include things like addiction, weight problems, physical pain, self-sabotage, financial issues, and heart problems. These are easiest to recognize and often most bothersome, because they are so real and present. Yet while they may seem to be problems in themselves, oftentimes they are simply expressions of a deeper issue. Ideally, over time you will identify the deeper issue and use that as your tapping target.

That said, it's sometimes easier to tap on an obvious symptom or side effect—and this can produce great results on its own. For example, my friend Arielle came to me complaining of migraine headaches. The pain wouldn't let up, no matter what she tried. We spent no more than 30 minutes tapping, focusing purely on the physical symptom—the headaches.

The setup statement we used was *Even though I have these headaches, I deeply and completely accept myself.* We then tapped through the points using reminder phrases like *These headaches, these painful headaches,* and so forth.

We didn't focus on the underlying emotions behind the headaches or on any limiting beliefs that might have been causing them. We talked about when the headaches started, but only briefly. We simply tapped on the symptom—this is referred to as "symptom tapping"—and the headaches went away!

But when symptom tapping doesn't get the job done, you'll know you need to go further down the tapping tree, to identify a deeper target that will yield the relief you're looking for. A good first step is to look at your emotional state.

Emotions

If Arielle hadn't seen results from tapping on her headaches, my next step would have been to ask, "What is the emotion behind these headaches? Exactly what do you feel when you think about these headaches?" She might have replied, "anger," "sadness," or "grief," and we could have then tapped on those emotions until they were cleared.

Sometimes there are multiple emotions behind a symptom. As we peel back the layers of the onion, different aspects of the target may present themselves. What starts as anger often moves into sadness, then into deep grief. We can always start by tapping on the emotions directly; if what's most pressing is an emotion, then that's where you should start. If you're angry about something, tap on it. If you feel rejected, helpless, or powerless, start tapping now.

A Deeper Emotional Experience

Sometimes it's easy to get stuck on the emotions we're most familiar with. For example, many of us end up tapping on feelings of anger and sadness, which are easy to recognize. But accessing a broader emotional vocabulary can help bring more specificity to tapping. Here are some key emotions many of us experience. Use this list to further connect with what's going on for you.

• Alienation	• Despair	• Frustration
• Ambivalence	• Disgust	• Fury
• Anger	• Distress	• Grief
• Anxiety	• Doubt	• Grouchiness
• Bitterness	• Dread	• Guilt
• Boredom	• Embarrassment	• Hatred
• Contempt	• Envy	• Homesickness
• Depression	• Fear	• Hope

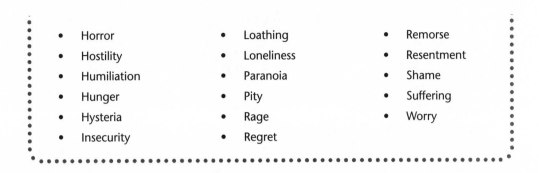

- Horror
- Hostility
- Humiliation
- Hunger
- Hysteria
- Insecurity

- Loathing
- Loneliness
- Paranoia
- Pity
- Rage
- Regret

- Remorse
- Resentment
- Shame
- Suffering
- Worry

Past Events

Another common category of tapping targets is past events. As we will discuss further in Chapter 5, there are two kinds of events: those that happen and are easy to move beyond, and those that affect us and stay with us. The difference between the two is whether or not we have processed them emotionally, energetically, and/or physically.

One person can think back to something that happened in high school—a bad breakup, for example—and be able to say, "Yeah, that was a tough experience, but it's done and I've moved on." She remembers the experience, but doesn't feel any emotion toward it. The next person thinks about her bad breakup in high school and has a totally different experience. She feels it in her gut; an intense sadness comes up, with regret and longing for that lost love. This is an experience that hasn't been processed. Addressing that past event with EFT will help her let go of the pain and move on.

Limiting Beliefs

A limiting belief is a false belief about ourselves or the world. Limiting beliefs are incorrect conclusions we draw based on events or experiences. For example, someone might have a limiting belief about his or her ability to succeed on a project because of a previous failure. We anticipate that the same outcome will happen in the future and thus limit our expectations.

As shown in the tapping tree illustration, our limiting beliefs are the root system for our life. Sometimes it's hard to wrap our heads around the idea of a "limiting belief" because until we recognize it as such, we just see it as "the truth"! We may believe we'll never lose weight because our parents never did or that we can't be wealthy because wealthy people aren't spiritual. Any idea that cuts off possibility is a limiting belief.

Some other common limiting beliefs include:

I can't do anything right.
I'm not safe.
I'm not lovable.
I'm different.
I'm not worthy.
I'm not good enough.

These beliefs are usually learned in childhood. We get them from our parents, teachers, and peers during our early years, and they color everything in our lives from there. The belief that "I can't do anything right" is going to have profound implications for everything we do. It's going to change how we behave, what we say, what we pursue, and much more.

Oftentimes tapping on childhood or past events will clear limiting beliefs. But if we are aware of what they are, we can tap on the limiting beliefs themselves.

Exercise: Create Your Own Tapping Tree

The Tapping Tree is a fantastic visual representation of what's going on in our lives. It's a wonderful tool for systematically working through different issues. It also makes it easier to see how a symptom might be connected to an emotion, event, or belief—how the "leaf" relates to the "branch," "trunk," or "roots." These connections and insights are vital for you to get the best results with EFT. As I've mentioned already and will continue to mention, it's crucial that you get specific when you tap, to really home in on what's happening, and the best way to arrive at that specificity is to dig deeper.

So take a few minutes now to draw your own tapping tree. You can print out a blank copy of this drawing by visiting www.tappingsolution .com/tree, or you can simply sketch it on a piece of paper. It doesn't have to be pretty, just be sure to leave plenty of space. Most of us have more stuff going on than this tree shows!

The Leaves: Symptoms and Side Effects

What symptoms are you currently experiencing? How does your physical body feel? What have you been diagnosed with? Do you have any pain in your body? Fill in all these visible, tangible issues as the leaves. For example, you might write in symptoms such as "extra weight," "pain in my back," "clinical depression," "low energy," or "lack of clarity." The best way to determine what to write here is to think about the issues you complain about most often. When someone asks, "What's wrong?" what do you usually say?

The Branches: Emotions

What emotions do you feel on a regular basis? When you wake up in the morning, how do you feel? When you go to sleep at night, how do you feel? Think back over the last day and write in any of the negative emotions you have experienced. Refer to the emotion list on pages 26–27 if you get stuck.

The Trunk: Events

What are the events, both current and past, that are still alive for you? What events have been a source of stress in the past week? The past year? The past decade? In Chapter 5, we'll dive deeper into how the past is affecting you, so don't worry about finding every single event for now. Just note the ones that seem most obvious and important.

The Roots: Limiting Beliefs

What beliefs do you have about yourself? About life in general or your life specifically? About money? About relationships? About your body? Don't worry if you struggle coming up with these now, because they often require deeper exploration. Remember, until we recognize them as such, limiting beliefs simply feel like the truth. Some good questions to ask yourself to start bringing up some of those beliefs are:

- What do I believe to be true about myself?
- What do I believe to be true about the world?
- What do I believe to be true about money?
- What do I believe to be true about relationships?
- What do I believe to be true about my body?

Again, we'll explore each of these in detail throughout the book. For now, just write what comes to mind.

When you're done, step back and take a look at your tree. This is a brief summary of your current challenges. I'm sure it's not comprehensive, but hopefully it serves two purposes. First, it will help you see some of what may be going on in your life so you can focus on the targets you want to address. Second, it will help explain how to approach tapping for the best results—understanding the aspects and layers of each issue and how one thing connects to another. These emotions, symptoms, events, and limiting beliefs are what we will be addressing throughout the book. We'll be clearing them once and for all, in order to make way for a newer, healthier, and happier you!

Negative versus Positive Statements

As I mentioned in Chapter 1, I frequently get questions about why tapping focuses on the negative rather than the positive. I wanted to talk a bit more about this since it's such an important topic.

Many people who have studied the Law of Attraction—which, at its simplest level, states that the ideas you focus upon expand—worry that by repeating "negative" reminder phrases, they're affirming and attracting more of them. But the reality is that these negative thoughts, experiences, beliefs, and symptoms exist, whether you consciously address them or not, and they affect you. Denying their existence doesn't make them go away. By taking some time to acknowledge them, bring them into the light, and teach your amygdala that they are not dangerous, you can clear them once and for all.

When weeds come up in your garden, it does no good to say, "There are no weeds, there are no weeds, there are no weeds . . ." It doesn't help to pretend they're not there. It doesn't matter how much you focus on the beautiful plants that are growing! The weeds aren't going to disappear until you get on your hands and knees and pull them out.

Taking the time to do the work—to pull the weeds—leaves you with a garden full of beautiful, healthy plants. The same is true for your psyche. When you take the time to pull weeds from the past, what you're left with is a healthy, vibrant, happy, and fulfilled self.

The other important point to note about EFT is that it's not a mind eraser. We are not erasing memories of the past; we are not erasing emotions. We are *processing* them. That is a vital distinction. After processing, we still have the lessons, insights, and growth from our experience. If, on the other hand, we bury an experience, trying to erase it without processing it, it stays stuck right where it is.

Often when I tap with a client about anger, that anger processes through the body and mind and turns to sadness. Then we tap on the sadness, and it might turn to a sense of loss. Then we tap on the sense of loss, and it might turn to gratitude for the experience and lesson. As that original anger is released, more positive feelings can become present.

If It's Not a One-Minute Wonder, Keep Tapping!

One of the amazing benefits of EFT is how quickly it produces real, long-lasting results that would take months or years to achieve through more conventional therapies.

The so-called one-minute wonders often happen when you least expect them. But no matter how frequently they occur, they're not the norm. We all have deep-seated emotional patterns that can be hard to break, and our brains are hardwired to resist change of all kinds. So often it's the ongoing commitment to tapping that yields the biggest, most profound breakthroughs.

For especially deep-seated emotions—the thickest, gnarliest roots in your tapping tree—your tapping journey may also occasionally take unexpected turns. If the thing you're trying to clear, usually an emotion, initially gets worse while tapping, you know you are on the right path. When you start opening up to your emotions, a lot of repressed material can start to surface. Try not to get discouraged; it's your body's way of telling you exactly *how much* emotional energy it's been storing around a particular issue. If you keep tapping, you keep clearing it. The results you can achieve in those cases, whether in minutes, hours, or weeks, are truly life changing.

You Can Do It

I know that, in the beginning, tapping can seem a little confusing and strange.

But once you learn the points and understand the process, you're going to experience rapid results in all the areas we'll cover in this book.

Love yourself enough to take at least 15 minutes to really experience EFT right now. Once you have an experience, be it a small shift or a massive miracle, then you'll know that this is worth learning and implementing in your life.

And just imagine . . . if this tool is everything others are saying it is—if you can experience the results that millions of others have experienced—what might your life look like on the other side?

What might it be like to release the physical pain you feel?

What might it be like to let go of old wounds, traumas, and stories that no longer serve you?

What could you create, accomplish, or contribute if you finally freed yourself from the limiting beliefs, the baggage, and the history that has been holding you back?

It all starts with these first steps—learning the tapping points and practicing tapping enough to feel a shift.

You can do it!

(Remember, you can see a video with further instructions highlighting the points and process at www.thetappingsolution.com/tappingvideo.)

CHAPTER 3

RELIEVING ANXIETY, FEELINGS OF BEING OVERWHELMED, AND STRESS

God grant me the serenity
to accept the things I cannot change;
courage to change the things I can;
and wisdom to know the difference.

REINHOLD NIEBUHR

Claire was on the brink of a meltdown . . . not that anyone around her could tell.

To the outside world, she was put together, happy; she had a good job, great kids, and a decent relationship with her husband. She was a loving, conscientious person, trying to make a difference in the world. In touch with her desire to improve herself and her life, Claire was aware of what she ate, thought, and did. She worked on herself, tried to lower her stress levels, and tried to be positive. But somehow, something was missing.

It started innocently enough: weird pains in her body. Her doctors could find no medical explanation. She had trouble sleeping through the night, had a general feeling of fatigue during the day, was carrying extra pounds she couldn't get rid of, no matter what she tried, and had an underlying feeling of anxiety and angst that just wouldn't release.

When she found the space to breathe and examine her life, all she could think was, *It's too much.*

It's too much responsibility. There are too many things to do. There's too much financial pressure. It's too much to take care of the kids and be a great parent. It's too much to try to be a loving wife. It's too much to eat perfectly. It's too much to look good, feel good, and keep up with the Joneses.

Modern life, with all its stressors—all the stuff we are intimately familiar with and know about—was overwhelming to her.

Sound familiar?

What's "too much" in your life? What's stressing you out the most? What do you feel like you just can't handle? What physical symptoms are showing up in your body?

Feelings of generalized anxiety, being overwhelmed, fatigue, and intense responsibility have become par for the course in modern life. "This is just the way life is," we tell ourselves. "It's hurried; it's busy; there's one thing after another, each stacking on top of the next, to the point where sometimes it's hard to breathe."

You know those times when you *do* take a deep breath? Try it now, and see what you find. The realization may run something like this: *Wow, I've been so stressed out. My body is running on overdrive, and I haven't noticed it. When was the last time I actually relaxed?*

We have developed patterns, ways of being and thinking, that simply do not serve us and are not sustainable. That's why we get unknown pains in our bodies; it's also why we come down with medical conditions that can be more easily blamed on biological problems like viruses, bacteria, or other outside forces. These patterns are why we walk around feeling stressed, anxious, and uncomfortable. They're why we have trouble sleeping and why we can't drop the weight we want to. That's why we feel like there's too much to do, like the stress will never end. It's why we can't be present in the moment or enjoy our lives.

Some of my clients argue that it's not their way of thinking or being that's the problem—the problem is *life itself!*

They say to me, "I could be happy if such and such changed" or "I would be happy if I had less to do" or "I would be happy if I had more money" or "I would be happy if I lost weight." Many of us simply believe that, until those things happen, we are not going to be happy.

Well, I've got some bad news. (I know, I'm just piling it on, right? The good news is coming, I promise!) The only way you're going to have more money, lose weight, be healthier, and feel more fulfilled is if you first change your patterns and ways of thinking. You must find a way to lower your stress levels, process your negative emotions, let go of the past, and stop repeating negative patterns. Only from there can you create the life you've truly dreamed of.

There was a time when this kind of stress reduction and pattern change might have seemed like a tall or impossible order, but now EFT tapping can make it all happen quickly.

In the first chapter, we saw the amazing effects that tapping can have on the body on a purely physical level, in terms of reducing the fight-or-flight response and calming the amygdala. The same goes for your emotional world. When you apply tapping to your existing patterns, beliefs, and emotions, your life changes almost instantly. It did for Claire—in seemingly miraculous ways, as you'll see on the following pages—and it can for you, too.

"Nothing Ever Works . . ."

When I began chatting with Claire about her life and everything that was going on, one of the first things she shared with me was her frustration about all the stress-reduction methods she had tried in the past, from yoga, to meditation, to affirmations, to positive thinking. She had a deep belief that, for her, "nothing ever worked." When we've been on a path of self-discovery and self-improvement for a few years and haven't seen the results we expected or were promised, it can be extremely frustrating! But that frustration—and the expectation of another negative outcome—is exactly what can keep us stuck. Oftentimes, we pile that frustration on top of negative feelings about ourselves and about our commitment to making change happen.

I know what I should be doing, but I never do it.
I've tried other techniques, but they don't seem to work.
It seems to work for other people, but it doesn't work for me.

I always start down a path, but never finish it. (We're going to change that pattern right now, so you can finish this book!)

It's important to clear this frustration, to clear your anxiety that the personal-development techniques you try won't work. It's in this clearing that you open yourself up to new possibilities. Otherwise the mind-set that "nothing ever works" or the belief that "I never finish what I start" will keep manifesting. And then you *won't* finish this book—even though the life breakthrough you're looking for might be in Chapter 9! Or you might read every word but not do the actual tapping, which is where all the magic lies.

So let's do some tapping right now to clear these negative expectations.

TAPPING SCRIPT: "Nothing Ever Works . . ."

(The tapping points chart can be found on page 21.)

You'll find throughout this book that I've made tapping scripts available for a variety of issues. All of them start with a "check-in" phrase, to determine if it's something you need to work on.

For example, this script's check-in phrase is *I'm frustrated because nothing ever works for me.*

Go ahead and say that out loud a few times, and then rate how true it is on the 0-to-10 scale, with 10 being "absolutely true" and 0 being "not at all true."

Generally speaking, if your truth level is a 5 or more, it's probably an issue you want to work on right away.

Remember, these are general phrases and ideas to get you started. If different language fits better for you, or if other ideas come up, feel free to follow your intuition.

Karate Chop: Even though I'm frustrated because nothing ever works for me, I deeply and completely accept myself.
Karate Chop: Even though I have a tendency to start something and not finish it, I deeply love and accept myself.
Karate Chop: Even though I'm anxious because nothing seems to work for me, I choose to relax now.

Eyebrow: Nothing ever works . . .
Side of Eye: All this frustration . . .
Under Eye: I'm frustrated because nothing works for me . . .
Under Nose: I've tried so many different things . . .
Chin: And nothing ever works . . .

Collarbone: This probably won't work . . .
Under Arm: This probably won't work for me . . .
Top of Head: All this frustration . . .

Eyebrow: Nothing ever works . . .
Side of Eye: I start things and don't finish them . . .
Under Eye: I'm anxious to try anything else . . .
Under Nose: Because I have so many experiences of things not working . . .
Chin: It works for other people . . .
Collarbone: But not for me . . .
Under Arm: All this frustration . . .
Top of Head: All this anxiety and frustration.

And now let's do a positive round. (Remember, go on to the positive statements only when you feel relief or if the statements feel at least somewhat true. Don't force the positive; keep tapping on what's stopping you or bothering you until the positive feels more natural. If during a positive round your mind says, "I don't believe you!" or "That's not true!" then you probably need to go back to the negative beliefs until they clear.)

Eyebrow: I choose to be open to the possibility that this can work . . .
Side of Eye: I choose to release any frustration in my body . . .
Under Eye: Things have worked for me before . . .
Under Nose: I have made lots of positive changes . . .
Chin: And I choose to make more . . .
Collarbone: I choose to believe in my ability to change . . .
Under Arm: I choose to release any frustration or anxiety in my body . . .
Top of Head: Letting it go . . . letting it all go.

For an extended tapping session on this topic,
visit www.thetappingsolution.com/tap1.

Identifying Cognitive Shifts and the "Apex Effect"

After doing this tapping script and bringing down her frustration, Claire went on to say, "You know what? That's not true that nothing ever works. I've had a lot of successes and have really changed my life a lot in the past couple of years. I'm hopeful that this tapping can help even more."

What had happened in the few minutes since Claire had told me, "Nothing ever works for me"? Had she been lying before? Did she change her mind in those few minutes?

What happened is that before, she was running a pattern and belief system that said, "Nothing ever works for me." Her brain and body were pulling up all those negative experiences from the past—all those mini traumas where she had let herself down, hadn't forgiven herself, and hadn't processed the experience. These experiences had created a limiting belief that she could not get past. By tapping on her feelings of frustration and on the story she was telling herself, we cleared the old thought pattern and allowed a new belief to spring forward.

When we use EFT on these feelings and experiences, a cognitive shift takes place that allows us to see more clearly, to reduce the noise in our head and in our body. Oftentimes, the shift is so profound that people almost don't remember what they thought before. As I said before, EFT isn't a mind eraser; it doesn't delete memories in any way, but it does clear the negative emotional and energetic patterns behind a memory. Thus it changes our approach and response to the event—and to life going forward.

At the most extreme level, this shift is called the "Apex Effect." The Apex Effect happens when a person's thought patterns shift so dramatically that they don't credit tapping as having made a difference. Some even say the belief was never a problem in the first place! Someone can be scared of spiders, tap to clear it, and then say they were never scared, because their mind has shifted so far from the fear that it doesn't seem real in their life anymore. This is one of the reasons it's always important to use the 0-to-10 scale after each round of tapping. It allows you to accurately gauge your progress and remember where you started.

Identifying Your Patterns

Throughout this book, we will explore your patterns regarding all sorts of major life topics, including weight loss, relationships, finances, and so forth. In this chapter, however, we're going to continue to address the more generalized patterns—the limiting belief systems and habits that are contributing to the stress in your life.

Stress itself is both the symptom and the cause of most of the challenges we face on a daily basis. Obviously, stress isn't pleasurable. It wreaks havoc on our body, raising cortisol levels (which helps put and keep weight on), blood pressure, blood sugar, and more. But beyond that, the stress response itself often leads to more stressful situations. For example, if stress is triggered by a colleague in a business meeting, you might then go home and take that stress out on the kids or your partner. The cycle continues.

So how do we end the stress cycle? The answer lies in shifting our fight-or-flight response, which we discussed in detail in Chapter 1.

. . . .

Tapping Tip: The Choices Statement

As we've learned, the traditional way of beginning a tapping round is with the setup statement, *Even though I _____* [fill in the blank with the problem], *I deeply and completely accept myself.*

I'd like to introduce you to an alternative called the "choices statement." The choices statement, developed by Dr. Patricia Carrington—one of the early pioneers in EFT—allows you to change the tail end of the setup statement to a choice. There are two main reasons to use the choices statement:

a. It provides an alternative if you have trouble saying "I deeply and completely accept myself."

b. The statement can feel very empowering, putting you in control of your own experience.

The choices statement goes like this: *Even though I_____* [fill in the blank with the problem], *I choose to _____* [fill in the blank with a positive affirmation].

For example:

Even though I'm angry about what happened at work, I choose to let it go now.
Even though I have this pain in my lower back, I choose to relax now.
Even though I'm frustrated about what I said to her, I choose to forgive myself now.

Use your own intuition as you decide whether the choices statement feels appropriate for a particular problem you're working with.

. . . .

"I'm Overwhelmed!"

Melissa had just achieved a major life goal, having finished her first book. She had been dreaming about writing it for years, so you'd think she would have been proud of herself—that she would be celebrating her accomplishment and taking the required steps to get the book out into the world.

Instead, she was stuck.

She hadn't done anything to promote her book in months. Copies of it were piled up in the garage. She wasn't moving on it at all, and when I asked her why, she said, "There's too much to do! I have to get a website designed. I have to set it up for sale on Amazon. I don't know how to do these things! I have a list a mile long that needs to get done, and I can't even get started!"

Talking to her further, I detected some subconscious sabotage and resistance to change, both of which we will discuss in Chapter 4. But before we could address such big topics, we needed to reduce her feeling of being overwhelmed. So I walked her through some rounds of tapping.

TAPPING SCRIPT: "I'm Stressed Out and Overwhelmed!"

(The tapping points chart can be found on page 21.)

Before you tap, ask yourself, "What am I overwhelmed about? What don't I believe I can get done? What exactly is stressing me out?"

Then try the check-in phrase *I'm overwhelmed and have too much to do*. Give it a number on a 0-to-10 scale, 10 being absolutely true, 0 being not true at all. Then join in, either tapping with the language below or using your own language. You might also want to identify the primary thought or event causing you stress, and give it its own number on the 0-to-10 scale. This is a way to drill even deeper into the issue, for greater results.

Karate Chop: Even though I'm stressed out, overwhelmed, and simply have too much to do, I deeply and completely accept myself.

Karate Chop: Even though my to-do list is a mile long and it's stressing me out, I deeply and completely accept myself.

Karate Chop: Even though I feel like I'm never going to get it all done and like I'm not smart enough, I deeply and completely accept myself.

Eyebrow: I can't get all this done . . .
Side of Eye: All these feelings of being overwhelmed . . .
Under Eye: I'm feeling so much stress and it overwhelms me . . .
Under Nose: There's simply too much to do . . .
Chin: I'm overwhelmed . . .
Collarbone: Too much to do . . .
Under Arm: And not enough time . . .
Top of Head: I just can't handle everything on my plate . . .

Eyebrow: How am I going to get all of this done . . .
Side of Eye: I can't get it done . . .

Under Eye: Because I have too much to do . . .
Under Nose: I need help . . .
Chin: There aren't enough hours in the day . . .
Collarbone: To get all of this done . . .
Under Arm: All these feelings of being overwhelmed. . .
Top of Head: All these feelings of being overwhelmed.

Keep tapping through negative rounds (think of them as "truth" rounds, because you're just speaking how you feel—your truth!) until you find relief. When you feel ready, move on to some positive rounds.

Eyebrow: I choose to relax . . .
Side of Eye: I have the resources to get this done . . .
Under Eye: I've done it before, and I can do it again . . .
Under Nose: I choose to release this feeling of being overwhelmed. . .
Chin: I have to do what I have to do . . .
Collarbone: And being stressed out about it doesn't help me . . .
Under Arm: Releasing these feelings of being overwhelmed . . .
Top of Head: Letting them all go.

Tap through those positive statements as many times as you want to.

Remember, we're doing very general statements here to start with. The more specific you can get about your own situation, the better results you'll have. For example, if as you were tapping on the above rounds, you realized that what is stressing you out most is one project you have at work, then tap specifically on that project and how you feel about it. For example: *Even though I'm really stressed out about this project at work, and it feels like it will never get done, I deeply and completely accept myself.*

Repeat the statement three times and then tap through the points.

Perhaps while doing that round, you'll begin thinking about the fact that you're angry. You feel like your boss doesn't recognize the amount of work you're putting into this project. In that case, you might say, "Even though I'm angry that I'm not being recognized by him for all the work I'm doing, I deeply and completely accept myself."

Repeat the statement three times and then tap through the points.

Continue until you feel clear on the issue. Sometimes it's a struggle for people to decide when they're done or when to stop tapping. I usually recommend that they keep going until they get an issue down to a 1 or 2 on the 0-to-10 scale. A 0 is obviously preferable, but sometimes issues can linger a bit and fade further in a few hours.

There's no right or wrong either! If you tap for 15 minutes on some deep hurt you're feeling, bringing it from a 10 to a 4, and you just can't tap anymore, that's okay! Listen to your intuition, to your body. Do the best you can. Sometimes you might have to sit with that for a day or two, to process it further until you're ready to go back to it.

For an extended session on this topic, visit www.thetappingsolution.com/tap2.

Melissa's Results

After doing just 15 minutes of tapping with me, Melissa said, "You know, there really isn't that much to do for the book. What there is to do, I can handle. I just have to take it one step at a time and know it's not all going to get done at once."

A very different perspective indeed! So what happened? She still had just as much stuff to do after the tapping as before. Nothing changed there. So what *did* change? She quieted the noise in her head that was telling her the situation she was facing (everything she had to do for her book) was dangerous and overwhelming. Her mind and body had created a threat (the fight-or-flight response discussed in Chapter 1) where there really was none. She was of course in no physical danger, but her mental patterns around her issues were such that they were stressing her out and keeping her stuck.

I say it all the time: using EFT makes us more *resourceful*. We feel like we have more bandwidth to face the world around us. It's as if the brain turns on and lights up, the body aligns, and we can actually cope! It brings us to a place of peace and understanding—about ourselves, about others, and about our life situations.

Why is it that one person can go about a busy day in a peaceful state of mind, enjoying the challenges and moving effortlessly through tasks and events, while another person with the same number of tasks and challenges feels panicked, stressed out, and overwhelmed?

It's because one person has developed healthy, nurturing beliefs and ways of thinking—while the other has not. With EFT, we can change those unhealthy habits and patterns. We can stop reacting and start being. We can reduce the noise in our head and let go of the stress, feelings of being overwhelmed, and anxiety. When we do, as Melissa proves, we become so much more resourceful. We are able to move forward, and we are able to enjoy our lives!

· ·

Tapping Tip: What Are You Most Overwhelmed By? Talk and Tap

Those new to EFT often get stuck with the "what to say" part of tapping. They complain that they don't know if they're doing it right and don't know what language to use. One fun and easy way to get around the question of "what to say" is simply to talk in conversational language about your issue while tapping through the points. Rather than following the exact tapping protocol, you can tap the sequence while talking freely about the topic causing you distress.

For example, imagine you are on the phone with a friend and you are telling her about the awful day you had at work. You can just start tapping, right there on the phone! She doesn't need to know what you're doing. As you vent to her, you're calming your body and processing the emotions through tapping. You're also getting all the benefits of tapping without having to create a particular script.

There's nothing wrong with venting, letting off a little steam. The problem comes when you find yourself venting about the same thing over and over again, with no change and no resolution. Add tapping to the venting and a few things will happen:

a. You'll let go of the story much faster.

b. You'll begin to come to a new awareness about the issue.

c. You'll naturally come up with creative solutions.

I've had many people tell me that there's no solution to a particular situation. I nod and ask them to tap while telling me about their stress, or anger, or sadness. More often than not, they discover potential solutions they didn't even believe existed, right there in real time. So feel free to talk, rant, and rave, get it all out—just tap at the same time. You'll see how different it feels!

- -

The Stories You Tell

Lauren, a mother of two from Colorado, was struggling with some issues around her marriage, her weight, and generally feeling overwhelmed and depressed. She began our session by telling me what was going on in her life.

For 20 minutes straight, with barely a pause to catch a breath, she told me her story, focusing on a big, dramatic situation around work. I tried to interrupt her a few times to ask her how she felt, but I could barely get a word in.

Eventually, I put my hand up like a stop sign. That got a pause, and I lovingly but firmly said, "Lauren, no more stories. This is all one big, dramatic story, and it's not *you*."

She instantly got it. She stopped, took a deep breath, and said, "Oh, my God . . . all I do is tell these stories."

The issue wasn't what she was sharing with me; it was that she was so invested in her story. She had told it again and again—had thought about it over and over—and was replaying the same scenarios each time. She was not connecting with her feelings about the situation, and she was telling the story not from a place of analyzing it or looking for a solution, but rather for the sake of the story itself.

We all get caught up in our own personal soap operas, with their characters, drama, and rights and wrongs. We tell stories where other people have "done things" to us. Where the world is treating us harshly and no justice seems to be served. We tell stories that are full of anger, heartache, jealousy, fear, and every other negative emotion. We tell these stories to validate what we've done and what other people have done to us.

But after we've told these stories, what do we have? What have we gained?

Lauren's life wasn't going to change unless she stopped telling those same stories again and again. Now that she recognized that, we went on to tap on her habit of telling stories—rather than the issue about work, which is what she'd originally come to me about. We used these statements:

Even though I keep telling these stories and I'm all caught up in the drama, I deeply and completely accept myself.

Even though I keep running the same patterns again and again, I deeply and completely accept myself.

We then focused the tapping on her *emotions* about the story. It's not about ignoring the story altogether; it's about processing it in a positive direction. So when I asked Lauren how she felt about what was going on, she was able to slow down, connect with her heart, and say, "I feel like all this drama is about other people, the things I do for them. I feel resentful. I never put myself first."

This was a big life issue for Lauren, and we explored other places in her life where she wasn't taking care of herself, where she was putting others first and both parties were suffering for it. You know how, when on a plane, you're told to put on your own oxygen mask before helping someone else? It was true in Lauren's life. She recognized she needed to prioritize herself before giving to others. But would she actually do it?

One of the exciting things about EFT is its flexibility. It can be very successfully combined with other systems and processes, including guided visualization. I decided to try a combination with Lauren.

I told her that it sounded like she was running a computer program called Putting Other People First and asked her if she would like to install a new program called Putting Lauren First. She instantly connected to the analogy and agreed that she was running the wrong program and was ready to try something new.

Through a guided, closed-eye visualization, where she continued to tap through all the points, I took her through "uninstalling" her old program and "installing" the new program. The mind works in mysterious ways; I don't know why, but again and again, I've gotten great results from walking a client through such a process. Step by step, Lauren removed all the old files—her old habits—and installed new, healthier ones.

Did it work? We had met on a Friday, and here's a portion of the e-mail I got from her on Monday:

> It was a great weekend. . . . The coaching session helped catapult me into a new place! I have a new perspective of myself and others around me. It's like what I know in my mind "meshed with" what I feel in my heart. Some kind of true aligning. Before, I knew a lot in my mind, and I knew what I *wanted* to feel in my heart, but had a hard time bringing the two together. Now . . . there is no gap between what I know is right for me and *feeling* it is right for me. The emotion is aligned with the decisions in my head!

Looks like Lauren is telling a different story!

Ask Yourself . . . Questions about Your Story

What are the stories you're telling that you want to let go of?
What's the new story you want to tell about yourself and your life?
What are the old programs you're running that you want to delete?
What are the new programs you want to install?

"I'm Stressed Out about the World"

Most of us would be well served to never watch the news again. The amount of negativity, fear, and plain misinformation is terrible. At the same time, burying your head in the sand and not having any idea what's going on in the world might not be the best move either. So what to do? Is there a way to be informed and to focus on the issues that matter without getting so caught up that we're affected in a negative way?

I believe there is—and that EFT can help. The reality is that if we find ourselves stressed out about the planet, politics, wars, and other issues that matter to us, we are damaging our bodies and becoming less resourceful.

Getting upset about an important environmental issue doesn't do anything about the issue itself. Many of us have a false belief that nothing will change unless we become upset. The reality, however, is that we help effect change by *positive action*—not by being stressed out about the issue.

I witnessed this reality just a few weeks ago, through a close friend who cares deeply about animals. She'd become aware of a neighbor who was mistreating many dogs and a horse. She had called the proper authorities, but for certain legal reasons, they were powerless to do anything.

Together, we tapped through the emotions surrounding the situation: her anger, feelings of powerlessness (a common theme with world issues), sadness for the animals, and so forth.

When we were done, she felt more at peace and was able to look at what was happening from a new perspective. She still continued to care, but she was no longer miserable while she was doing it. That difference, that small distinction, is massive. We'll see specifically in the chapter on relationships how, when we change our beliefs, our state, and our approach, people around us change. The same thing is true when it comes to changing the world.

TAPPING SCRIPT: What's Stressing You Out Most?

(The tapping points chart can be found on page 21.)

Take a moment to think about what's going on in the world that's stressing you out. Then let's do some tapping to relieve it.

Karate Chop: Even though I'm stressed out about _____ [fill in the blank with your world issue], I choose to relax now.
Karate Chop: Even though I can't stop thinking about _____ [fill in the blank with your world issue], I deeply and completely accept myself.
Karate Chop: Even though I'm really worried about _____ [fill in the blank with your world issue], I choose to feel safe now.

Eyebrow: I'm so stressed out about this . . .
Side of Eye: It's not right . . .
Under Eye: All these problems in the world . . .
Under Nose: They stress me out . . .
Chin: All this worry . . .
Collarbone: All this anxiety . . .

Under Arm: About this problem . . .
Top of Head: And about the world.

Eyebrow: I need to worry about these problems . . .
Side of Eye: If I don't worry about these problems, who will?
Under Eye: I have to worry . . .
Under Nose: All this worry . . .
Chin: All this stress . . .
Collarbone: Nothing will change unless I worry . . .
Under Arm: Nothing will change unless I stress . . .
Top of Head: All this worry.

Keep tapping until you find some relief, and then do some positive rounds:

Eyebrow: I choose to relax . . .
Side of Eye: I choose to let go . . .
Under Eye: I can relax and still effect change . . .
Under Nose: I can let go of these negative emotions . . .
Chin: And still care . . .
Collarbone: I don't have to be stressed out to care . . .
Under Arm: I don't have to be stressed out to effect change . . .
Top of Head: Letting it all go.

For an extended tapping session on this topic,
visit www.thetappingsolution.com/tap3.

A New Perspective

You might have noticed a theme in this chapter: when we're looking at the anxiety, feelings of being overwhelmed, and pressures of modern life, what EFT does is provide us with a *change in perspective*.

We're not magically changing the situation—if I find something that does that, I'll be sure to let you know—but we're changing our perspective and reaction to it. One of the amazing things I've found in doing this work for the past ten years is that when you change your perspective, often your feelings, reactions, and the situation itself naturally change, too—most of the time for the better.

So use tapping to bring down the noise in your head and in your life to find a clearer perspective and begin telling a new story. It's possible to move through our busy lives, in a busy world, with grace, joy, and peace. EFT can make this a reality.

Exercise: I SHOULD . . .

The word *should* is a staple in most of our vocabularies. Unfortunately, it's an extremely loaded word—with guilt, fear, shame, regret, and other negative emotions attached to it. Often we don't even notice how we're subtly putting ourselves down, stressing ourselves out, and increasing our sense of being overwhelmed when we say, "I *should . . .*"

I should exercise more.
I should eat better.
I should work harder.
I should be thinner.
I should spend more time with my kids.
I should read more.
I should be a more attentive parent.
And it goes on and on . . . and on.

The problem with the word *should* is that it implies that we are not enough as we are. It shames us and focuses on our failures. If the statements in the list above used the word *choose* instead of *should,* they would feel—and be—a lot more empowering.

I *choose* to exercise more.
I *choose* to eat better.
I *choose* to work harder.
I *choose* to be thinner.
I *choose* to spend more time with my kids.
I *choose* to read more.
I *choose* to be a more attentive parent.

Feels better, doesn't it? So let's find out what the big *should*s are in our lives, tap on them, and then replace them with positive choices.

Grab a piece of paper and a pen or pencil, and make a list of everything you believe you "should" do. Use the list above to prompt you, but go beyond it into your personal experience. Knowing most of us, this won't be a hard list to make!

Once you have your list, we're going to tap through all of the *should*s, one by one.

So if one item is *I should exercise more,* tap on the karate chop point and say, "Even though I should exercise more, I deeply and completely accept myself." Repeat this three times.

Then continue to tap through the points, repeating at each one, "I should exercise more."

Keep going until you feel a shift, when the statement no longer feels true. From there, tap through the sequence again while making a positive choice, such as "I choose to exercise more." (That, or another statement that feels right. You might shift your thinking and decide you're already exercising enough!)

Go through each of your *should* statements, tapping on them until you feel a shift and then tapping in the new, positive emotions. If you have a lot of *should* statements, you might want to break them down and tap a few at a time, and then go back to more later or the next day.

Once you've tapped through all the statements, notice what you feel. If you're like most of my clients, you're going to be surprised by the amount of self-love, compassion, and overall peace you feel as you release all the *should*s in your life. If you find any of them creeping back in over the next few days or weeks, tap on them again!

A life free of *should*s is a life full of choices. When we choose, we are at our most empowered, free and joyful.

Further Exploration

Want to get a real grip on your daily stress? Get a free daily stress-relief meditation (normally sold for $19.95 and free to all purchasers of this book) at www.thetappingsolution.com/stress.

CHAPTER 4

OVERCOMING YOUR RESISTANCE TO CHANGE

Death is not the biggest fear we have;
our biggest fear is taking the risk to be alive—
the risk to be alive and express what we really are.

DON MIGUEL RUIZ

Now that we've quieted some of the mental noise of stress, feelings of being overwhelmed, and anxiety, we'll spend the rest of the book looking at how you can use EFT to create change in all areas of your life.

Because that's why you're here, right? You want to change. Whether it's to lose weight, heal a physical condition, improve your financial situation, improve your existing relationship, or attract a new one, you're here to shift something. That's the focus of this chapter: change.

But before we can start to effect real change, we need to look at a nagging little problem many of us have. Underneath the desire to change the circumstances of our lives, many of us harbor a sneaky saboteur: *an underlying resistance to change.* Inherently, most people don't like change. It's easier for things to stay the same. It takes less effort—it's what we know, so oftentimes some part of us *wants* to stay stuck. Like the proverb says: better the devil you know than the devil you don't. It can feel easier to deal with a situation that's familiar, even if it's not ideal, than to take a risk with an unknown person or thing. So when we start contemplating change in an aspect of our lives, resistance can come up quickly.

I can hear you now. "I don't have a fear of change! I *want* to lose weight! I *want* to make more money! I *want* to heal my body!"

I believe that you *consciously* want these things. I also know that, as humans, we often have subconscious or semiconscious beliefs, fears, and blocks. We say we want things to change, but somehow we remain stuck. We don't move forward, or worse, we backslide and lose ground.

Fear of Getting What You Want

Every human being wants to succeed—on the conscious level. Unfortunately, our unconscious often has its own agenda. The conscious mind is made up of the things we're aware of—the thoughts we have on a daily basis, the decisions we make, and so forth. The unconscious mind, on the other hand, is there behind the scenes, running the show. It's the hidden driver of our thoughts and decisions, and it mostly runs on experiences and programming from childhood.

How many times have you worked at changing something (like starting to exercise) only to find it didn't last? And then you got down on yourself, calling yourself names and coming up with unflattering reasons why you didn't and wouldn't do what it took to get the job done. The more you do this, the worse it gets. And the more experiences you have of failing, the less confidence you have the next time around, perpetuating that downward spiral.

Ask Yourself . . . Struggling with Change

Not sure if you struggle with change? Here are a few of the ways fear of change shows up. Recognize any of them?

- **Self-sabotage:** When things start to go well, you find some way to screw up.

- **Procrastination:** You find yourself not getting started or not following through.

- **Perfectionism:** It's got to be absolutely right before you can go forward.

- **Lack of clarity:** You don't start because you're not sure what you want.

- **Indecision:** Not deciding keeps you from moving forward.

If you have any of these patterns in your life, it's important to take a closer look at whether you might be resisting change. Unless you address that resistance, the struggle will continue.

A Downside of Losing Weight?

Marie had been saying for years that she needed to lose weight. She'd tried every diet on the planet, succeeded for a little while, then put the weight back on. She always fluctuated in the same range—a seven-pound variance.

When we began working together and talking about her weight, she said, "I can't seem to lose any more weight once I hit 130 pounds. It's like an alarm goes off, and I immediately sabotage myself. I either stop exercising, or start eating more food, or get off the diet I'm on. I find a way to put weight back on again, no matter what."

She knew something was going on psychologically, because it made no sense to always get stuck at that number. She had no conscious awareness or thoughts when she hit that weight that said, "Stop exercising! Stop eating well!" but she knew enough to know something was going on, because the pattern kept repeating itself.

I asked her some of the power questions you can also use to identify resistance to change (we'll cover them on the following page), and the one that immediately resonated with her was "Who will be hurt or upset if you lose all the weight you want and move past the 130-pound block?" She instantly replied, "My sister."

When I asked her to share more, she told me that, growing up, she always idolized her older sister. And she remembered clearly one day when her sister, obviously in a bad mood and with her own issues, said to her, "You are too pretty and too thin, and you make me feel like a fat cow."

This wasn't the only instance when her sister made her feel bad for standing out, but it was the most powerful memory. This memory, along with more recent confessions that Marie's successes made her sister feel like a failure, added up to Marie acquiring a belief that it wasn't safe or fun to be thin and pretty! So sure enough, she gained weight until she was in a "safe" zone. For her, unconsciously, it was more important to have her sister like her and approve of her than it was to be "thin and pretty."

Once she had this awareness, she could tap on the original event with her sister and her emotions around it. In the process, she changed her belief systems about losing weight. What's more, she also used tapping as a catalyst to change her relationship and response to her sister, which brought about healing in much deeper ways.

The beauty of identifying patterns such as these is that often they go beyond the original issue—here, it was weight loss—to affect many areas of our lives. When we can heal these relationships and patterns, dramatic change is possible.

Let's Take a Closer Look

We can think of ourselves as having two sides or parts. One part of us wants to experience personal growth, to be more of who we can be. But then there's another part that is governed by our need for certainty and familiarity. Change, either welcome or unwelcome, is unknown—and unknown means uncertain. Our response is to question our ability to handle the unknown. Our mind takes an inventory of past events and uses them to project the probability of success in the future. Depending on the information it gathers, we either move forward—or the fear response is triggered and forward progress is circumvented.

Ask Yourself . . . Change

Here are some great questions to ask yourself in order to identify
whether you have a resistance to change. Think about the change you're
trying to make and then ask yourself:

What will happen if this changes?
How will other people feel about it?
What pain might I experience if I make this change?
What will I lose if I make this change?

Resistance to Change

Understanding your resistance to change is vital, regardless of what it is you're trying to change. The underlying patterns are the same whether you are trying to heal
your body or make more money. That's why, throughout the book, we'll keep ref-
erencing these ideas to make sure you've cleared your resistance to change on each
particular subject.

I personally experienced resistance to change in a big way around growing my
business and having more financial success. A few years after college, I hit my stride
with a growing web development and marketing consulting business. I was earning an
annual income that was triple what most of my close friends were making.

To personally celebrate this success—and also to have a great time with friends—I
put together a weeklong vacation for 12 of us: two stunning villas in Mexico. We had
the time of our lives; it was a trip I'll never forget. It was a positive experience that re-
inforced my commitment to success. But the next year, when we tried to put the same
trip together again, those villas weren't available. As it turned out, each person was
going to be responsible for paying more.

I tried to round everybody up, but several people said they couldn't afford it. In my
enthusiasm for the trip and my friends, I tried to convince people how important it was
to get away, to be together, and to have another great experience. The response I got,
from one friend in particular, was, "We don't all make as much money as you do. We
can't just do whatever we want to do."

It wasn't a pleasant conversation. I walked away feeling bad for being enthusiastic—
and bad for making more money than my friends. Was my financial success making
people mad at me? Jealous? Was I losing friends because of it?

At the time, I wasn't confident enough—and my sense of deserving financial rewards wasn't strong enough—to take the shock of having conflict with my friends over finances. (I hadn't tapped through all those issues yet!) Sure enough, within 12 months, my finances turned around completely. I incurred a massive amount of personal debt, clients who were supposed to pay me didn't, and jobs I needed fell through. I found myself in a very different place—a place where I could commiserate with my friends. We were all in the same boat, and nobody could be jealous of me or my financial success.

It wasn't until I realized what had happened, learned EFT, and tapped through my issues—my sense of deserving, my comfort with making more money than my friends, my sense of being okay with being different—that I was able to truly get back on my financial feet and once again create prosperity for myself.

Ask Yourself . . . Peeling Back the Layers

One of the ways we can help peel back the layers so we can see our hidden agendas is to ask ourselves a powerful question:

- What's the *upside* of staying stuck where I am (or keeping the problem)?

Be willing to play with this question. Really give some thought to how staying in your current situation is serving you. This may require reaching into your subconscious mind, perhaps closing your eyes and digging a little deeper than usual.
Now ask yourself:

- What's the *downside* of things changing (or getting over the problem)?

Again, allow yourself to entertain the idea that there are some downsides to things changing.
Here are some responses I've heard from my clients. See if they resonate with you. What's the *upside* of things staying as they are?

- *I won't have to change anything.*
- *I get to keep doing what I've been doing.*
- *People won't expect more from me.*
- *I'm familiar with it.*
- *I won't be making someone else uncomfortable.*

What's the *downside* of things changing? What will be different?

- *I'll be noticed, more visible.*

- *I won't be able to handle it.*
- *There will be more responsibility.*
- *People will expect more from me.*
- *I'll have to work hard to keep it.*
- *I won't be able to keep it.*
- *I won't have time to relax.*
- *What if I put all this effort into it and it doesn't work out?*
- *They can judge or criticize me.*

You've just discovered some reasons why you *wouldn't want to change*—and reasons why you've had to work so hard to get the changes you have made to stick. No matter how many reasons you have for wanting what you want, the reasons you have for not wanting those changes are more powerful. They win out every time! We'll tap on this resistance to change in just a moment; for now, just let yourself become aware of these issues and how they might be operating in your life.

Who Am I Trying to Protect?

Protection is a central issue for all of us. Anything that feels like a safety risk activates the limbic centers in the brain, sending us into the classic fight-or-flight response. Our mind is weighing the risks associated with doing, having, or getting something new with change, which equals the unknown and uncertainty. One of the questions it's asking is "Will this change be good for me?" If the answer is "No, this change *isn't* good for me, because it will be too much responsibility," then subconsciously you'll be looking for a way to keep the change from happening.

The brain is hardwired to look for danger and to focus on the negative, for the obvious reason that our body wants to stay physically safe. Our ancestral, ancient brain is watching for that tiger, looking for that bear, and it is programmed to notice danger first—before it looks for the "good in life." Can you imagine telling our ancient ancestors to stay positive? To not be so negative and fearful about the tiger attacking them? Or, even more dramatically, asking, "Did you know that if you focus on the positive things in your life, the tiger won't get you?"

That would have been an absurd statement back then. Thankfully, our modern world is much changed, and we have the leisure to focus on needs beyond basic survival. However, our brains haven't fully caught up with this change.

TAPPING SCRIPT: Anxiety about Change

(The tapping points chart can be found on page 21.)

If you're like most of us, your anxiety has started to rise just *talking* about change. Well, there's no time like the present to do a little tapping. Choose something you want to change in your life, and test the check-in statement *I feel anxiety about changing* _____. Give it a number on the 0-to-10 scale and start tapping.

Karate Chop: Even though I don't feel safe enough to change right now, I still accept myself.

Karate Chop: Even though I'm not willing to dig deep and clear out these issues, I'm accepting myself and that this is where I am.

Karate Chop: Even though I now know that I have reasons why it doesn't feel okay to change, I'm open to accepting myself and these feelings.

Now tap through the points:

Eyebrow: I don't want to talk about change . . .
Side of Eye: I don't even want to tap about change . . .
Under Eye: I just want to be left alone . . .
Under Nose: But it's not comfortable being where I am either . . .
Chin: It's scary to look at this . . .
Collarbone: I'm not sure I'm willing to do it . . .
Under Arm: I'm not sure it's safe to do this . . .
Top of Head: I get pretty anxious just talking about change.

And a positive round:

Eyebrow: There are some things I'm ready to change . . .
Side of Eye: Maybe I'm more ready than I thought . . .
Under Eye: What if I really start to like the changes I'm making?
Under Nose: What if I'm already making small changes?
Chin: And it's easier than I thought . . .
Collarbone: I wonder what changed . . .
Under Arm: That's making it so easy for me to decide . . .
Top of Head: That it's okay to start making changes now!

Physical Pain to Prevent Emotional Pain?

Joan had developed severe back pain, which kept her virtually incapacitated and unable to work. She was on disability, and she was honest in sharing with me that while she was in a lot of pain, there were some good things about her situation.

She got a steady disability payment, which—while it wasn't much—covered her bills. Her last job before the injury had been a miserable one, with a boss who was borderline abusive. When I asked her to think about her back healing, she instantly started stressing out about going back to work. There were clearly some connected issues there.

We tapped through her anxiety about going back to work, her comfort with being on disability, how her life would change if the pain subsided, and the upsides and downsides of it all. Even before we addressed the physical issue, tapping on her resistance to change dramatically reduced her pain.

She wanted to know if some part of her was causing her pain in order to keep herself from having to work. I suggested that, rather than causing, she might have been *contributing* to the pain. To accuse oneself of causing such a thing is a heavy burden that none of us needs to carry. One of the challenges I see when people start exploring the connection between emotion and physical issues is that it can be easy to add guilt to the already-heavy burden—which creates even more distress.

Instead, we can explore these issues, this resistance to change, with compassion for ourselves—knowing that we are doing the best we can with the resources we have. Ultimately, as we've already discussed, our bodies and minds are just trying to keep us safe. Once we recognize our need for safety, we can directly address our resistance to change, clear it with tapping, and then actualize the change itself.

So—what do you do after you make the discovery that you're trying to keep yourself or someone else safe? Start the tapping, of course!

TAPPING SCRIPT: It's Not Safe to Change

(The tapping points chart can be found on page 21.)

The check-in phrase is *It's not safe for me to change.* Give it a number on the 0-to-10 scale, and start tapping.

Karate Chop: Even though it isn't safe for me to change, I'm accepting how I feel.

Karate Chop: Even though I won't be able to keep myself safe if I make this change, I'm open to a new perspective.

Karate Chop: Even though I've been holding myself back from making this change because I need to protect myself, I'm accepting that this is where I am, and I'm open to seeing this change with new eyes.

Now tap through the points:

Eyebrow: It doesn't feel safe to make these changes . . .
Side of Eye: I won't know how to protect myself if I make them . . .
Under Eye: I know it would be painful . . .
Under Nose: And I want to protect myself . . .
Chin: I'm not sure how to keep myself safe if I make this change . . .
Collarbone: It might be really hard to keep myself safe . . .
Under Arm: I don't know if I know how to keep myself safe . . .
Top of Head: I don't know if I can learn to keep myself safe.

And now a positive round:

Eyebrow: What if I could be safe and make this change?
Side of Eye: What if I have more resources than I thought?
Under Eye: Perhaps it's not as hard as I thought . . .
Under Nose: There's a chance that I'm already doing some of it . . .
Chin: Sometimes I do feel more relaxed . . .
Collarbone: Maybe I can find ways to do that more often . . .
Under Arm: I can make changes and protect myself . . .
Top of Head: I love feeling my confidence grow daily.

For an extended tapping session on this topic,
visit www.thetappingsolution.com/tap4.

What Do You Really Want?

We all say we want change, but as we've explored in this chapter, the conscious desire isn't always steering the ship. So what if you could get your unconscious concerns in alignment with the part of you that *is* ready for change?

Imagine how effortless change would be then. If you don't get in alignment with the change you desire, it's either not going to happen or it will feel like an uphill battle. Losing weight becomes a miserable experience where you deprive yourself and hate going to the gym. Making more money is a burden if it involves countless hours of work you despise. Change simply doesn't feel good if we're not in alignment with it.

However, once we identify our limiting beliefs (both real and imaginary) and tap on them, we can move toward our goals with ease and joy. Take, for example, the belief that losing weight is going to be miserable because you have to go to the gym and you hate the gym. You could either tap on your hatred of the gym, or you could tackle the belief that in order to lose weight, you have to go to the gym and be miserable. If you tap on the latter, you might discover something new. Maybe you'll realize, "Actually, I could start playing tennis, which is a great exercise that I love." Now you're aligned with the process of change, because it feels fun and safe.

Be kind to yourself when addressing your resistance to change. Recognize that it's an ongoing process and you're not going to find every little bit of resistance at once. But even uncovering just one layer of resistance can open a door. Change is one of the great truths of life. We're always toggling between our desire for certainty—keeping things the way they are—and our desire to grow and change. Tapping can really help, but it's an ongoing process. You'll make a change, get comfortable with the new circumstances, desire to grow again, encounter your resistance to change, tap through it, make the change, get comfortable with it . . . well, you get the idea! This is why it's a great idea to bookmark this chapter. Then, you can come back and repeat the tapping scripts on a regular basis to keep your change muscles flexible.

Exercise: Digging Deeper

Try this little experiment to see if you're fully lined up to experience the change you desire.

Imagine that you've achieved the things you have been wanting. Maybe you are now at your goal weight and looking hot, or you've got that successful business and it's making millions. Maybe you have your health back and you're ready to get back into life, or maybe you've met the new love of your life.

Now see yourself driving up to a beautiful home in a big expensive car, dressed to the hilt, smiling from ear to ear, and feeling good about life. As you walk in the front door, you enter a room filled with all your friends and family. You have gathered them here to share with them about your good fortune.

How does it feel?

- ❑ Completely relaxed, never felt better.
- ❑ Some discomfort, not really sure about all of this.
- ❑ Whoa! This is uncomfortable!

What is their reaction?

- ❑ Everyone is so happy for me!
- ❑ They look concerned and uneasy.
- ❑ They look mad!

What is your reaction?

- ❑ I'm elated; this feels as good as I always thought it would!
- ❑ It's really uncomfortable.
- ❑ I want to get out of here!

If you answered the first one each time, then good for you! Chances are, you're moving forward toward your goals with ease and joy. If you answered yes to either the second or third answer, then congratulations to you as well. Now you know there are some hidden obstacles to achieving the success you desire. With that knowledge, you can do something about it—like tapping!

CHAPTER 5

TAPPING THROUGH YOUR PAST

The knowledge of the past stays with us. To let go is simply to release any images and emotions, grudges and fears, clingings and disappointments that bind our spirit.

JACK KORNFIELD

Judy was angry at her father.

He never hugged her. He never showed her any physical attention. He didn't show up at parent-teacher conferences. He favored her brothers over her. He never held her hand.

Judy's anger, her rage about how her father treated her, her sadness about how he *should* treat her, the depression she experienced because of it—all these emotions—were affecting her deeply.

This situation would have been bad enough if Judy were a teenager, living at home with her parents. What made it worse was that Judy was 63 years old. She'd been angry, hurt, and upset at her father for more than 50 years.

How can this be? Why is it that we store these emotions, these memories, these tragedies for so long? And why do they matter so much?

Shouldn't we just let go of the past and move on? Why are we harping on things that happened so long ago and don't seem relevant anymore? Why is a 63-year-old so upset at her long-deceased father?

We'll explore these questions and more as we look at how events from your past might be affecting your present—and your future.

Be forewarned, part of you is going to want to skip this chapter. Looking at the past can be difficult. It's much easier to talk about your current stress, the things you have going on in your life now, than to look at your childhood and the relationships you had or have with your parents.

But the relief you'll feel—and the change you'll experience when you finally process and release these events and memories—will be astounding. I've seen more dramatic, lasting results from addressing childhood issues than virtually any other work. More often than not, what you think of as your current issues—your extra weight, your trouble with finances, your relationship problems—are rooted in experiences of your childhood.

Childhood Trauma and the Body

Childhood trauma, unresolved events, and unprocessed emotions don't just affect us emotionally and spiritually; they have profound effects on the physical body. The Adverse Childhood Experiences study, or ACE, is a research project undertaken by Kaiser Permanente and the Centers for Disease Control. A huge study examining the medical histories of more than 17,000 adults, the ACE study found direct correlations between unresolved childhood emotional trauma and several physical conditions. These include heart disease, cancer, diabetes, stroke, high blood pressure, bone fractures, depression, and drug use.

Compared to a person with an ACE score of 0, a person with high numbers of adverse childhood experiences is nearly three times more likely to smoke and a whopping 30 times more likely to attempt suicide. Many of the participants in the study were older than 60, showing that these childhood events were affecting the physical body decades later.

Many other studies have confirmed these findings, including Renee D. Goodwin and Murray B. Stein's 2004 study "Association Between Childhood Trauma and Physical Disorders Among Adults in the United States," which states that:

Childhood physical abuse, sexual abuse, and neglect were associated with a statistically significantly increased risk of a wide range of physical illnesses during adulthood. After adjusting for demographic characteristics, lifetime anxiety, and depressive disorders, alcohol and substance dependence, and all types of trauma: results showed that childhood physical abuse was associated with increased risk of lung disease . . . , peptic ulcer . . . and arthritic disorders . . . ; childhood sexual abuse was associated with increased risk of cardiac disease . . . ; and childhood neglect was associated with increased risk of diabetes . . . and autoimmune disorders.

Dr. Gabor Maté, a physician and best-selling author, speaks to this issue when he says:

In most cases of breast cancer, the stresses are hidden and chronic. They stem from childhood experiences, early emotional programming and unconscious psychological coping styles. They accumulate over a lifetime to make someone susceptible to disease. . . . Research has suggested for decades that women are more prone to develop breast cancer if their childhoods were characterized by emotional disconnection from their parents or other disturbances in their upbringing; if they tend to repress emotions, particularly anger; if they lack nurturing social relationships in adulthood; and if they are the altruistic, compulsively caregiving types.

As these examples illustrate, research continues to point toward a mind-body connection, and it is starting to reveal more about how our emotions show up in our physiology.

The Big *T* and the Little *t*

You might have read the above couple of paragraphs and thought, *This doesn't apply to me, I didn't experience any abuse.* But sometimes it's not the huge traumas that affect us most. As my friend and EFT expert Carol Look says, "There's trauma with a big *T* and trauma with a little *t*."

Big-*T* trauma includes major events in our lives—an accident, an earthquake, 9/11, a house burning down. Then there's also little-*t* trauma: traumatic experiences that accumulate over a long period of time. Often we're not even aware that they are occurring. If you grew up in a household with an alcoholic parent who constantly berated you or made you feel unsafe, if you were bullied in school, or if you were neglected by your family, then you likely experienced a long string of small traumas that can add up to major trauma in adulthood.

One word of caution as we explore this topic: while EFT is very safe and effective, it's up to you to decide which memories you are comfortable exploring. If just thinking about something that happened in childhood makes you shiver, it might not be a good idea to start tapping on it by yourself. For major abuse, turn to a therapist who uses EFT or to an experienced EFT practitioner with whom you feel comfortable and who has experience with these kinds of issues. You can find a list of practitioners at www.thetappingsolution.com/eft-practitioners.

The same caution goes if you have a friend or family member whom you want to help with EFT. You can certainly teach them the process, tap with them on all sorts of issues, and provide great support and assistance to them. If, however, it feels like the tapping is going somewhere that doesn't seem safe, where you don't have enough experience—or if it feels outside your comfort zone—get help.

Our Current and Future Reality

The physical effect that childhood experiences can have on the body is clearly demonstrated in the studies we've discussed. But the effects of childhood trauma go well beyond the physical body. They impact the whole of who we are. Our patterns, beliefs, habits, and emotional reactions are formed through, and are thus deeply affected by, childhood experiences.

A vast majority of our understanding of the world is formed before the age of seven. During this period, events make a lasting impression; in essence, they shape our personality—our beliefs about the world and how we approach it. Why is it that one person cruises through life feeling content, joyful, fulfilled, and excited, while another struggles, never feeling safe, feeling that the world is a dangerous place, that happiness is difficult? More often than not, childhood experiences determine these characteristics.

Sonia, a massage and EFT practitioner from Florida, came to me to work on some financial issues she was having. She had a laundry list of limiting beliefs about money, her skills, and how the world operated. She had done tapping on some of them but felt she hadn't gone deep enough or addressed the root cause. She'd feel better for a while but then go back to her old patterns.

When I spoke to her and read her intake form, it became clear that while she certainly had a lot of limiting beliefs about money that we could work on, she still had some deep wounds from a tough childhood. Her mother had been an alcoholic, and the situation at home was always extremely difficult. She shared with me one specific memory that had been coming up over and over again—a vivid scene where she recalled walking into the bathroom and seeing her mother bleeding, having slit her wrists. Her father was there as well, stemming the bleeding and making sure her mother didn't die. The memory was vague for Sonia, but I could tell it was still affecting her emotionally.

I told her that while we could certainly work on her limiting beliefs about money, my intuition told me to focus on this event and other childhood trauma first. I asked her if she felt safe going there and if she was ready to take a close look at it, and she firmly said she was. I always find it's better to give a client the choice when addressing difficult issues, rather than just diving into them. That initial affirmation of personal strength and power can often be the driving force for the rest of the session and can improve results.

She began tapping, moving through each point at her own pace. As she tapped, I asked her to describe, to the best of her recollection, what happened with her mother. She described her memory of the scene. I probed her about what she felt, saw, smelled, and so forth, to get as many details as possible. When she was done telling the story, I asked her to tell it to me again. And then again, and then again. Each time I probed for more details, more emotions. At one point I said to her, "What did this event teach you about life?" And she responded, "That I'm never safe. That my mom can die at any time, and I always have to worry about her."

- -

Tapping Tip: The Movie Technique

The Movie Technique was developed by EFT founder Gary Craig as a way to address specific events while not getting caught up in more global issues. Imagining that you are narrating a movie about an event pretty much guarantees that you are dealing with that specific event. A movie has a beginning and an end. There are central characters who do and say specific things, and there is a usually a crescendo, or peak moment. Use the movie technique to work through a specific memory or event from your past that still holds an energetic charge.

One of the really great things about this technique is that at no point in this movie is it necessary for you to tell or say the details out loud: *you can do the whole thing in your head while tapping along.* The critical part is that the details of the movie engage all five senses. Focus on the sights, sounds, emotions, and physical feelings, and what the characters are thinking, and, if appropriate, smelling or tasting. The following questions will help you to set the stage for your movie.

How long will the movie last? You want to make sure it is short—three minutes or less. Often the key traumatic event in the movie takes only seconds. If there are several peaks or traumatic moments in the movie, break down the experience into as many three-minute movies as necessary.

What will the title be? Create a name specific to that movie segment.

Now that you have a specific event that has been turned into a short movie with a title, run the film in your mind. Evaluate the intensity you experience as you imagine the scene, on a scale of 0 to 10. If it feels unsafe to feel the event or emotion too deeply, you can also *guess* what your intensity would be were you to vividly imagine it.

Next, do several rounds of tapping while running the movie in your mind.

Check back on the intensity. Typically it will have come down by several points.

Then run the movie in your mind again. This time, start from a point that has no intensity or a very low intensity—and *stop whenever you feel any intensity arise and begin tapping.* This is very important! Most of us have lived with trauma for so long that we don't even notice how we push ourselves through the story, regardless of how it feels. Not anymore! With EFT, when we recognize these moments of intensity, they provide us with the perfect opportunity for tapping.

Run through the movie in your mind again, beginning to end, stopping to tap on any intense aspects as they come up. Continue until you can play the entire movie without any charge arising.

Finally, run the movie one more time. Exaggerate the sights, sounds, and colors. Really *try* to get upset about it. If you find some intensity coming back up, stop and tap again!

Note: It can be helpful to speak the events of your movie out loud, narrating it as if you were telling the story to a friend. Be sure you stop at any point that is upsetting—even just a little bit—and tap again until you are at a zero. Then continue the narration of the movie where you left off. If it feels more comfortable for you, you can tap in silence, just seeing the movie in your mind, or you can use language to describe what you see and what you feel. It's up to you!

• •

Sonia and I tapped on the memory, running the event again and again until she could witness it without an emotional charge. In this particular case, I had her tap while keeping her eyes closed. That can help people relax and access the memory more fully. If you find yourself distracted, try closing your eyes while tapping.

Once we both felt that the event in the bathroom with her mother was clear, I asked Sonia to share more of her childhood memories with me, and we tapped on those as well. I asked her to bring to mind all the times she could remember her mother being drunk, all the times Sonia worried about her dying, every scene she could think of around this difficult childhood, and put them in a visual pile in front of her. From there, we tapped on that pile rather than each individual event.

It was an emotional session, with a lot of tears—followed by the joy of relief at the end. So what happened from these 45 minutes spent tapping on these old memories? I'll let Sonia tell you in her own words:

> After a very intense session with Nick, I felt exhausted that evening. I was very quiet; I felt soft. My family actually noticed how quiet I was. I was at peace with the quiet. I went to bed fairly early, and it seemed like all night I thought or dreamed, "I am safe in my body." This was a piece I worked on with Nick. It came to mind over and over; I just kept affirming it over and over, but not like I was trying. It happened naturally.
>
> I had a very emotional week. I was very tired, like I needed sleep, a lot of sleep, but it was a healthy need. I felt tender; I felt like I was so clear with myself. My eating preferences just shifted. No sugar cravings. My attention was present, and I felt clearly supportive to each person I encountered.
>
> I also wanted to share a few things that have opened up this week. Around money, no charge or angst about it. Not when I think about it, talk about, or make it. I have been searching for a group of women to work with, and I was invited to a gathering Friday night with 25 women. It was so powerful. Out of that, I have been asked to do a small class on EFT with four to six of these women. One of them is already a client.
>
> I have created the title for my book. I am also working on my website, bio, etc., and I have ordered business cards for EFT coaching.
>
> It has been an amazing experience. I look forward to life every day. Looking from joy, love, and happiness, my body, mind, and spirit are all different.

If you're anything like me, you just read the above e-mail from Sonia and wondered, "Really??? All of this happened from one 45-minute session?" I'm still amazed that results this powerful happen this quickly, but sometimes they do! As we saw in Chapter 1, this work is literally retraining the brain and body. When you get to the root cause, the results can be astounding.

You might also be wondering how it is that we worked on a childhood event and Sonia's current experience around money changed completely. While there are no definitive answers explaining exactly how this happens, it's my belief that when we address and heal powerful root issues and beliefs, such as *I'm not safe in my body*, it has a cascade effect on the rest of our lives.

It's as if a defective operating system of a computer is completely replaced with a new, healthy, well-functioning system. Have you ever found that after a few years your computer runs slower, crashes more frequently, and doesn't function as well? These traumatic events from childhood do the same thing!

A person who is walking around with the belief *I am safe in my body* is going to approach the world from a very different place than someone who doesn't believe that. That person will be more confident in approaching others, as Sonia was in sharing her business at the women's event. They're going to be much more willing to put themselves out in the world, to be vulnerable in relationships, and to be willing to risk and dare, because they're operating from a place of safety.

Professional Profile: Eric Robins, M.D.

Dr. Eric Robins, a board-certified urologist and surgeon in private practice who is affiliated with a major hospital in the Los Angeles area, has successfully used EFT with his patients for the last 13 years.

Even before medical school, Dr. Robins had an interest in alternative medicine. A few members of his family had chronic illnesses that were not responding to the allopathic model. As he started his residency, he developed chronic fatigue—another disease that responds best to alternative modalities.

Taking his first class on EFT in 1998, he decided to test it on himself. He was looking to increase his energy level, and the results he experienced amazed him. Shortly after that class, he noticed that some of his private-practice patients were getting urinary tract infections while others were not, even though all were sexually active. What he discovered was that the patients who developed UTIs usually had emotional trauma of some sort, and he recognized that for them to get results and heal, he'd have to do something to heal that trauma. Enter EFT!

He estimates that about 90 percent of his patients have emotional issues or past traumas that either contribute to their illness or hinder the healing process. This, along with his own personal experiences with EFT, led him to look more closely at psychological release methods. Ultimately, he started using tapping while working with patients.

"EFT is the best mind-body technique out there," he says, because it is "quick and easy for use in a clinical environment."

Dr. Robins's passion for helping his patients was evident in my conversation with him. He shared with me his first experience of using EFT with a family friend. This man was a Vietnam veteran and suffered from severe PTSD.

"He had horrible night terrors," Dr. Robins told me. "We started tapping on the specific memories from Vietnam that were the most traumatic. We tapped on those memories until he got to a neutral place, where they weren't affecting him emotionally any further. Months later, I ran into him at a family function, and his wife shared with me that the night terrors had disappeared, and he was doing much better."

As we spoke, Dr. Robins clarified that if a patient comes to see him, he has a professional obligation to first rule out any physical cause using conventional medical tools and resources. However, his general belief is that the body has an amazing power to heal itself, and if a patient is able to clear emotional and traumatic issues that are held in the body, then the physical issues can heal.

Another incredible result Dr. Robins witnessed concerned a patient in his early 40s. This man had urinary retention problems and wasn't responding well to treatment or medication. Within five minutes of meeting with the patient and his wife, his wife revealed a traumatic incident that happened to the patient when he was five years old. It was a terrifying medical procedure that left this man in a deep state of fear, both conscious and unconscious.

Immediately Dr. Robins started tapping with the patient, clearing out the emotional trauma and memories of that initial experience. His body had remained in a state of hypervigilance and panic, and it was affecting him physically. Within two weeks, his initial problem, which medical treatment and medication weren't able to help, was fully resolved.

Imagine if doctors around the country and world used Dr. Robins's approach to healing. Not only would they help their patients get healthier and healthier, but the whole medical model—with its associated exorbitant financial costs and oftentimes disappointing results—could change dramatically.

The Things That Were Left Unsaid

Sonia and I focused on releasing the charge from specific memories. That's just one approach to healing childhood issues. Another effective approach is to give a voice to what we wanted to say as children but couldn't. Children are often told to be quiet, not to speak unless spoken to, that their opinions don't matter, and so forth. And often a child doesn't have the verbal cognition to express what he or she is feeling—much less share it with an authority figure.

Remember Judy from the beginning of the chapter, and her anger at her father? When she shared with me how she felt, I asked her to say, out loud, "I'm angry at my father" and rate the truth and intensity of the statement on the 0-to-10 scale. As you can imagine, it was beyond a 10 for her. Even as she said the statement, I could feel her anger bursting forth. So we did the most basic tapping: *Even though I'm angry at my father, I deeply and completely accept myself.*

We then tapped through the points with the statement *I'm angry at my father.*

As we went through the points, I didn't have to encourage Judy in any way—she was speaking it out loud, with force. I told her to keep tapping through the points, again and again, and keep repeating the same statement, *I'm angry at my father.*

She continued for at least 20 minutes, saying the same exact statement with no prodding from me. I was astonished by the intensity of emotion and how much she just wanted to keep saying it. It was also interesting to see that, as she progressed through the statements, I could sense her emotions changing. At first, the anger was real, raw anger. As she continued, it subtly changed until she was saying the first statement, but the emotion she was feeling was sadness.

Almost like a child who throws a temper tantrum and gets out all this bottled-up emotion, then collapses, exhausted, Judy had to express what she had kept inside for so long. The good thing is that she did this while tapping, thus clearing the emotional charge, relaxing the body progressively, and retraining her limbic system toward a new response.

At one point, when Judy was calm, I asked her to switch her statement and pretend that she was talking to her father. I had her imagine being able to tell him, with no consequences, exactly how she felt. She shared her deep sadness, her grief for the lack of love she felt from him. She shared how hurt she was, how she was only a small child who wanted love. She asked him, "Why? Why did you not love me the way you loved my brothers?" She cried, and tapped, and spoke her truth, and finally found the voice she never had. She told her father, "I am worth something! I deserve to be loved!"

I followed up with Judy a few weeks later, and her response was one I see often with childhood work. She said that she felt lighter than she ever had, happier and more free. She had even been thinking about her father and how much she loved him! Truly, when we heal the past, our whole experience of life can change.

- -

Tapping Tip: The Things Left Unsaid

I've found that one of the most powerful processes when working on childhood issues is to go back in time and say what you wish you could have said.

Start by going back to the memory of the event or experience. Replay it in your mind, as you did with the Movie Technique discussed on pages 66–67.

Then, whenever it feels right, say out loud what you wish you could have said back then. Tap along as you speak. Follow your intuition and speak your truth. You might even hear the other person speak back to you; if so, simply respond in turn. Continue tapping and talking until you feel you're complete and the situation has been resolved and healed.

- -

Going through this process also helps people get clear on whether they want to, in present time, say something to the people involved. For example, I worked with a client who was sexually abused by her brother. We went through the process as she envisioned saying exactly how she felt, even speaking it out loud. She spoke about how much she had been hurt by his actions and how it had affected her whole life.

After we went through it, she told me that she'd been wanting to say that for years, and it felt so good to get it out. She also said that she hadn't yet made a decision about whether to confront him in person, but she felt much more able to consider it after our work together. She felt that she could make the decision that was best for everyone involved.

When It's Really Stored in the Body

My experience of working with a young woman by the name of Rachel made it clearer to me than ever that we store trauma in the body. Rachel came to me concerned about intimacy issues with her husband. She loved him dearly, they had what seemed like a wonderful life together, but she really struggled with being intimate with him. Whenever he touched certain parts of her body—including her genital area, but also the outside of her legs, her back, the sides of her hips—she recoiled.

She felt terrible about it, and her guilt only added to the issues that this problem was causing. When I asked her if she had any memories of events that might have caused this freeze response, she said that she had vague recollections but couldn't get any further than that. This is often the case with childhood trauma. People say, "I just don't remember." I've learned that sometimes you have to get creative in approaching the issue.

On a whim, I had her draw a picture of herself and mark the spots on her body that felt uncomfortable. This was purely intuition; perhaps I was trying to channel her inner child by having her draw!

. . . .

Tapping Tip: Creativity and Intuition

The basics of EFT are, well, basic! They're simple and easy to learn. But once you have them down, feel free to get creative in your use of the process. Follow your intuition as to what you or someone you're helping needs.

. . . .

Once Rachel marked the spots, I had her number them from least sensitive to most sensitive. We began tapping with the least sensitive and simply saying, *Even though I don't want to be touched on my arms, I deeply and completely accept myself* and *Even though I panic when someone touches my arms, I choose to relax now.*

I had her visualize someone touching her arms, and we kept on tapping until she could hold that picture without any feelings of panic or fear. We then proceeded to do the same thing for all the spots on her body. She said she felt relaxed and much lighter and better. Then I asked her if she really wanted to get to the root of it, and she said, "Yes!"

A word of caution here: what I did next is not traditional. Then again, *I'm* not traditional! I work with people on a coaching basis; I'm not a licensed therapist. I'm simply someone who cares deeply and has a certain level of mastery working with people using EFT. I also happened to have a very close relationship with Rachel, so there was some leeway to try things that might be a little outside the norm. But regardless, I'm committed to helping people, and I'll do whatever it takes to get the result.

To really test how Rachel was doing and to clear out the trauma on a deeper level, I asked my wife, Brenna, to help me. Brenna also had a close relationship with Rachel and was in the house that day. I asked Rachel if it was okay for Brenna to gently touch her on the arms. Rachel agreed, and Brenna touched her arms while Rachel tapped. At first Rachel recoiled slightly, but then as she continued to tap, she relaxed.

We kept going, round after round, until there was no sensitivity in her arms. At the end, she said, "That feels really nice!"—the appropriate response to a loving touch. We proceeded to go through several other sensitive parts of her body (only focusing on those that were appropriate to address in this setting, of course). One spot we worked on was the sides of her rib cage. Rachel shared that if someone tried to tickle her there, she would get borderline violent and extremely angry.

First I had Rachel tap, visualizing someone tickling her. When she felt comfortable enough, I had Brenna try to tickle her. Rachel laughed a little, but then when Brenna grabbed her in a certain way, I could see fury in Rachel's face. She knew it too—she'd gotten triggered. We continued to tap and tap until that cleared. Then Brenna tested it again, grabbing Rachel's sides, with no negative response.

The last part of her body we worked on was the outside of her legs. This is where it got tricky. As soon as Brenna touched the outside of Rachel's legs, she immediately went "out of body"—disassociating from the experience. Her body froze; she couldn't think and couldn't feel. Something had been activated in a deep way, and she was stuck. Continuing to tap didn't seem to move the issue. She was just too disassociated. I had to get her back in her body and try again.

Fortunately, her body was fine with being tickled now—so I had Brenna do that, which made Rachel laugh and brought her back into her body. We continued to tap, and then Brenna went back to the legs. When Rachel told me she had "left her body" again, we went back to tickling. Back and forth, back and forth, until she was able to stay in her body while the outside of her legs were being touched.

Eventually she was able to be fully comfortable with the experience. Once again she said, "That feels nice!"

I'm covering this story in such detail because I've seen so many people, particularly women, who have really painful issues around their bodies being touched in intimate ways. To forfeit that feeling of safety around human contact, sexual or platonic, is a major loss. Our bodies are meant to be held, touched, and loved. It's been clearly demonstrated that babies who aren't held enough aren't as healthy; they don't "thrive" the way those who are cared for and nurtured do. Very little changes as adults, though we like to pretend it does. Issues of intimacy are also paramount in having healthy primary relationships, as we'll cover further in the chapter on relationships.

So how is Rachel doing now? It didn't take long for her to experience great results from this work. She called me the next day, excited to share that—ahem—she had had a *wonderful* time with her husband the previous night. She felt more loved, cared for, and safe than ever before!

Having Compassion for Yourself and Others

If there's one thing I've gained from working with people on their childhood traumas, it's a deep level of compassion. I've heard so many stories and so much pain from so many people. Now when I see someone in the world acting out—being violent, unhappy, or rude; letting people down; or hurting me or the world in some way—I know they've likely experienced deep trauma. In almost all cases, they are simply reacting, doing the only thing they know how to do.

That doesn't mean we should excuse negative behavior. But it does open the door for a deeper level of compassion and understanding. When your life partner isn't physically open with you, you can ask, "What happened?" instead of feeling rejected, angry, and upset. When someone lashes out at you in anger, you can ask, "What happened?" as opposed to lashing back at them. We all have stories to tell that need healing. We can use EFT to finally let them go, to heal and create a new future for ourselves and for our loved ones.

And let's not forget having compassion for ourselves and for our journey. Instead of beating yourself up for reacting a certain way, for not being perfect, for not being able to have the control in your life that you want, ask yourself, "What happened?" and give yourself love and compassion in response.

Exercise: Personal Peace Procedure

The Personal Peace Procedure was developed by Gary Craig and involves making a list of every bothersome specific event in one's life and systematically tapping on them. As you discover, neutralize, and eliminate the emotional baggage from your specific events, you will have less and less internal conflict in your system. Less internal conflict translates into a higher level of personal peace and less emotional and physical suffering. The steps are as follows:

1. Make a time line of your life, chunking time into segments. For example, birth, zero to five years old, six to ten years old, etc.

2. Fill in the time line with a list of all the bothersome events you can remember from that period. Don't be surprised if you find yourself with a list of a hundred items or more! If you've been living on this planet for more than a few years, you've most likely acquired a variety of bothersome moments. Include anything that has a "charge" of a 4 or higher on the SUDS. You can tap on smaller issues later, but for now, work on the big ones. (And you'll often find the small ones fade away when you work on the big ones.) Don't forget to include relationships with siblings or anyone else who lived in the house with you; your school experience from kindergarten through college; and other traumas, illnesses, accidents, hospitalizations, and so on. Consider the nature of the relationships in your life—with your mother, your father, friends, and other significant figures. What did you learn or tell yourself about these events and relationships? What did they teach you about yourself, others, or the world? Remember, you can tap and clear the negative lessons you took on as a result of these events. While making your list, you may find that some events don't seem to cause you any current discomfort. That's okay; list them anyway. The fact that you remember them suggests a need for resolution.

3. Give each event a 0-to-10 rating, with 10 representing the highest level of emotional intensity.

4. Starting with the 10s, apply EFT to each event. Be sure to notice any specific layers of memory or emotion that come up, and tap on those as well. You might start by working on one issue from an event, such as anger, and then find that another aspect comes up, such as sadness.

5. As you tap, new memories or concerns might arise; give them a number and add them to the list.

6. Develop a daily practice, working on two or three events from your list each day. In this way, you can easily address your entire list of specific events in three months. Take notes in a journal to record any changes you notice, such as how your body feels, how often you get upset or triggered, and the shifts and changes in your relationships. Revisit some of those specific events and notice how those previously intense incidents have faded into nothingness.

CHAPTER 6

HEALING THE BODY

Emotions are at the nexus between matter and mind,
going back and forth between the two and influencing both.

CANDACE B. PERT

"Ha ha, very funny, Nick."

That was my sister's first reaction to tapping. I'll admit, as her older brother, I'd earned her skepticism—having played countless practical jokes on her over the years. This time was different, though. This time I was actually trying to help.

She'd come to me complaining of a sore throat and sinus headache. She was achy, low on energy, short of breath—you know what it's like. This was ten or so years ago, when I was just getting into this "strange tapping thing," and I asked if she'd be willing to try it. It was when I showed her the points and how to tap on them that her skepticism kicked in. How could tapping her head, face, and chest do anything for a common virus? I assured her that tapping was legit and that it really *could* help her feel better. And—with raised eyebrows—she agreed to try it.

We began tapping on her symptoms, and that provided some relief—from a 10 in intensity down to an 8. It was progress but not good enough, so I asked her what had been going on recently. Had anything been stressing her out?

"Well," she said, "Alex"—our brother—"hired me to paint his room, and I really don't want to do it. I mean, here I am, 21 years old, and I'm painting my brother's room. It's depressing. I really, really don't want to do it."

We began tapping on her emotions around painting Alex's room. Within minutes, her sinuses and throat were clear and pain free. Just like that, from an 8 down to a 0!

Year after year, session after session, I've seen it happen. I call results like Jessica's "one-minute wonders" (they're often more like 15-minute wonders, but who's counting?). They seem to happen most often with basic physical symptoms, like a sore throat, physical pain, a headache, and so on. But in terms of what tapping can do to help heal the body, these symptoms are just the tip of the iceberg. As you'll see throughout this chapter, EFT is an equally powerful tool for advancing healing from serious illnesses, diseases, and chronic conditions.

Tracking the Mind-Body Connection

The first question people ask is, "How is this even possible?" How can tapping on meridian points help unclog your sinuses, much less promote healing from serious diseases?

It's a question I'll explore in detail later in this chapter. First, we need to clear out some clutter and touch on the core concept that makes all of this possible— the mind-body connection.

The very idea of a mind-body connection has been largely dismissed by conventional (as in Western or "modern") medicine since the time of René Descartes (1596–1650), French philosopher and mathematician. As history tells it, in order to get his hands on human bodies—dissection being blasphemous at the time— Descartes had to make a deal with the pope that he would study the physical body only. The mind, and its band of merry men we call emotions, would be considered separate. (The Church reportedly feared that any study of moods or emotions might tread on followers' faith, potentially threatening the Church's considerable power at the time.)

That bargain between Descartes and the Church effectively divided the body and mind into separate camps, cutting the cord for centuries. From that point on, commonly accepted Western wisdom dictated that the body did one thing and the mind did another. Sure, they existed within the same physical space, but they didn't intermingle. End of story.

Centuries passed; medicines were concocted, manufactured, and prescribed. Then came the 1960s. Suddenly, the counterculture movement began inspiring people to explore Eastern philosophies, many of which focus on an understanding of the human body and mind as one. Before long, the supposed separation of mind and body came into question.

In the decades since, that momentum has continued to build. Alternative therapies like massage, acupuncture, holistic medicine, and—increasingly—tapping, have become more accepted. A 2009 study by the National Institutes of Health (NIH) actually found that Americans spend $34 billion annually on "complementary and alternative medicine (CAM)," which is the umbrella term for alternative health treatments and therapies.[1] Clearly, a large number of Americans are seeking new, more integrated approaches to health and wellness.

Demystifying the Mind-Body Connection

Okay, so what are we *really* talking about when we say "mind-body connection"? Is this "real science," or is it a bunch of hocus-pocus?

Actually, you've seen the mind-body connection in action since you were too young to grasp the concept. Think back to your early school years for a moment. Remember the first time the teacher called on you and the entire class turned around and *stared* at you? I'll bet you did what I did—you blushed. The embarrassment you felt emotionally caused the blood vessels in your face to dilate, turning it that infamous shade of beet red.

Blushing is so socially accepted that we forget to ask the pertinent questions: How *do* those blood vessels know you're embarrassed? How do they pick up on your emotions at that precise moment?

Enter Candace Pert, doctor of pharmacology, author of *Molecules of Emotion*, and internationally renowned speaker. Thanks to her, we can now begin to answer questions like that (and many others!). During the 1980s, while she was a section chief at the NIH, she was among the pioneers of what is now known as "psychoneuroimmunology." Basically, she discovered a scientific basis for what she calls the "bodymind."

Thanks to Pert's extensive research, we have a much better understanding of the influence of the unconscious mind on psychosomatic illness, happiness, and wellness. You can almost guess her theory on "psychosomatic illness" by dissecting the word *psychosomatic. Psycho,* of course, references the psyche or mind, while *somatic* refers to the body. Translated literally, it means "mindbody."

In the 1970s, Pert made a discovery that laid the foundation for the rest of her amazing career. She was able to measure a molecule on the surface of cells called *opiate receptors*. (For scientists, measurement is the gold standard. By measuring the opiate receptor, Pert was proving its existence.) As she explains in *Molecules of Emotion*, these receptors are like keyholes. They bind with very specific keys, called *peptides,* which, she explains, "are indeed the other half of the equation of what I call the molecules of emotion." When the opiate receptor, which floats on the surface of a cell like a lily pad on a pond, binds with its perfectly fitting peptide, that cell's behavior can change. In other words, at any given moment, a cell's behavior can shift based on which peptide "keys" are attached to its opiate receptors. "On a more global scale," Pert explains, "these minute physiological phenomena at the cellular level can translate to large changes in behavior, physical activity, even mood."

Over the years, Dr. Pert has become an icon among alternative healers, conventional doctors, and many others, speaking internationally to massive crowds. It's her scientific achievements, though, that continue to open new possibilities for how we explore, understand, treat, and heal our bodies. Pert herself is candid about the fact that she never set out to defy or disprove Western medicine. She simply wanted to open the conversation and incorporate the "bodymind" into the Western approach to healing and treatment.

Stress Goes Chronic . . . and Gets Physical

We've already gone into great detail about how stress can affect our emotional and psychological state. But it has an enormous impact on the body as well. With Pert's "bodymind" concept in hand, let's take a closer look at stress and its effects.

In Chapter 1, we looked at the body's stress response—how the amygdala, that almond-shaped structure in your brain, senses danger and rings your internal alarm bells, prompting your body to release adrenaline and the stress hormone cortisol. That process is known as the fight-or-flight response for good reason: on a biological level, it was designed to protect you from specific, brief danger, like that tiger chasing your ancient ancestor. The extra adrenaline and cortisol released during fight-or-flight gives your body the quick boost it needs to either stay and fight the danger—or run like the wind. Your blood pressure and heartbeat rise, and more oxygen- and energy-rich blood becomes available to your brain and your muscles. Your senses sharpen, your body becomes more agile, and you're able to defend yourself (or climb the nearest tree) at top speed.

Today, people are experiencing something very different—*chronic* stress. As far as your body is concerned, you're perpetually being chased by a tiger! While it has a host of built-in protective systems, from the immune system to the blood-brain barrier, your body just wasn't engineered to spend so much time defending itself—never mind that today the danger is endless worry over mortgage payments, work stress, or keeping up with your incredibly packed schedule. For most of us, the list of stressors gets long fast, and when one goes away, another quickly takes its place. It's as if the moment you outrun that first tiger, another one appears.

Your body, of course, can't stay in the heightened fight-or-flight state of alertness forever. What happens is that chronic stress begins to disrupt natural processes like homeostasis, which allows our bodies to balance "bad" stress with "good" stress (yes, some stress is actually good for your health[2]). In homeostasis, the stimulating and tranquilizing chemicals naturally found in your body can more or less even out. With chronic stress, your body can't achieve homeostasis, leaving you hormonally and chemically off kilter.

Biologically speaking, being imbalanced—or unable to achieve homeostasis—is not a good place to be. Chronic stress has been linked to heart disease, sleep problems, digestive issues, migraines, depression, obesity, poor memory, sexual dysfunction, infertility, body aches and pains, skin conditions, and lowered immune response . . . the list goes on!

Quick Stress Facts

According to the American Academy of Family Physicians, two-thirds of office visits to family doctors are for stress-related symptoms.

According to one study, middle-aged men under severe stress who lacked emotional support were five times more likely to die within seven years than those who had the same amount of stress but had close personal ties. A different study also indicated that stress-management programs may reduce the risk of heart problems, including heart attack, by up to 75 percent in people with heart disease.[3]

The Roots of Dis-Ease

Under chronic stress, your body is more apt to enter a state of *dis-ease*. Unable to achieve its natural balance, it can't function the way it should. The ripple effects can be profound. And yet Western medicine has trained us to focus on symptoms rather than root causes like stress.

Why "Dis-Ease" . . .

What most call "disease" I refer to as "dis-ease." I spell it this way for two specific reasons. First, it helps highlight what the word actually means: that your body is out of balance and not at ease. Second, medical doctors and the pharmaceutical establishment have created a monopoly on the treatment, cure, and management of "disease." So I will leave "disease" to the medical approach and offer tapping as a different model—one that can certainly be combined with conventional medicine—for treating and healing "dis-ease."

Think back to the last time you had a cold. Your sinuses were blocked, you couldn't stop coughing, and your throat was raw. You were miserable, and you just wanted it to be over, right? To help your body heal, you probably tried to get extra rest and took vitamins, herbs, or over-the-counter medications. Your friends, colleagues, and family probably supported your efforts and reassured you that your cold would be gone soon.

You may have vaguely attributed your condition to being "stressed out," but while you quickly got busy decongesting your sinuses and quieting your cough, it never really occurred to you to address your emotions. What if, instead of the "nighttime sniffling, sneezing, coughing, aching, fever, best-sleep-you-ever-got-with-a-cold" medicine, your body actually needed the "release your fear, guilt, anger, and whatever other negative emotions you're experiencing right now" medicine? That's what seemed to heal my sister's cold—tapping on her *feelings* around painting Alex's room.

It's tempting to dismiss the "common cold" as no big deal, but the truth is, Western medicine has yet to cure it. Scientifically, the common cold is still somewhat of a mystery. I have yet to hear about a medicine, herb, or other treatment that could have given Jessica total (and lasting!) relief in a matter of moments.

Let's take that idea further. If blocked emotional energy could contribute to serious, even life-threatening dis-eases, what else might be possible? What if EFT, which, as we've already seen in Chapter 1, has been found to lower levels of the stress hormone cortisol, could promote healing in people suffering from dis-eases far scarier and more limiting than the common cold?

Managing Fibromyalgia: Finding "Happy Knees"

Remember Jodi from the introduction? Her fibromyalgia was causing her terrible pain when we met her at her home in Texas. During the course of a typical night, her pain would wake her 15, even 20 times, and she had to give up her beloved nature walks because the pain was too intense. She had gone to doctors for a solution but hadn't gotten relief. The cortisone injections they gave her helped only for a short period of time before she had to go back for more.

Fibromyalgia is one of those mystery dis-eases that affects millions, yet hasn't been fully explained. Questions about its root causes—and how to cure it—continue to puzzle modern medicine. When Jodi finally joined us at the four-day event in Connecticut where we were filming *The Tapping Solution*, she was at the end of her rope.

The cameras started rolling as Rick Wilkes, the EFT practitioner who would be her coach for the weekend, guided her through the initial tapping session. He began by asking Jodi if anything significant had occurred prior to the onset of her fibromyalgia. Yes, she answered. She'd learned that her daughter, who had long battled with addiction, was HIV-positive and pregnant. It was a time that she could describe with a single word—*sad*. When Rick asked how her inability to take nature walks felt, she again replied, "Sad."

Rick dubbed her knees "sad knees," and then led her through tapping rounds, focusing not just on her pain and symptoms, but on her emotions. Within the first day of tapping, Jodi was able to climb a flight of stairs without pain. Afraid to consider the possibility that tapping could alleviate her pain entirely, she dismissed the event as one of the rare times when fibromyalgia symptoms magically but temporarily vanish.

After a surprisingly restful and pain-free night's sleep, Jodi returned on day two for more guidance and tapping. By the end of the fourth day, Jodi found herself not only enjoying a nature walk but also being able to comfortably, painlessly pace herself ahead of our entire group. To my delight, her dramatic transformation was all caught on film. Overwhelming evidence of how quickly someone can heal!

Today, years later, Jodi's life is barely recognizable. Pain-free, regularly sleeping through the night, and "up and down the stairs all day long," she is able to enjoy in its entirety a two-story house that she and her husband built. She writes frequently and at length now and has several books she wants to publish.

Prior to tapping, Jodi, like so many chronic-pain sufferers, focused all her energy on staying active—hoping to defy her dis-ease and avoid her pain. With EFT, she learned to slow down and listen to her body, which, we quickly learned, was storing her emotional anguish. Her knees had assumed the burden of the guilt and sadness she felt over not being able to "save" her daughter from addiction and the circumstances that followed. Through tapping, Jodi was able to release those emotions, clearing that energy so her body could heal itself.

One of the reasons for Jodi's continued success with her fibromyalgia is her ongoing commitment to tapping. Each morning and sometimes through the day, she uses EFT—not just to help her accomplish positive goals but also to clear any negative emotions she experiences. "No sense storing [negativity] and having it come up as an illness later," she says.

Is EFT a Cure?

Looking at Jodi's transformation, it's tempting to claim that EFT "cured" her fibromyalgia. In the space of a four-day tapping retreat, she eliminated her chronic pain, regained her ability to be physically active, and began to sleep soundly through the night for the first time in eight years.

Scientifically speaking, no one can claim that tapping is a cure, whether for fibromyalgia or any of the other dis-eases we'll discuss in this chapter. The human body is incredibly complex, and any number of factors contribute to the millions and billions of changes, positive and negative, that are taking place inside us at any given moment.

What *is* clear is that tapping is an incredibly powerful tool for releasing the *emotional energy* that gets stored in our bodies. As you've seen, that emotional energy may be manifesting itself in our physical bodies in more obvious ways than we recognize—not just through the cold or flu you "caught," but through everything from mysterious aches and pains to serious dis-eases.

Slowly but surely, Candace Pert's findings on the "bodymind" are showing us that the physical body may be in closer, more intimate contact with our emotions than we and Western medicine have imagined. As focused as we are on germs (Americans spend almost $1 billion annually on antibacterial soaps[4]), our bodies may be less sensitive to microbes than to what we are *feeling*.

Do You Create Your Own Destiny?

When you start talking about how emotional energy promotes healing in the body, there's a temptation to leap to the conclusion that emotions create dis-ease. Again, that's not a fair statement. What we're discussing is the mind-body connection—how the mind affects the body and the body affects the mind. A friend, the best-selling author Kris Carr, shared with me a great word regarding this topic: *participate*. Rather than saying our mind *creates* dis-ease, she suggests that it's more accurate to say it *participates* in dis-ease. We *participate* in our own reality—physical, emotional, and otherwise.

On the other hand, we can participate in healing—but that doesn't mean dis-ease won't occur. Just because you "feel good" about breathing in toxins, that doesn't make those toxins good for your body! That said, if you happen to breathe in some toxic air, your body will do a much better job of detoxing and coping with it if you're calm and relaxed as opposed to stressed out and worried about it. Once again, you can *participate* in your health and well-being by handling your stress, anxiety, and other emotions through EFT.

Getting Back to Sleep

By the time Donna arrived at the tapping retreat, she was physically, mentally, and emotionally drained. After being diagnosed with breast cancer six months earlier, she'd undergone a bilateral mastectomy and 33 rounds of chemotherapy. The reason she'd come to learn EFT, however, wasn't to find a cure. Donna's goal was simple—to sleep. For four consecutive months, ever since beginning chemo, Donna had suffered from chronic insomnia, often going for four full days without sleep. Other nights she'd wake up at least three times; "and that is with two sleeping meds plus an antidepressant," she explained.

Not surprisingly, she'd gone from being an active, high-energy, "type-A" person to someone who could barely leave the house. She wanted her two kids to have their "old mom" back.

"Less anxiety and an inner peace and confidence would be a gift, too," she said. Since her diagnosis, she continued, "I have retreated from my previous lifestyle and social life. . . . It would be great to have the energy and confidence to rejoin the world again."

Donna had already tried several alternative treatments, including Reiki, acupuncture, and craniosacral therapy, as well as conventional talk therapy—all of which she had hoped would help bring her peace of mind and, by extension, a good night's sleep. Unfortunately, none of them had done this.

At the recommendation of her therapist, Donna had come to our EFT retreat, hoping to tap her way out of insomnia and into a new and more fulfilling life.

"The cancer has been a blessing to me in many ways," she explained. "It has helped me to find a balance in my life that was lacking. It has helped me to realize what is truly important to me." Her goal, she added, was to find a "new normal" and learn to "live up to my potential with a joyful soul."

Watching Donna speak, we were all touched and inspired, but also somewhat worried. You could sense her resolve, but her voice was thin and fragile. It was as if she had never truly inhabited her own body. She was physically present but absent in many other ways.

Hoping to get at the underlying causes of her anxiety and sleeplessness, we decided to probe deeper into her feelings, hopes, and dreams. When asked what she wanted in life, she responded, "I want my kids to be happy." When asked to imagine telling her family that she was going to take a few hours to do something nice for herself, she became noticeably uncomfortable.

To help her reconnect with herself, we began leading her through tapping rounds that focused on claiming and expressing her personal power. She also tapped on wanting to feel like a "real" woman again after her double mastectomy, and of course on the sleep issues that had brought her to us in the first place.

In short, the tapping worked. That first night, Donna slept soundly, without waking. For the rest of the retreat—and afterward—she continued to enjoy solid sleep. "Being able to sleep changes everything," she said, smiling.

Donna's tapping also allowed her to begin connecting with the one person she'd forgotten to notice—herself. "I wish I could tell others that they don't have to feel the pressure of always being 'positive.' I now realize the importance of expressing my feelings, tapping, and then letting them go." EFT, she adds, has "made an immense difference in my life."

Ending Insomnia

Seeing Donna after our tapping retreat, you could feel her renewed energy right away. She seemed fully present, as if through tapping (and being able to sleep again), she'd reconnected her body and mind into a cohesive "bodymind." She'd also achieved her goal of joining the world and was once again able to attend her children's events. But for the first time, she was also willing to skip some of them in order to give herself the time and attention she needed.

If you want to hear more about EFT and insomnia, rest assured—we'll go into more detail in Chapter 12.

Putting Cancer into Remission?

EFT expert Lindsay Kenny shared with me her experiences with Leah, a 50-year-old former teacher who had recently been diagnosed with lung cancer. When they first met, Lindsay asked Leah if anything had happened in her life just prior to her lung cancer. Leah said no, that she had a comfortable life, a happy marriage, and had never experienced any real trauma. The moment she finished speaking, though, her husband, Dick, chimed in. About six months before Leah's diagnosis, her sister Beth had died from a respiratory ailment.

At the mere mention of Beth's passing, Leah began to cry. Clearly this was a traumatic event; it was surprising (or was it?) that she had not made the connection.

They continued discussing her memories and feelings, and it quickly became clear that Leah had been holding on to more than grief for the past two and a half years. Beth, Leah felt, hadn't given her own life a chance. She had refused all treatment. Having lost her husband a year before her own diagnosis, Beth had lost her will to live.

Lindsay couldn't help but wonder if Leah's powerful, unresolved emotions had contributed to her lung cancer, so she spent an hour tapping with her and her husband about her feelings over Beth's passing. Leah shared not just her grief and loss but her feelings of anger and betrayal as she watched her sister refuse treatment—essentially choosing, in Leah's mind, to abandon herself, her life, and her sister.

By the end of that first hour of tapping, Leah had neutralized the trauma of Beth's passing and her emotions around that memory. She had also chosen to forgive Beth for declining treatment and for dying.

It was great progress, but of course, Leah still had lung cancer. There was more tapping to do. To clear more negative energy and promote healing, Lindsay taught Leah and Dick a simple protocol. Instructing her to tap on each point, she had Leah ask her body to send healing energy to her lungs, repair the damage inflicted by her cancer, eliminate all cancer cells, boost her immune system, and restore her health. Finally, she instructed Leah to tap while thanking her body for responding.

Leah and Dick left feeling relieved and enthusiastic about their experience and about the potential of EFT to help her heal. Lindsay told them to use the tapping healing sequence at least three times a day and to continue to use tapping to process all other negative emotions.

Four months later, Leah reported an astonishing result: her lung cancer was in complete remission, and she'd been able to avoid chemotherapy, radiation, and surgery! She'd continued tapping and made other simple lifestyle changes. She told Lindsay that she believes EFT, positive thinking, and asking her body to heal are what saved her. Having been given a very low probability of survival by her traditional doctors, Leah had found new ways to boost her body's healing power.

Lindsay reported to me recently that Leah's health remains steady, and her cancer is still in remission. It's important to note that while these results are incredible, calling them "typical" would be an overstatement. Cancer is an incredibly complicated dis-ease of the physical, emotional, and often spiritual systems. It would not be fair to say "tapping cures cancer." But tapping through emotional issues, traumas, and overall stress can help the body heal. When the body heals, the body can cure *itself* of cancer.

It's impossible not to be inspired by Leah's story. As many times as I've seen tapping defy the odds and promote healing in the body, it's also true that each physical body, human being, and diagnosis is unique. That Leah went into remission after using tapping and lifestyle changes doesn't translate literally. While tapping is an incredibly powerful therapy, it's not a replacement for Western medicine. In many cases, EFT is used in combination with surgery, chemotherapy, and other conventional and alternative treatments. In some cases, it's the addition of tapping that enables patients to access the full healing power of their own bodies.

Healing Through Positive Emotions

We touched on this topic in Chapter 2, but I want to take a moment to discuss again negative versus positive emotions as they relate to healing. A lot of this chapter has focused on releasing negative emotions. Many people worry that by focusing on their anger, grief, stress or anxiety while tapping, they might be attracting negativity into their lives.

As we've seen in this chapter with Donna, Leah, and Jodi, dis-ease may partially result from trying to deny emotions and experiences like grief, anger, resentment, and personal need. Again, there's actually nothing wrong with *experiencing* negative thoughts, emotions, beliefs, and symptoms. I'd argue that it's human to experience all of those at various times. It's when those negative emotions get *stuck*—when they have no outlet—that your body can enter a state of imbalance that may contribute to dis-ease and prevent healing.

Once your negative emotions, beliefs, and experiences have been processed and released, you're free to *feel* and *be* positive again—not in the forced way Donna had tried to be positive before she began tapping, but in a deep, authentic, powerful way. *That* is when the true force of positive energy shows up in your life—when it's coming from your core, not when it's masking stress or helping you avoid difficult emotions, memories, and circumstances in your life.

A New Vision for Western Medicine

Imagine visiting a medical professional and being able to get to the root of your problem in a matter of minutes—as opposed to going through an endless battery of tests, taking ongoing medications (each with its own side effects and problems), and possibly never truly resolving your physical issue. As more and more medical professionals recognize the importance of the mind-body connection, that reality—one of true healing—is becoming increasingly possible.

Doctors, psychologists, psychiatrists, and other clinicians around the world are embracing EFT and incorporating it into their practices. They're doing this for one primary reason: EFT works.

Modern medicine in the United States is taught from the standard, or allopathic, approach. The general philosophy is that the body needs medication or surgery to heal a set of symptoms. Unfortunately, medication and surgery don't have the success rates we might hope. They can also cause undue stress and further trauma to the body. Anybody who's been deep in the medical "system" can attest to the toll this approach can take, emotionally and physically.

But there is hope. Dedicated professionals, whose primary concern is doing whatever it takes to help their patients heal, are turning to EFT and incorporating it into their practice. I've personally seen an attitude shift in the medical profession over the past few years—from skepticism to eager enthusiasm when it comes to using EFT.

While I believe that EFT is safe and effective for anyone to use, it's very encouraging to see professionals incorporating it into their practices. You don't have to be a doctor or a psychologist to use EFT for yourself or with others (I'm neither!), but certainly the experience and knowledge that such professionals bring to an EFT session can help.

When I work with people, I bring my years of experience in personal development, counseling, and mind-body techniques, as well as my own intuitive ability to know what people need and how best to help them. So whether you explore healing through EFT by yourself, with a dedicated EFT practitioner, or with a medical or alternative practitioner who incorporates tapping into his or her practice, the reality is that this powerful tool is available to you now and hopefully soon will be available to millions of others.

Exercise: Create Your Healing Tapping Tree

Using the ideas we've explored in this chapter, let's return to the exercise you did in Chapter 2, the tapping tree. This time we'll focus on creating a tree to help your body heal. Some of what you put in your tree in Chapter 2 may reappear in your healing tapping tree, and that's fine. The point is to take a few moments to examine how you can use tapping to improve how your "bodymind" functions. Even if you feel healthy, take a few moments to think about the rare times when you do get a headache, the flu, or some other symptom.

Grab a piece of paper and a pencil or pen, and draw your own healing tapping tree. (You can get a blank copy of the tapping tree drawing to print out and fill in from www.thetappingsolution.com/tree). Your tree doesn't have to be pretty; just copy it as best you can and leave plenty of space—as you may recall from your previous tree, most of us have more stuff going on than we think!

The Leaves (Side Effects)

What symptoms or side effects are you currently experiencing? How does your physical body feel? What have you been diagnosed with? Do you have any pain in your body? Fill in all these visible, tangible issues as the leaves.

The Branches (Emotions)

What are you feeling on a daily basis? When you wake up in the morning, how do you feel? When you go to sleep at night, how do you feel? Think back over the last day and write in any negative emotions you have experienced. Do you feel any specific negative emotions about your body? About your dis-ease? About your overall health?

The Trunk (Events)

What are the events, both current and past, regarding your physical body or dis-ease, that bother you? When did your problem start? What was going on around that time?

The Roots (Limiting Beliefs)

What are your limiting beliefs in terms of your health and wellness? What's the story you tell about your body? About your dis-ease? What did your doctor tell you that you now believe to be true? What do you believe about your physical condition? Honesty is crucial here, so again, forcing yourself to be positive will work against you (and your body). Get real and get it all out. Then you can move on to create the deep and authentic positive energy your body needs to help itself heal.

When you're done, step back and take a look at your tree. This is a brief summary of your "bodymind" right now. These emotions, symptoms, events, and limiting beliefs are what you will use tapping to clear once and for all, in order to make way for a healthier, more energetic, and vibrant you!

Tapping Through Your Tree

Your healing tapping tree is a great visual reminder to tap on more than your symptoms. To harness the full healing power of tapping, you have to tap through your entire tree, starting with the symptoms, and progressing all the way down through your limiting beliefs. As we've seen throughout this chapter—from Jessica's cold to Jodi's fibromyalgia, Donna's insomnia, and Leah's cancer—it's that *entire* process, including tapping through the roots (the beliefs that may have contributed to your dis-ease) that enables your body to heal.

CHAPTER 7

RELEASING PHYSICAL PAIN

If there is a single definition of healing it is to enter with mercy and awareness those pains, mental and physical, from which we have withdrawn in judgment and dismay.

STEPHEN LEVINE

My sister vehemently disagreed with me.

"But Patricia's pain isn't some psychological issue! It says here that she fractured her L1 vertebra. She has rods and bolts in her back! How could tapping possibly help?"

We were sitting around a table in July of 2007, reviewing applications for the documentary retreat. We had a stack of paper in front of us—people desperate for anything to help them relieve pain, lose weight, overcome grief, and much more.

Patricia, whose application Jessica was reading, had been in a terrible boating accident where she shattered her L1, one of the large lumbar vertebrae of the lower back. Surgeons had succeeded in stabilizing her back with four titanium rods and eight sets of screws and bolts. But the remaining pain was excruciating. She was taking morphine, Percocet, Norco, and Valium. She had trouble sleeping, so on top of everything else, she took Ambien to get a good night's rest. Even with all the meds, she was regularly in pain and stressed out about her difficult situation.

The argument I was having with my sister was whether EFT would work on pain that had a clear physical cause. It was her understanding at the time that EFT was most effective for psychological or psychosomatic pain issues—stemming from repressed emotions—but I knew there was more to the story than that. Using my project-manager/big-brother veto, I overruled Jessica's protestations and accepted Patricia into the four-day event.

She showed up for the weekend in considerable pain, after riding in the car for six hours. It was evident that as much as she was trying to keep her spirits up—she was naturally a determined and positive person—the pain was simply wearing her down. She had shared with us on her application that "it still feels like I'm living a bad dream that I'll wake up out of. . . . Everything has been modified . . . and I'm still adapting, adjusting, and trying to find the right balance." She went on to say, "I hate that I always have to ask, *How will this activity/event/decision affect my back?* I'm much slower than I used to be, and that's frustrating. I'm afraid that people may perceive me as being handicapped. The accident has totally redefined my life, and I resent that but try to focus on the positive."

Tap on the Diagnosis

EFT expert Rick Wilkes, who was one of the facilitators at the *Tapping Solution* event, spent the weekend working with Patricia to relieve her pain and help her move forward in life.

One of the first things he addressed was everything the doctors had told her about her back—about what was possible and not possible. The diagnosis and prognosis, especially since we are often most vulnerable at the time we hear them, can have devastating effects on our bodies and our futures. When we hear "you'll always have pain" or "you'll never be active again," the body internalizes that limiting belief on a subconscious level. On the conscious level, we often operate as if it's the truth as well.

Patricia loved doing yoga before the accident and was told she would "never do yoga again." Emotionally, this devastated her—sending negative chemicals coursing through the body, and it limited what she thought was possible. Perhaps if she had never been told that, she might have attempted to do yoga—slowly stretching, opening up, and healing. But her doctors' pronouncement ended that possibility in her mind.

Until she tapped, that is! Rick expertly guided her back through everything the doctors had said to her and how she felt about it. They systematically tapped to clear the negative emotions she felt and to address the subconscious messages her body was storing.

This tapping, along with other approaches we'll cover in the rest of the chapter, had incredible results. By the end of the weekend, Patricia felt no pain in her back. The constant heaviness from the rods and screws was gone. And, perhaps most important, she felt hopeful for the future and excited about what was *possible* for her—she was no longer focused on everything she *couldn't* do! After the event, she got off all pain and sleeping medications and started doing yoga again. An incredible result!

Try It Yourself: Tapping on the Diagnosis

When you think about any pain you might be experiencing, ask yourself,

What do I know to be true about this pain?
What have my doctors told me is going on with my body?
What did I read online about what's going on with my body?
What do I believe to be true about my condition?

Take a few minutes and answer these questions, preferably on paper, in as much detail as possible. We'll use this list as the basis to begin tapping. Your list might look like this:

- I have a slipped disc in my back. (Feel free to get as specific as possible—i.e., I have a slipped disc in my third vertebra that is degenerating and now causes a throbbing, red pain.)
- The doctors told me it would always hurt.
- The doctors told me eventually it will need surgery.
- The doctors told me it is degenerating and will likely get worse.
- The only way the pain goes away is if I take pain medication.
- I believe I'll have this pain forever and it will only get worse.

Go back through every item on your list, and give it a number on a 0-to-10 scale, noting how true it feels to you. If you absolutely, positively *know* you have a slipped disc in your back and that's the truth, give it a 10. If you fully believe it will always hurt, give it a 10. If part of you doesn't believe that, it might be a 7 or 8.

Now take a moment and rate the overall pain you're feeling. Give it a number on the 0-to-10 scale.

We're going to take these statements and, the first time through, combine them into one tapping round.

TAPPING SCRIPT: Tapping on the Diagnosis

(The tapping points chart can be found on page 21.)

Karate Chop: Even though I have a slipped disc in my back, I deeply and completely accept myself. (Repeat three times.)

And now moving through the points:

Eyebrow: This slipped disc . . .
Side of Eye: This slipped disc in my back . . .
Under Eye: It's throbbing and painful . . .
Under Nose: The doctors told me I have a slipped disc . . .
Chin: The doctors told me it would always hurt . . .
Collarbone: The doctors told me it would eventually need surgery . . .
Under Arm: The doctors told me it would likely get worse . . .
Top of Head: The only way the pain goes away is if I take pain medication . . .

Eyebrow: I believe I'll have this forever and it will only get worse . . .
Side of Eye: This slipped disc in my back . . .
Under Eye: This painful slipped disc . . .
Under Nose: This throbbing, red-hot pain . . .
Chin: I believe it will only get worse . . .
Collarbone: I believe what the doctors told me about my back . . .
Under Arm: The only way the pain goes away is if I take pain medication . . .
Top of Head: This painful slipped disc.

Take a deep breath . . . and let it go.

For an extended tapping session on this topic,
visit www.thetappingsolution.com/tap5.

Remember, this language is just an example for you to see what tapping a diagnosis can look and sound like. The key is for you to come up with your *own* language, to speak your truth, and to follow your intuition on the issue.

So now, as always, we're looking for two things:

1. Where are the numbers now—how did the pain shift?

2. What came up?

Check in on your original pain number. Has it gone up? Down? Has the pain shifted? Has it moved in the body? Write down your new number.

Then go back through the original statements and see how those numbers have shifted. Do you still believe you'll be in pain forever? If you believe it a little less, if a glimmer of hope has appeared, write down the new number. Do you still believe everything your doctors told you to be true?

Then ask yourself, "What came up for me during that tapping?" Did you find yourself getting very emotional when you said, "The doctors told me it would eventually need surgery"? That's a clue that there's more there to be tapped on. What phrase stuck out the most? What new thoughts/ideas/emotions came up? Write those down and then use them as the basis for the next round.

You can tap again on all the same statements, going through them until they all clear and feel good, or you can shift to new statements—whatever is most present for you.

What you'll find as you tap on the current situation and diagnosis is that you free yourself from the shackles of what others told you and what you believe about your pain. As we saw with Patricia, this release can have nearly miraculous effects.

As hard as it is for a little sister to admit, Jessica has since acknowledged that I was right about accepting Patricia into the event.

"I didn't believe Patricia could get rid of her pain," she says. "But now I know how much our beliefs affect our pain levels. And that the body is miraculous in its ability to heal when we get out of the way!"

When We *Become* Our Pain

Patricia's story still amazes me. Even though I had hoped her pain would improve by coming to the event, a part of me, just like Jessica, doubted we could help her, since she had such a physical, tangible issue. Often we hold on so tightly to the "truth" of physical pain and dis-ease—to what we know about it, to what others have told us about it—that it becomes part of our identity, part of who we are. We are no longer ourselves, we are no longer our hopes, dreams, goals, and desires. Instead we *become* the pain. We become the diagnosis; we are ruled by everything that's wrong with us as opposed to everything that's right with us.

The medical system, as well-intentioned as it is, doesn't help in this sense. The Western medical industry is constantly looking for and reminding us about what's wrong with the body—the "likely" future negative scenarios—as opposed to what's *right* with the body. Can you imagine a doctor saying to you, "My diagnosis, from a purely medical perspective, based on the X-rays I see, is that you have a slipped disc in your back. That being said, I do want you to know that I've seen many X-rays with slipped discs where there was no pain. I've also seen slipped discs that healed on their own. Remember, the body has an innate ability to heal, and I have faith that you can move beyond this. Tell me a little more about the things in life that you're excited about. What might your future look like once this pain goes away?"

What would that attitude, approach, and messaging do toward healing the body, toward providing people with hope and possibility, and toward giving us the native energy we need to move forward? Doctors in their white coats have incredible authoritative power. What they say is often taken in directly by the conscious and subconscious minds and can go on to rule our reality.

So until the medical industry changes its tune, use EFT to tap through any and all limiting beliefs about your body and its ability to heal.

Professional Profile: Dr. Erin Shannon

Dr. Shannon is a traditionally trained doctor of clinical psychology who was disappointed with the lack of effectiveness of the traditional therapies that she was taught. During her doctoral program at a VA Medical Center in St. Louis, she got frustrated seeing doctors work with patients for years, and even decades, with no concrete results.

Years later, she painfully watched her mother die from a brain tumor, feeling helpless at how little she could do. The only things that seemed to ease her mother's tremendous pain were alternative therapies, including Reiki and other energy healing modalities. While Dr. Shannon was initially skeptical—her medical training had taught her that such techniques had no validity—she couldn't deny the results she was seeing and the relief her mother was experiencing.

Like any good clinician and researcher, she began to take a closer look at how the brain and body worked together to produce these results. Mind-body research had been a key part of her work during her postdoctoral fellowship at the Washington University School of Medicine departments of psychiatry and genetics, which was funded by the National Institute of Mental Health. Dr. Shannon was intent on discovering how the brain and body were related from a neurological perspective.

As she began exploring alternative therapies, she encountered a mound of user testimonials and a growing body of research on EFT. Curious, she decided to incorporate it into her practice. As is often the case with traditionally trained therapists, she was blown away by how quickly she got results.

Nowadays she usually starts her sessions tapping with a patient. She takes them through the routine of tapping and goes to work immediately on any pressing issues so the patient can walk out of her office feeling better. After teaching the basics, she assigns homework for continued tapping. Giving her patients this tool facilitates the kind of success that her practice is known for in the conservative Midwest.

Dr. Shannon is an advocate for EFT and believes that it should be taught to every medical professional because of its simplicity and high-quality results. For a professional who dedicated years of study to becoming a doctor, she struggles with why more medical professionals, including M.D.s, psychologists, and psychiatrists, aren't more eager to learn this powerful healing technique.

The advice she gives to her patients is to give it a try. There's no harm—it doesn't cost you anything, and it's not going to hurt you in any way. The technique is so simple that anyone—including a highly trained medical professional!—can use it.

Anger and Pain: A Surprising Connection

When I first met John, he was subdued, quiet, and obviously in a tremendous amount of pain. A Vietnam veteran who had suffered 30 years of chronic back pain, John was another one of the people chosen to attend our four-day EFT event. Nick Polizzi and I flew to Minneapolis to film "before" footage of John, showing him in his home environment. There, we documented what was going on with his body and his life.

You could tell John was a kind man, but he was in a lot of physical and emotional pain. His wife, Pearl, shared with us that John rarely laughed. She revealed that the kids would always ask, "Where's Dad?" to make sure not to cross him.

His back pain was the result of an accident in 1974 that had given him a severely herniated disc. He'd had four surgeries over the years, with little to no results. He had trouble sleeping through the night and suffered with high blood pressure, diabetes, tinnitus, and more.

As with Patricia, John had been told by medical doctors that there was something physically wrong with his back—that he would always have pain, that he would need more surgery, and so forth. Steve Munn, the EFT expert who hosted the event at his retreat center in Connecticut, took a different approach.

"What emotion is in your back?" he asked. "What story are you holding on to there?" John didn't hesitate.

"Anger," he replied.

He went on to recount (and tap through) how his father had beaten him repeatedly with a heavy leather strap as a child. He continued to tap with Steve on various emotions and events related to his father. Beyond his anger and sadness about his father, John tapped on his guilt about what he had done in Vietnam, his anger toward the people in charge then and now, and even his deep fear of rats!

And, as you can see in the movie, John was astonished to discover his back pain disappearing—after 30 years.

Perhaps the most revealing result of John's experience with EFT isn't the disappearance of the back pain. Instead, it's what his daughter now says about her father.

"I feel like Dad is a new person," she says. "I love this new person!"

Pearl agrees. "He smiles and laughs!"

What Emotion or Event Is Creating Your Pain?

Take a moment and tune in to any pain you might be feeling in your body. If you're free from pain, look for some stiffness, tightness, or other constriction. Then ask yourself, "If there is an emotion in my _____ [name the part of your body that hurts], what might that be?" You can also ask yourself, "If there is an event or story in my _____ , what might that be?"

Listen to your body and just allow an answer to come forward. There's no right or wrong here; you might be surprised with what you hear. Once you have an answer, give it a number on the 0-to-10 scale, and let's do some tapping on it!

Use the example script on the next page, filling in the blanks with your specific emotion and event.

TAPPING SCRIPT: The Emotions in Our Pain

(The tapping points chart can be found on page 21.)

You've likely never had your doctor ask you "What emotion is in your pain," but after you see and feel the results of tapping and focusing on that, you'll see that there's much more to pain relief than we've traditionally acknowledged.

Karate Chop: Even though I have this _____ [insert your emotion here] in my _____ [insert your body part here], I deeply and completely accept myself.
Karate Chop: Even though I have all this _____ in my _____ about what happened, I deeply and completely accept myself.
Karate Chop: Even though I have this _____ in my _____, I choose to release it now.

Eyebrow: All this _____ in my _____ . . .
Side of Eye: I'm holding on to so much _____ . . .
Under Eye: This _____ about what happened . . .
Under Nose: I can't let go of this _____ . . .
Chin: All this _____ in my _____ . . .
Collarbone: I have all this _____ about what happened . . .
Under Arm: All this _____ . . .
Top of Head: This _____ in my_____ .

Eyebrow: Releasing all this _____ in my _____ . . .
Side of Eye: Letting it go . . .
Under Eye: It's time to let go of what happened . . .
Under Nose: And it's time to let go of this _____ . . .
Chin: Letting it go . . .
Collarbone: Letting all this _____ go now . . .
Under Arm: All this _____ . . .
Top of Head: Releasing all this _____ in my _____ .

Take a deep breath . . . and let it go.

For an extended tapping session on this topic,
visit www.thetappingsolution.com/tap6.

Now, as always, tune in and ask yourself, "What changed? How strong is my emotion now? Did the pain go up or down? Did it move? Did something else come up?"

Use that information to formulate another tapping round, and keep going until you find relief.

Ask Yourself . . . Questions about Your Pain

- When did the pain first start, and what was going on in your life at that time? For example, "It was ten years ago, and that's when I changed jobs."

- Who comes to mind when you think of this pain? For example, "This neck pain might represent that pain in the neck, my mother-in-law."

- How do you feel about having this pain? For example, "I'm angry that I've had it for so long."

- How do you feel about yourself with this pain? For example, "I feel like I'm not enough, since I can't find a solution."

- Who would you be without this pain? For example, "I'd be a totally different person, able to do so much more . . . but with a lot more responsibility than I have now."

- Does this pain have a message for you? For example, "It's telling me to slow down."

- Describe the pain. What quality/texture/color/size does it have? For example, "It feels red and small, but the whole area is swollen."

- What's the upside of holding on to this pain? For example, "I don't have to go back to work."

- What's the downside of holding on to this pain? For example, "I can't live the life I want to live."

Answers to these questions are all clues to finding the underlying issue. The examples are just that—examples—so use them if they help, but if you don't connect with them, answer the questions for yourself. Use the answers to develop tapping phrases.

It's Not Always What We Think

This time, the pressure was on me.

I was working with the girlfriend of a potential business partner, someone who could help promote EFT in a big way, and I just wasn't seeing the usual results.

Amy had complained of sciatica pain for the past several years. She was a toned, athletic young woman who loved to run and was severely hampered by her pain. I asked her when it started, and she knew exactly.

"I was at a wedding. I was dancing and had a bad fall," she reported.

When I asked her what was going on emotionally at that time, she had a quick answer to that as well: "It was an awful night. I got in a huge fight with my ex-boyfriend, and everything seemed to go wrong from there."

It would seem from her answers that tapping on the original event and emotional conflict would resolve it, so that's what I was trying to do. (I had already begun with the global tapping on the pain and hadn't seen a shift.) So we went through the original event, all the emotions, all the memories. While she certainly felt better about the event, it wasn't doing anything to shift the pain, which surprised me. It seemed the pain might not have been related to the fall at the wedding after all.

Never one to give up easily, I asked her, "What's the most stressful thing in your life right now?"

She answered, "Work. I hate it."

She shared with me how miserable she was in her job, how she didn't like the work she did or the people she worked with. She just wanted to get away, she told me. So we began tapping, starting with, *Even though I hate work and it really stresses me out . . .* To both of our surprise, her pain shifted dramatically after just one round! We went on to tap longer on her work stress until the stress—and her sciatica pain—abated.

She was in shock as she turned, stretched, and tried to otherwise activate her sciatica to no avail. It was truly gone. Somehow it had been connected to all her stress at work.

So when you're stuck or don't know what to tap on, don't be afraid to take a leap. Try something else. Just the process of tapping can often relax the body and mind enough that different ideas, impressions, and leads come your way. Through trial and error, you can determine what's really going on and how to clear it.

Incredible Results with Headaches

People who are curious about EFT often want to know, "How quickly will this work? Do things really go away in just one minute? How often will I have to do this?" The answer is different for everyone—and the approach changes for everyone!

EFT expert Carol Look reports a similar experience with the doorman at her apartment building. He often complained to her about recurring migraine headaches, so she offered to tap with him about it. Again, they focused purely on the physical symptoms. They touched on the overall stress in his life, without getting overly emotional or specific. He saw immediate results, and for the next seven years that he worked at her building, he reported never having a headache again!

As you can see, simple tapping on the symptom can have profound results. At other times, as we've seen, it's necessary to dig a little deeper. My best friend, Nick Polizzi, had suffered from migraine headaches for his whole life. We did some tapping on the symptoms, and he saw some relief, but they kept coming back. It wasn't until we dug deeper and he connected the migraines with some unresolved feelings and events with his father that the headaches stopped for good.

The bottom line is, it's impossible to say how quickly the pain will go away. Will it be a one-minute miracle? Maybe. Will it take working with a trained practitioner to get to the root of the problem? Maybe. What I can tell you is that the results I've seen, again and again, are so astounding, so groundbreaking, that if you feel any physical pain, you owe it to yourself to explore tapping. Start with 5 to 15 minutes of tapping on the symptom. Hopefully, you'll get relief. But if not, don't give up. Make that commitment to going a little deeper, to asking yourself those power questions on page 104 and finding out what's *behind* the pain. I promise the upside is worth the effort.

You Don't Have to Say It's Gone Just to Please Me

I often have the opportunity to share EFT with live audiences around the world. When it comes time to demonstrate the technique, I ask for three volunteers to come up onstage and work with me. It's a testimony to the power of EFT and its consistent results that I'm willing to work with people in front of an audience of hundreds. If tapping didn't work, I'd have more than a little egg on my face by now!

Yet again and again, I've seen incredible results, especially with pain relief. Pain is such a tangible experience—you either feel pain or you don't—that it serves as a great demonstration. Still, as often as I've seen miraculous results both in front of audiences and in private sessions, I'm always amazed when it works yet again.

I tell people, "You don't have to tell me the pain is gone just to please me. Is it really gone?" And of course, they reply that it's truly gone away.

Part of the reason it continues to be hard for me to believe it moved that quickly is that we don't have an existing framework or known paradigm that says, *pain can go away and not come back*. Sure, we believe aspirin can get rid of a headache through a purely chemical interaction, but we didn't grow up with people telling us, "Just tap and make it go away" or "Sweetheart, what emotion might be at the root of this pain?"

All of that is changing, of course. We have more and more experiences that show us that the body *can* heal, that pain relief *is* possible, and that it's not all about the diagnosis of what's "wrong." The possibilities emerging in the realm of pain and healing are exciting. You owe it to yourself to take the time, do the tapping, and find relief.

Exercise: Feeling into Your Body

As we've learned in this chapter on pain—and the previous one on the mind-body connection—our bodies are more than skin and bones. They are our allies, providing us with incredible feedback and information about our whole lives.

Take a moment now to feel into your body. Look for places where you feel tension, stress, or pain. Roll your neck around and feel for any tightness. Inhale and notice how deep the breath is. Is there any constriction in your lungs or chest?

Now that you have a sense for the physical tension, stress, or pain in your body, ask yourself, "What is this about? What is my body trying to tell me? If there were an emotion in my body, an event, a belief, what would it be?"

When you have an answer, do some tapping on it. Tap both on the symptom you feel—the pain, stress, or tension—and the emotion associated with it.

Watch how the whole body releases and relaxes when you tune in, tap, and let go. Keep tapping until you feel deep relaxation in your body and enjoy the sensation!

CHAPTER 8

LOSING WEIGHT AND LETTING GO OF FEAR, GUILT, AND SHAME AROUND FOOD

Our greatest weakness lies in giving up. The most certain way to succeed is always to try just one more time.

THOMAS A. EDISON

Marie couldn't decide what she was more stressed out about: her extra weight or what to do in order to lose that weight.

She had tried every diet, every exercise program—and nothing seemed to work. When we met, she was ready to give up. Was losing a few pounds worth the misery she was putting herself through?

Marie's problem is one that I see again and again. Her situation gives rise to a few questions: What happened to food? What happened to the joy of eating? What happened to eating meals in peace? What happened to feeling grateful, nourished, and warmed by a meal made with love? At one point in our history, food was a friend, a provider, a sustainer, the root of life. It contained within it our memories, our families, and our heritage. But recently, food has turned into something else. For many of us, food is less a source of nourishment than a source of . . .

STRESS. FEAR. ANGER. GUILT.

Cravings. Weight gain. Toxins. "Do I eat this?" "Don't eat that!" "I feel guilty about eating this." "I can't believe I ate that!"

My question is, when did food become such a pain?

But back to Marie. Why was she not losing weight? Why was she so miserable when it came to eating?

As far as I can see it, there are two factors at play when it comes to weight issues, both of which can be significantly impacted by tapping. The first factor is the reality of our current food landscape. Food has, in many ways, become "stuff in a box." This is a subject that hundreds of books have been written about, so I'm not going to go into detail here. But suffice it to say that we are truly, deeply disconnected from our food. Once we started processing, packaging, freezing, and shipping our food, our relationship to what we eat changed in a dramatic way—and not for the better. Most of the stuff we're eating either barely qualifies as food or is outright harmful to our bodies.

I wish I could say that tapping will make any food you eat healthier. But even with an elevated consciousness, positive thoughts, and a high vibration, you can't turn that McDonald's cheeseburger into something nourishing for your body.

I could go on and on about how much better off we are to start with good, fresh, local, organic food that is full of nutrients and life force. Food that can actually help us, rather than be a burden on our systems. But again, that's a different book. Here I want to address something that tapping really *can* help with: the confusion Marie suffered around what she should and should not be eating.

We've heard so many different theories. We've been told, "Make sure to eat this!" by one expert, while the next expert insists, "Whatever you do, don't eat that!" It's enough to make our heads spin. It's gotten to a point where what we choose to eat is of far less consequence than the poison pill of negative emotions and stress that we swallow along with the food.

Marie recounted her 20-year endeavor to lose weight. For a decade, she was obsessed with "fat-free" and ate all sorts of stuff out of a box. In her mind—because of what the media and "food" companies told her—eating fat-free foods would help keep the fat *off.* It was obvious to Marie that this wasn't working, but she kept doing it. She thought that there must be something wrong with her or that she wasn't doing enough, because everyone in the commercials selling the fat-free stuff looked happy and skinny.

Next, she went on the diet roller coaster: Atkins Diet, South Beach Diet, grapefruit diet, Blood Type Diet, and on and on. With each new diet book she bought and tried, her confusion and frustration grew. "Didn't the last book say the exact opposite of this?"

After Marie recounted her history, I knew the first thing we had to do was quiet down some of the mental noise she experienced around food and dieting. Just as in Chapter 3, when we tapped on the general feelings of being overwhelmed and anxiety of modern life, most of us have some global tapping to do around food and dieting. Without this initial tapping, we're often so stressed out and unclear that it's hard to find the right setup statement.

So let's do some general tapping now, to ease that burden a bit before we get into the specifics.

TAPPING SCRIPT: Stress about Food

(The tapping points chart can be found on page 21.)

Let's see what your starting point is around food. Say out loud, "I am stressed out, anxious, and overwhelmed about food and what to eat and not eat."

On a 0-to-10 scale—10 being 100 percent true and 0 being not true at all—how true does that feel? It doesn't have to be exact or perfect, just write it down.

Now let's getting tapping!

Karate Chop: Even though I'm really stressed out about what I should and shouldn't be eating, I deeply and completely accept myself.

Karate Chop: Even though I can't stop worrying about what's good for me and what's bad for me, I deeply and completely accept myself.

Karate Chop: Even though I've heard so many different things about food and I'm overwhelmed and don't know what to do, I choose to relax now.

Eyebrow: All this stress around food . . .
Side of Eye: Should I eat this?
Under Eye: I can't eat that!
Under Nose: This is good for me . . .
Chin: That's bad for me . . .
Under Arm: Or is it?
Collarbone: I just don't know what to eat . . .
Top of Head: So stressed out about eating . . .

Eyebrow: I've read so many different things . . .
Side of Eye: Everyone seems to disagree about what to eat!
Under Eye: I'm confused, scared, and stressed about food . . .
Under Nose: All this stress around food . . .
Chin: Releasing all this stress around food . . .
Collarbone: All this anxiety around food . . .
Under Arm: I shouldn't eat this . . .
Top of Head: I shouldn't eat that . . .

Eyebrow: Should, shouldn't, should, shouldn't . . .
Side of Eye: So much confusion . . .
Under Eye: Such a burden . . .
Under Nose: So much anxiety . . .
Chin: So much stress . . .
Collarbone: All around food . . .
Under Arm: This stress around food . . .
Top of Head: Releasing all this stress around food.

If you're still feeling strongly negative, or if other things have come up, tap on those specifically. Otherwise, let's do some positive tapping.

Eyebrow: I choose to relax around food now . . .
Side of Eye: I choose to feel safe around food now . . .
Under Eye: Food is safe . . .
Under Nose: I am safe . . .
Chin: I am at peace and easily choose the foods that best nourish me . . .
Collarbone: I relax around food, enjoying every bite I eat, regardless of what it is . . .
Under Arm: Once I choose to eat something, I relax and release any guilt, fear, or anxiety around it.
Top of Head: I choose to relax around food.

Eyebrow: My body knows exactly what it wants and needs . . .
Side of Eye: I attract all the right information to choose the best food for me . . .
Under Eye: Food is safe . . .
Under Nose: I am safe . . .
Chin: I choose to relax now . . .
Collarbone: I let go of any fear, guilt, or anxiety around food . . .
Under Arm: Letting it go . . .
Top of Head: Letting it all go.

Take a deep breath . . . and let it go.

For an extended tapping session on this topic,
visit www.thetappingsolution.com/tap7.

How are you feeling? Let's check in. Say out loud, "I am stressed out, anxious, and overwhelmed about food and what to eat and not eat."

How true does that feel? Did your original rating number go down? What else came up when you were doing the tapping? Remember, when you're doing "global" tapping like this, you really want to pay attention to specific things that come up along the way. I can't instruct you to tap on specific experiences you've had, because I don't know what they are! But you do—so as anything pops up, tap on it and release it. The more specific you get, the more the global tapping will stick.

Marie and I spent most of the session tapping on her stress about food and dieting. I had her recount her experiences of the past 20 years, focusing on her emotions along the way. For example, she told me that when she was on the South Beach Diet, it was a particularly hard time in her life and she remembers looking at the book in anger. So I had her recall that memory and tap on that. On and on we went, detailing her emotions, specific memories, and anything else that came up about her weight-loss journey.

. . . .

Tapping Tip: Have You Been Doing the Actual Tapping?

I don't mean to be harsh, but if you've been reading this book and *not* doing the tapping, you're wasting your time. The difference between tapping and other systems is that tapping can make change *happen*—this isn't just intellectual exploration. I don't want you to walk away knowing more about food and your experience with it; I want you to walk away *being different* around food and your experience with it. So get tapping!

. . . .

When we were done, Marie reported that she felt lighter than she had in years. And she was not just emotionally lighter; she was shocked that her body itself felt so much better. She had an enthusiasm and passion that was missing at the beginning of the session. As happens with EFT, the cognitive shift was profound.

"You know, the last 20 years of dieting have been tough, but I've learned so much," she said. "I know what works for me now, and I know what makes me feel good. I also know what I have to do to lose this weight. And if it doesn't happen immediately, that's okay, too!"

As I shared with you in the pain-relief chapter, I'm always surprised when people say their pain is truly gone. And I feel the same way when this kind of cognitive shift happens. People come from such a different perspective after EFT—a perspective that is wise, compassionate, and peaceful. Often it feels like I'm talking to a new person. In reality, it's the person who was always there but was being drowned out by the noise of negative experiences, emotions, and beliefs.

When I checked back in with Marie a few weeks later, she was happy to report that she had lost seven pounds with little effort beyond tapping. But even more than the weight loss, she emphasized that she felt more peaceful about food and her weight than ever before. She reported, "When I think back on how stressed out, angry, and confused I was about food, I can't believe it. I feel like I have my life back. Even people around me are noticing a new vibrancy and energy in me!"

Ask Yourself . . . Go Back in Time

Most of us have a long and rocky relationship with food and our bodies. If you relate to Marie's story, then you might want to try the same exercise she and I did together. You can write this out with pen and paper, or you can also do it verbally with a friend.

Think back through your experiences with weight loss. When did you first notice that you weren't happy with your body? What diet or exercise did you try? What came next? What happened next? What else did you try? How did you feel during that time? What beliefs did you adopt during this process?

Step by step, remember what this journey looked like. Tap on any relevant events, emotions, or beliefs that come up. If you're doing this with a friend, simply tell your story. Keep tapping on each important point in the story until you feel that the emotional charge is gone.

This is quite a long story for many of us, so feel free to take notes on what comes up to ensure that you clear it fully. It might not happen all at once—you might spend a week or a month tapping on each element—but stick with it. You'll be amazed by how you feel when you're done!

I can't emphasize this enough: the stress you feel about food and weight loss itself can be the very thing that keeps you stuck. Yes, there are often other limiting beliefs, which we'll explore later in this chapter, but start by letting go of the overall stress and feelings of being overwhelmed. As we'll see in the next section, that very stress can be what is making you gain weight—or not be able to lose it.

Why Does Tapping Help with Weight Loss? The Stress Connection

When Marie stopped stressing out about food and weight loss, she lost weight. Why? Well, the stress response can cause a massive cascade of events in your body, including:

- On average four times less blood flow to your digestive system

- Less oxygen to your gut

- Lower absorption of nutrients

- Less enzyme production in your gut. (As much as 20,000 times less! This is one of the reasons why, when you eat a meal while you're stressed, you'll often feel bloated and uncomfortable.)

- Increase in excretion of important nutrients, such as vitamins and minerals

- Decrease in gut flora population

- Increase in cholesterol

- Increase in cortisol and insulin levels

The last item is particularly important for weight loss, because when your cortisol is consistently elevated, it's hard to lose weight or build muscle. In fact, you're more likely to *gain* weight, particularly around your midsection.

When Marie relaxed and stopped stressing about food, her body responded. I think I'll have to put out the next diet book, and here's what it will claim:

Following this diet, you'll lose weight, increase the oxygen to your gut, increase the absorption of nutrients, increase enzyme production (so you won't feel bloated), increase retention of vital nutrients, increase healthy gut flora population, lower your cholesterol, and lower your cortisol and insulin levels. What is this magic diet? What do you eat? *Whatever you want!* Just *relax* while you're doing it. . . .

It'd be a short book, but it would be guaranteed to work for those who follow it!

You don't have to wait for the book to come out; you have everything you need here. When you lower stress levels (and obviously it's not just stress about food—that's what we've been focusing on here, but lowering stress about anything and everything is important), then you'll lose the weight.

That's why people who use EFT on their general stress and feelings of being overwhelmed, traumatic events in their past, and other problems in their lives often lose weight without even trying!

EFT for Food Cravings

I shared in the last chapter that when I am speaking in front of a live audience, I often work on EFT for pain because the results can be so dramatic and easy to witness and measure. The other problem I often turn to is food cravings, because those are also easy to witness and measure.

Working with food cravings in front of a live audience follows a similar trajectory every time. First, we all have some good laughs as I introduce a bag of candy, chocolates, cookies, or other treats people often crave. This can be particularly amusing when I'm speaking in front of a very health-conscious crowd and they admit they are craving this junk food! I pass around the bag and have people pick their favorite. I have them look at it, smell it, and do whatever else it takes to bring their craving levels up. Then I ask for a few volunteers who want to work live onstage to reduce those cravings.

I first ask the volunteers to describe the intensity of their craving on a 0-to-10 scale—and what, in particular, they are feeling or noticing about the candy or chocolate. I immediately get answers like this:

"The craving is a 10. It smells so good . . . can I have a little bite? I love Snickers, and I'm so hungry!"

"It's an 8. I didn't eat much at lunch, and this would really fill me up."

"It's a 10. I can't stop thinking about it—are we going to get to eat these at the end?"

We all have some more laughs, as it becomes obvious that the volunteers are desperate to eat these treats!

And then we begin some very general tapping—*Even though I really crave _____, I deeply and completely accept myself*—and we tap through the points for several rounds.

This generally dulls the edge of the craving—that almost crazed desire for the food—and it's what you can use whenever you're having a craving. Start with the most general and basic tapping to calm down the body.

Once we do a couple of rounds of tapping, you can see the volunteers on stage take a deep breath and settle into their bodies more. The next question I usually ask is, "If there was an emotion behind this craving, what would it be?"

. . . .

Tapping Tip: Working with Cravings

You can often get amazing results and relief from a craving simply by tapping *Even though I have this craving for _____, I deeply and completely accept myself,* repeating the same rounds again and again until the craving subsides.

But it's important to go to the next level—looking at the emotion behind the craving. If we don't get to the root of the craving, to what's causing it in the first place, it's likely to come back a few hours or days later.

Sure, you can tap it down each time. But why not handle the emotion right up front and get rid of the craving once and for all?

. . . .

As people tune in to the emotions behind the craving, that's when the laughter often turns into tears. Many of us use food to suppress or dampen negative emotions, events, and the overall stress in our lives. John, who came up onstage to work on his food craving when I was teaching at Omega, shared that behind the craving he felt a deep sadness. Mark, another one of the volunteers, shared that he didn't understand why, but when he thought about the craving and what was behind it, he felt anger.

And Rick (yes, the three volunteers who came up that particular weekend were all men—a rarity!) told us how he felt fear of the unknown.

We went on to focus on those emotions and the events and patterns behind them, virtually ignoring the food cravings altogether. The stuff we covered is what we've addressed in the rest of this book: the childhood issues, the stress, the feelings of being overwhelmed, the fear. After tapping for about 20 minutes, I asked all three men to check back in on their food cravings. Lo and behold, they were gone!

As my friend Carol Look likes to say, "It's not about the food!" The food is covering up or masking what's really going on underneath. When you address the underlying patterns, emotions, events, and beliefs, that's when your relationship with the food can shift toward something much healthier.

Exercise: Curbing a Craving

If possible, get your food of choice in front of you so you can see it. And if you crave something other than food—a glass of wine or a cigarette, for example—you can use that instead. If you don't have your craved food around, create a mental picture of it in your mind.

How does your craved food smell? Hold it in your hand—how does it feel? Stand back and look at it; take in all aspects of it. Is there something about the way it looks that really does it for you? Use these elements as part of your tapping.

Walk yourself through the process of acquiring the food. Do you have to go somewhere to purchase it? Do you have to unwrap it? (Some people get excited just hearing the crackling of the wrapper.) Is there a sound that goes along with it (the sizzle of cooking, the crunch when you sink your teeth into it)? Use all these aspects as part of your tapping.

After you've done a round of tapping and the intensity of the craving has dropped, go back and smell it again. Has the smell changed in any way? If you can, take a small nibble or sip. Has the taste changed in any way? Did your craving go up again, or do you find that you could take it or leave it?

Sometimes cravings pop up when we're stressed. The next time you find yourself suddenly hit by a craving, stop and do a little detective work. Who were you just with or what just happened before the craving hit? What was the topic of conversation? What were you just thinking about? Many times we're reaching for that craving without even being aware that something specific triggered it. When you identify the trigger, you can tap directly on the feelings generated by it—and most likely skip the craving altogether.

You Gotta Move Your Butt . . .

Sharon, a mother of two from Maine, shared with me that she was happy with the progress she was making in losing weight. She had found an eating plan that she felt good about, and it was working, though not as fast as she wanted it to.

After we did the necessary tapping on her stress and feelings of being overwhelmed about dieting, weight loss, her body, and so forth, I asked her, "What are you doing for exercise?"

She looked down sheepishly and said, "Oh . . . I don't really like to exercise."

I smiled back at her, not saying anything, as she went on.

"I know, I know. I need to exercise, it's good for me, and I'll lose weight much faster and feel better," she said. "I used to love to run, but now I'm so heavy and clunky that I just feel awkward when I try."

We had our starting point for tapping: *I just feel awkward when I try to run.* I had her measure how true that felt on a 0-to-10 scale and she replied that it was an 8. So we began tapping on the statement *Even though I feel awkward when I try to run, I deeply and completely accept myself* and continued for several rounds. She then said, "It's really my legs that feel clunky and heavy." So we tapped on that until she said, "My body feels lighter . . . I can do it, I can run a bit." (Notice how so many people in this chapter use the word *lighter* when describing their body after tapping with relation to weight loss! A coincidence? I don't think so!)

There are three ways I generally address resistance to exercise:

1. **Describe how you're feeling when you think about exercise, and tap on that.** So you might say "I feel lazy and don't want to move" or "It's too hard, and I hate sweating" or "It's too much work to exercise." Whatever your mind tells you is what to tap on. See the "Ask Yourself" box on page 120 that lists other obstacles that might be in the way when it comes to exercise.

2. **Simply tap on, *Even though I don't want to exercise, I deeply and completely accept myself.*** While it's always better to get specific, when I'm feeling lazy (sometimes I don't want to dig deep and find the root cause of everything in my life!), I use a global statement like this. Doing a couple of rounds of this one gets the energy going and the next thing I know, I'm on the treadmill or doing yoga.

3. **Identify the root cause.** This is obviously the most effective and lasting way to approach your resistance to exercise. I'll share an example of a root cause below in Sharon's story. And in the next couple of pages, we'll address all sorts of root causes regarding weight loss, exercise, body image, and more.

Ask Yourself . . . Limiting Beliefs about Exercise

Do any of these apply to you? Identify them, measure them, and then tap on them!

- If I start exercising, I'll always have to exercise.

- I'm not really the jock type.

- It will take too much time.

- I can't afford a personal trainer.

- I can't afford a gym membership.

- I'm too busy.

- I travel a lot for my business and can't keep a routine.

- I'm too tired—I don't have the energy to work out.

- If I have more energy, I'll have to take on more responsibility.

These are just some examples. Work with these or find your specific limiting beliefs.

After we did the general tapping with Sharon on how her body felt heavy and clunky and she felt more ready to exercise, I wanted to dig deeper on the issue. So I asked her to close her eyes and visualize herself standing in front of a mirror at her perfect weight, having achieved her goal of fitting into the "skinny jeans" she told me she had. I could see her smiling as she pictured herself fitting into the skinny jeans, until I asked her, "Is there any downside to being at this weight?" The smile faded as she quickly replied, "My husband will pay more attention to me, and I don't want that. "

Sharon was in a difficult relationship with her husband. The intimacy had faded, and she generally wasn't happy being with him. She had been considering divorce for several years but had stayed with him because she had two kids at home and felt it was better for them if their parents were together. She was scared that by losing weight—looking and feeling better—she would attract his sexual attention again, and she had no interest in being with him in that way.

Her relationship issues certainly needed to be addressed at some level, but since we were focusing on her weight and resistance to exercise, we began by tapping on that:

Even though I don't want to lose weight because then my husband will be attracted to me, I deeply and completely accept myself.

Even though it's not safe to fit into my skinny jeans, I choose to feel safe now.

Even though I don't want my husband to notice me, I deeply and completely accept myself.

After several rounds of tapping, I asked her to visualize that same picture— standing in front of the mirror in her skinny jeans—and to share with me what she saw and how she felt.

"I can easily tell my husband that I'm not interested and feel safe doing so," she said. "And who knows? Maybe if I look and feel better, I will have more energy for the relationship and things might improve."

The next step for Sharon would be to look at her relationship—her feelings toward it and toward her husband—and to clear out the stress and negative emotions surrounding it. But she took a first step at the very least, getting herself moving forward, both literally and energetically!

A few weeks later, Sharon reported in:

I started running. Many days I can go the first 11 minutes without stopping and walking. But today, I went 15 minutes straight! This felt like a huge accomplishment, because on the route I run, the minutes from 12 to 15 are a gradual hill. I felt awesome doing it!

I also weighed myself today. I am at a 13-pound weight loss total and have stayed there for over a week, and it was over New Year's! I'm happy with that!

Ask Yourself . . . Upsides and Downsides of Exercising

Remember Chapter 4 where we addressed the upsides and downsides to change? See if any of the statements below apply to you. If so, tap on them. What's the downside of working out or exercising?

- I won't have any time left to relax.
- It's expensive—I'll have to buy equipment or new gear, or join a gym.
- More energy means taking on more work and responsibility.
- I won't have time for anything else.
- I could get injured.

What's the *upside* to staying where I am?

- I don't have to juggle time with the family.
- I get to relax and unwind.
- I won't be expected to try new and unfamiliar things.
- I won't have to embarrass myself and feel awkward in those classes.
- I won't have to feel like a failure when I quit again.

Once you've identified your particular downsides and upsides, you can tap on them specifically.

Your Weight Loss Picture: The Tapping Tree

Remember our tapping tree? We're going to do one for weight loss, to identify the side effects, emotions, events, and beliefs that you have around weight, food, your body, exercise, and more.

You can get a blank tapping tree at www.thetappingsolution.com/tree, or you can draw your own.

On the following page, I've listed some examples of what might fit into each category. Use these as a launching point for filling in your own tree.

The Leaves (Side Effects)

10 extra pounds
Low energy
Cellulite
I'm fat!
No muscle
Clothes don't fit
Tire easily
Can't catch my breath
Poor self-image

The Branches (Emotions)

Anger
Sadness
Embarrassment
Self-reproach
Failure
Fear of judgment

The Trunk (Events)

The time John told me I was fat
The time my mother told me to stop eating so much
The time everyone got asked to the dance and no one asked me to go
The time I couldn't fit into my favorite jeans
The time my husband said I didn't look the way I did 20 years ago
The time my trainer said I wasn't working out hard enough

The Roots (Limiting Beliefs)

I can't lose weight—I've tried before.
It's hard to lose weight.
It's in my genes.
I'm just "big-boned."

You have to be deprived to lose weight.
I'll be vulnerable if I lose weight.

Remember, beliefs are built from experiences and messages received over the course of a lifetime. We use this "evidence" to continue to support our beliefs. When we take the "legs" out from under the belief through tapping, we can start to create new beliefs that support new decisions about how we nourish and move our bodies.

On the following pages, I'll expand on some of these limiting beliefs in more detail, and you can determine whether they apply to you.

Limiting Belief Number 1—I Can't Lose Weight

If you have tried unsuccessfully to diet many times before, you may find yourself struggling with a strong belief that you can't lose weight. You may believe that you can lose only so many pounds or that you can't lose any at all. When it doesn't feel like you can succeed, it's easy to develop a "why bother?" attitude. This will override your desire to eat healthily and to exercise, until it seems like a constant battle to make any progress!

Even though I've tried before and it didn't work . . .
Even though it's impossible for me to lose weight . . .
Even though I don't see the point in putting myself through this again—why bother . . . ?

Or maybe you think you can't lose weight because everyone in your family struggles with weight, so it's just the way it's going to be for you. Or you were once told that you have a slow metabolism, and ever since then, you've believed your body doesn't *want* to lose weight.

Even though no one else in the family can lose weight and neither can I . . .
Even though my metabolism is so slow that I can't lose weight . . .
Even though my body is different than everyone else's and mine just holds on to the weight, I deeply and completely accept myself.

Limiting Belief Number 2—It's Hard to Lose Weight

It's easy to see why this would be a belief—after all, there's tons of evidence to support it! All one has to do is revisit the effort it took to follow the last diet plan—especially if it entailed preparing foods that you weren't familiar with, measuring and weighing everything you ate, and learning new cooking methods. And on top of it, you have to exercise! You have to create new habits, and we all know how hard it is to change habits (another limiting belief). The reasons *why* you want to lose weight and be healthy lose their steam compared to the *why nots!*

This is a perfect place to tap, because tapping will help with the frustration that often accompanies the early stages of learning something new. Tapping on the feelings that come up when you're outside your comfort zone allows you to hang in there long enough for the new thing to become the familiar thing!

Even though it's too hard to lose weight . . .
Even though I don't want to work that hard . . .
Even though it's going to take too much effort to figure it all out . . .
Even though I don't think I have what it takes to stick with it, I deeply and completely accept myself.

Limiting Belief Number 3—You Have to Deprive Yourself to Lose Weight

You're probably thinking that this belief is the truth because it's your experience—and it's also what every diet out there reinforces. Even if you've tried a diet that permits you to have a treat here and there, you will most likely have to cut back on certain things. For most of us, this brings up a wealth of feelings—all of them perfect tapping targets! Tap for the fear, the frustration, the anger, and the rebellion. Go ahead and have a good rant while you're tapping!

Even though I can't lose weight unless I give up sweets entirely . . .
Even though I can't eat as much as I want to . . .
Even though I felt deprived the last time I lost weight and I'll have to do it again . . .
Even though I'm afraid to feel deprived . . .
Even though it makes me mad that I can't have what I want, I deeply and completely accept myself.

Limiting Belief Number 4—I'll Be Vulnerable if I Lose the Weight

Remember in Chapter 4, when we uncovered all those hidden reasons why making a change could be risky? Those hidden *why nots* play a big role in weight loss. Unless you do the work to release them, you will not have the success you are hoping for.

Although on the conscious level we may want the weight loss, the subconscious may be harboring its own reasons for keeping the weight on. These are not always obvious and may require some detective work to bring into the light. For example, if you have a history of trauma or abuse, the weight could be serving as a defense mechanism. It can feel safer to be protected with those extra pounds. When you start to lose the weight, you can end up feeling vulnerable and exposed.

Even though I'm afraid of getting unwanted attention . . .
Even though I won't be able to protect myself if I lose the weight . . .
Even though if I don't have this extra weight they will be able to hurt me again . . .

We absolutely have a need to protect ourselves; it's part of our survival plan. If losing weight seems to threaten your connections with other people, you better believe it will be a struggle to get healthy. The changes we make affect those around us and oftentimes result in others trying to sabotage our best efforts.

Even though my mom/husband/best friend will be angry/jealous if I lose the weight . . .
Even though my family always gives me a hard time if I don't eat with them . . .
Even though I want to be like everyone else and order dessert when we go out . . .

Maintaining a stable identity is one of the strongest drives in our nature. It's a delicate balance that can be easily disturbed by making a big change. Who will you *be* when you lose the weight? What did you say you would do in your life when you lost the weight—go back to school, jump out of a plane, start singing onstage? What if you're not ready to do those things? Here's a strategy: tap on the beliefs that are keeping you from living a healthy life. Then you can make a separate decision—and do a separate round of tapping—on whether or not you want to make those other changes.

Even though I'm afraid that I'll have to make major changes in my life when I lose the weight . . .

Even though I don't know who I would be if I lost the weight . . .

Even though I'm afraid that I'll still be unhappy when I lose the weight—and then what?—I deeply and completely accept myself.

These are just a few of the most common limiting beliefs people face when they want to lose weight. It's likely you resonated with at least one or two of them. If you didn't and you have weight you'd like to lose, go ahead and dig deeper in your own experience to find out what's going on with you specifically. Digging deeper might involve journaling, speaking to your parents about what you were like as a child (and their experience of your weight gain or loss) talking to a friend, etc.

Exercise: Your Weight-Loss Tapping Tree

Go ahead and fill out your weight-loss tapping tree. Remember, you can get a blank tapping tree at www.thetappingsolution.com/tree. There's likely a lot to fill in, so try not to get overwhelmed! Rather, take it one step at a time and know that tapping through the different elements on this tree will make a dramatic difference. Not just in your weight-loss journey, but in all areas of your life.

CHAPTER 9

CREATING LOVE AND HEALTHY RELATIONSHIPS

Our parents, our children, our spouses, and our friends will continue to press every button we have, until we realize what it is that we don't want to know about ourselves, yet. They will point us to our freedom every time.

BYRON KATIE

It was love at first sight.

Actually, that's not true. "First sight" happened when she was ten years old. Years later, I found out that it might have been love at first sight for *her*—she had a huge crush on me—but I was a too-cool 18-year-old who (for many reasons) didn't notice my younger sister's best friend.

When we reconnected 15 years later, it was definitely *like* at first sight. Or at least, *interested but not sure* at first sight.

And then tapping changed everything.

Okay, let me back up a bit and explain what happened. A few years ago, I found myself single for the first time in six years. I was coming out of a committed relationship with a wonderful person; things just hadn't worked out the way we'd wanted them to. While I knew that going our separate ways was ultimately the right decision, it didn't make the process any easier.

Knowing something—reasoning that it's the right move, even intuiting that you're going in the right direction—doesn't necessarily make the heart hurt any less. When a relationship ends, so many pieces of your life have to be put back together. There is so much change, so much uncertainty. There's not an adult alive who hasn't felt heartbreak and everything that goes with it. That's exactly where I found myself back then.

The beautiful thing about using tapping in a situation like that is that it ties in perfectly with the natural healing process. I don't believe that you can break off a long-term relationship, do tapping for an hour, and feel fine the next day. But I do believe that you can use it to move much more quickly through the grieving process and through the process of letting go.

Without tapping, you might obsess about a previous lover for months or years. You might be stuck feeling anger at your former partner and carrying the baggage—the pain and negative experiences—into your next relationship. Tapping can help you forgive, let go, and move on.

So there I was, single again—and wondering what was next. How do I move forward? Do I date again? What went wrong in my last relationship? Do I need to change? Was it my fault?

The usual practice is for people to ask themselves these questions again and again, with no real answers, conclusions, or closure. But of course, I asked myself these questions and used EFT to move forward. For example, when I started thinking about dating again, certain thoughts, beliefs, and emotions came up.

I'm 31 years old—where do I even go to date?
Do I have to go online? It's so embarrassing to have to fill out a profile and pick a picture. Ugh. I just don't want to put myself out there again . . .

So I tapped.

Even though I'm stressed out about dating again, I deeply and completely accept myself.
Even though I'm not ready to put myself out there . . . do I have to go online? It's so embarrassing . . . I deeply and completely accept myself.
Even though I don't want to put myself out there again, I deeply and completely accept myself.

Note that the tapping I did is the simplest form you can do: take exactly what you're thinking and turn it into tapping phrases.

Once I did the tapping, I felt myself relax. Soon the cognitive shift happened. "You know, it might be fun to go on some dates! I'm sure I'll meet interesting people. If it's a disaster, at least I can have a good laugh about it with my friends!"

I used EFT extensively during this time period to heal, to let go, and to move forward. I tapped on a huge variety of issues. Once I had spent a few months getting myself back on my feet, tapping every day, building a new life, I found myself ready and willing to get back out there. I'll spare you the details of the first dates, because there are no lessons in there—none related to tapping, anyway! But with the newfound energy I got through tapping—and a true alignment to move forward in my life and find the perfect person for my self—a strange idea came to mind.

Ask Yourself . . . What Are Your Fears about Dating?

Take a look at the list of limiting beliefs below and see if any of them resonate with you. You can try saying them out loud to check in on them and give them a number on the 0-to-10 scale, with 10 indicating that they feel totally true for you.

- Why bother? It never works out anyway.
- I'm not attractive/thin/rich/interesting enough.
- It will take too much time.
- I don't know how to do this dating thing.
- I have trouble meeting people.
- I'm too picky/old/set in my ways/busy.
- I have children.
- My job is too demanding.
- I have no time to go out.

Remember the girl I mentioned in the beginning of the chapter, the one I had known for 15 years? Her name was Brenna, and she had been my sister, Jessica's best friend that whole time. We had known each other but only in passing. I would see her at the house when I came home to visit my parents and Jessica, and I would hear what she was up to every once in a while. Even though I found her attractive, we were never really close. But for some reason, I thought to ask Jessica how Brenna was doing—and if she was dating anyone. A little hesitant, Jessica said no, she was single. I asked what she thought about us dating.

At this point, the eight-year age difference meant very little. I figured I might be able to make use of the fact that she had a crush on me when she was ten. While Jessica was initially uncomfortable at the thought of her best friend and her older brother dating, she said she thought we would be a good match in a lot of ways.

On an impulse, I reached out to Brenna by e-mail. We spent some time chatting and connecting again, until a series of circumstances brought us together just a few weeks later. We met at an event in New York where I was speaking about tapping. Brenna had volunteered to help EFT expert Carol Look, who was running the event.

There was definitely a spark or two in the first few days, but I wasn't convinced.

"Brenna is great and right for me in so many ways," I shared with Carol, "but I just don't think she's the one. I can't explain it, but her heart doesn't feel open to me. I need someone who can be fully loving and engaged in a relationship."

As it happened, the day after I shared this with Carol, Brenna came up to me and asked if I would spend some time tapping with her one-on-one. She wanted to do some work around a previous relationship. I agreed, taking off my "I kind of like this girl" hat and putting on my "I'll do anything to help this human being heal" hat, and we started tapping.

She shared with me that her previous relationship had been very painful. In a nutshell, her boyfriend had been deceptive. He'd cheated on her, had been in another relationship at the same time, had never given her any real closure, and had generally been a jerk! I could see the pain she felt when she talked about it.

We began tapping on exactly what happened—on the story. This is often the easiest way to release the top layer of pain and hurt to uncover what's really going on. Oftentimes when we do this—when we tap while sharing what happened in the past—we start to recognize that the issues go deeper than the actual events. We begin to uncover the deeper wounds beneath.

As she shared with me what happened and her feelings about it, she told me that she felt humiliated about the way he had treated her. As soon as she said that word, *humiliated,* I could tell that it captured her deepest hurts and core wounding. So we began to tap on that feeling specifically.

Even though I'm so humiliated about what happened, I deeply and completely accept myself.

That word was such a trigger that we focused on it again and again, tapping through multiple rounds with the exact same phrasing. Whenever you're tapping, look for key words and phrases that really strike a chord. Just as with Judy, who you'll remember was so angry at her father—and that feeling was all she had to work on to get a massive clearing—Brenna felt *humiliated* about what had happened. Focusing on that word brought a flood of tears and, eventually, a huge sigh of relief.

From there, we proceeded to tap on the beliefs she had formed from that experience, beliefs like "I can't trust men." It's easy to see how such a painful experience can generate that belief. If it's not cleared and healed, the person will either re-create the same situations again and again or stay out of relationships in order to avoid the pain.

It was beautiful to see how Brenna relaxed and let go of the past. She shared that she felt so much better and thanked me for my time. But to me, that wasn't the most exciting and fascinating part of what happened. What really blew me away was what happened at dinner just 30 minutes later.

Remember how I shared that my reservation about Brenna was that I didn't feel her heart was open enough? As we sat down for dinner that evening, I was shocked to notice how much I could feel her heart open. My feelings started changing immediately. It couldn't have been more than ten minutes into dinner that I said to myself, "This woman is amazing—I'm falling in love with her."

What had changed in that hour-long tapping session that so dramatically affected my feelings toward Brenna? And why is this lesson so important for you? Before we tapped together, Brenna was scared of being hurt again. She was carrying her past negative experience into her current reality, and it was affecting how she acted, the choices she made, the things she said, and so forth.

As for me, I had been scared to go out in the world, to be single again, to get my heart broken again. But I tapped, and the next thing I knew, Brenna was in my life. Brenna felt similarly. She was afraid of being humiliated again, afraid that she couldn't fully trust me. So she tapped, and the next thing she knew, we found ourselves in a loving, committed relationship.

What was most interesting to me about this whole experience was how dramatically different I felt about Brenna when her heart opened and she released the past. Nothing changed about how she looked, what she did, her personality, or who she was at the core. She simply released old fears and opened a part of herself and her heart. That changed everything for me.

Brenna and I got married on September 22, 2012. If our story isn't a testimony to the power of tapping, I don't know what is!

Baggage Check

We all understand the term *baggage* as it relates to relationships. "She has so much baggage." "I wouldn't date him, he comes with way too much baggage." Here, "baggage" points toward previous negative experiences, events, and beliefs that are brought into a current relationship.

Why do we never refer to a child as having baggage? Because most of them don't! "Baggage" is everything we've been talking about throughout this book—the negative emotions, defining events, and limiting beliefs that we have collected throughout our lives and that we carry around with us at all times.

Before Brenna and I got together, we both had baggage from our previous relationships. And if we hadn't used EFT to release that baggage, we may not have gotten together at all. Worse, we might have gotten together in an unhealthy way, bringing all our crap from the past into the current relationship.

Why do we attract the same kind of person again and again? Why do our relationships often seem to get worse as we get older? You'd think wisdom would come with time and experience, but instead, many people become more jaded and angry the more relationship attempts they make. Again, it's all the baggage they pick up from relationship after relationship, experience after experience.

If we had a visual of the baggage we're carrying around, it would either make us laugh, cry, or both! Picture every negative experience, emotion, or belief you have about past relationships. If each of them were a bag you had to carry around with you everywhere you go, would you get very far?

It's really quite simple. You can either choose to heal, let go, and return these bags to where they came from, or you can feel burdened by them for the rest of your life. How healthy can you be in your current relationship—or how successfully can you find the right one—if you're carrying all this stuff around?

TAPPING SCRIPT: Relationship Baggage

(The tapping points chart can be found on page 21.)

This is a very general script to start bringing up and clearing issues from past relationships. Stay on the lookout for specific memories and ideas that come up, and tap on them, too.

Karate Chop: Even though I've got all this relationship baggage, perhaps I can accept myself anyway.

Karate Chop: Even though I've gathered all this baggage from all those other relationships, I'm choosing to find a way to put it down.

Karate Chop: Even though I've been carrying this relationship baggage with me—it sure is getting heavy—I'm just going to acknowledge that this is what I've been doing and accept myself anyway.

Eyebrow: This relationship baggage . . .
Side of Eye: All those old hurts and fears . . .
Under Eye: The pain and suffering . . .
Under Nose: All those tears . . .
Chin: I've been gathering all this baggage . . .
Collarbone: Carrying it with me into every relationship . . .
Under Arm: As a reminder to keep me safe . . .
Top of Head: But, boy, is it getting heavy!

Eyebrow: All these old ghosts and memories . . .
Side of Eye: But what if I could find a way . . .
Under Eye: To put down some of these old bags . . .
Under Nose: I'm ready to travel lighter . . .
Chin: What if I could be curious about this whole relationship thing?
Collarbone: I wonder what possibilities that would open up?
Under Arm: I'm so glad I've decided to put down some of this old baggage . . .
Top of Head: I'm ready to travel lighter.

For an extended tapping session on this topic,
visit www.thetappingsolution.com/tap8.

Now let's take a look at some of the other common baggage many of us carry.

Baggage from Our Parents

Our parents are often the first example we have of what a relationship looks like. Especially because they surround us in our formative years, there's a strong tendency to model what they do and say.

At the most extreme level, patterns of abuse—verbal, physical, and emotional—tend to be repeated again and again, from generation to generation. If a child saw his father beat his mother when he was angry, then the child learns, often subconsciously, that this is an appropriate response or behavior. Of course, there are countless examples of the opposite happening, of those who vow never to be violent the way their parents were. But that choice often requires significant growth in the individual and healing of the generational pattern.

Even if there wasn't abuse in the family, children pick up the subtlest patterns of relating and carry them into the future. Does the father go quiet and close down after the end of a stressful day at work? Does the mother nag her husband to get things done? What does the child learn from witnessing all this? She learns that this is how things happen in life.

You might be familiar with the classic folk song, "Cat's in the Cradle" by Harry Chapin, which tells of a father not being able to play with his son—not having time, because he's too busy with work. As the son grows up and the father retires, the father wants to spend more time with his son, to make up for the past. This time, it's the son who is too busy. The father then laments that his boy had grown up to be just like him.

We can use EFT to break these generational patterns, to avoid bringing them into our new relationships. One of the most effective ways to do this is to tap on childhood issues and experiences. Witnessing and remembering what happened between your parents—and tapping on the emotions, events, and beliefs that formed because of those events—can create a profound shift.

Ask Yourself . . . Baggage from Our Parents

What "lessons" are you carrying around? Do any of these statements feel true to you?

- Love hurts.

- You can never leave, no matter how bad it gets.

- You'll have to give up who you are to be in a relationship.

- You'll have to give up the things you love.

- The angry one has all the power.

- Never talk about your needs, and don't expect them to get met.

Not sure how to begin finding your family history about relationships? Here are a few good questions to get you started!

- How was love shown in your family?

- How were disagreements handled?

- If someone had a problem or needed help, how did they get support?

- Who had the power, and how did you know it?

- What did you hear about relationships, about how men and women were?

- How was affection shown between your parents? With other family members?

Now go outside your immediate family and consider the relationships your grandparents, aunts, and uncles had; ask the same questions. Often this helps us to see the patterns and beliefs that have been handed down for several generations.

Professional Profile: Dr. Joe Mercola

Next to Gary Craig, the founder of EFT, no one has done more to spread the word about EFT than Dr. Joe Mercola. Founder of Dr. Mercola's Natural Health Center in Chicago, Dr. Mercola provides medical information and resources to millions through his website Mercola.com, which he started in 1997. Today it is one of the most highly regarded websites for natural health. His background as an osteopathic physician (D.O.) is unique, because osteopathic medicine practices a whole-person approach. Studying both natural and traditional medicine, Dr. Mercola focuses on preventative health care.

He is also a huge proponent of EFT. His first exposure to EFT was when a woman assisted in helping him with a personal relationship breakdown. She introduced him to tapping, and they tapped on "not deserving." Immediately he found resolution—and weeks later, an amazing relationship! This personal experience with EFT left him wanting to learn more, and he began offering it on his website as a tool for others.

I distinctly remember sitting in the audience at a conference where Dr. Mercola was speaking about general health and wellness. He spent more than an hour detailing the most important actions to take for health, such as having adequate vitamin D levels; eating fresh, unprocessed foods; exercising; taking certain supplements; and so forth. After covering these topics in detail, he concluded his talk by saying that while all these elements were important for health, there was one crucial component that needed to be addressed first, because it has the biggest overall impact on health: childhood trauma! What was his tool of choice to address childhood trauma along with other emotional stressors? Why, EFT, of course.

Baggage from Past Relationships

Emily had been divorced for more than a year, but the pain was still excruciating. After a 15-year marriage, putting the pieces of her life back together was more difficult than she could have imagined.

In spite of knowing the divorce was absolutely the best decision for her, she still felt pain. While she had already experienced a tremendous amount of relief, growth, and positive change in the year since the split, she also still felt hurt. The thought of being in a relationship again terrified her—the potential for pain was too great. So she focused on her career to keep her mind off the past. She knew it was time to move on, but she just couldn't find a way to do it.

When we sat down to tap together, she shared everything that had happened and how she was feeling. I'm going to recount the highlights of the hour we spent tapping together, focusing on the tapping statements for each event or emotion. That way you can see both the progression and the evolution of the session—and identify what you can tap for yourself.

As you read this, think back to previous relationships where negative emotion remains—be it anger, sadness, or grief.

Tapping on Emily's Divorce

Issue 1—*There was no closure. We broke up, but then talked here and there and I didn't know the last time I would see him, and something feels incomplete.*

Rarely are breakups perfect. Things are left unsaid, the wrong things get said, or the timing is wrong. It helps to tap to release that regret.

Issue 2—*The memories are the most difficult. They sucker punch me in the stomach out of the blue.*

When we've built a life around someone, it can feel like we're on another planet when they're no longer there. Sometimes the littlest things can remind us of what was. If we don't heal the relationship, we'll continue to be triggered again and again. This is what was happening to Emily.

Issue 3—*I'm worried about him. I was always taking care of him. I feel grief and sadness that he is alone.*

The most nurturing of us want to give, help, and support our partner, even when it's hurting us or we don't get that nurturing back.

Issue 4—*I feel like I wasted 15 years not living my life in order to facilitate his happiness. I'm angry about that.*

Usually, people are angry first—then the anger turns into sadness. In this case, Emily had been focusing on the sadness of the situation, and when she tapped on that, anger rose up that she didn't even know she felt. Her nurturing and mothering instincts were not coming from a healthy place. When she tapped on them, her built-up resentment arose.

Issue 5—*The whole divorce was so messy. The day I was in court to finalize it was terrible. I feel ill just talking about what happened that day.*

At this point in the session, a specific, painful memory came up. Instead of doing the basic "even though . . ." tapping, I had her tap while telling the story, describing to me what happened that day, step by step.

Issue 6—*It's hard to have walked away. I want to be needed, and he needed me.*

Notice the awareness that Emily expresses. At this point, we'd done a lot of tapping on the anger, sadness, and specific painful events, and she was starting to recognize some of the subtler issues in the relationship. Identifying these and clearing the originating cause for them would make a massive difference as she moved forward.

Issue 7—*I'm turning 41. What now?*

At the start of the session, Emily wouldn't even have considered a new relationship. By this point, her mind had opened up to the possibility, and her limiting beliefs about it were coming up!

Issue 8—*I'm ready to let go of him.*

After doing some tapping on Emily's age and the possibilities for the future, she spontaneously declared, "I'm ready to let go of him."

The above shows how a tapping session can evolve, moving from one issue to another. In a more traditional healing process, each step might take months. With EFT, we're still going through the emotions and still learning the lessons from each step of the way—we're just doing it much faster.

Instead of being stuck in anger for months or years, we can process it in minutes and then take a look at what comes next and move through that step.

The opportunity here is to let go of the baggage of past relationships, let go of the baggage and generational patterns from our parents, and create a relationship that is healthy and nurturing at the deepest levels.

Tapping on Your Current Relationship

Obviously these same patterns—this same baggage—can show up in existing relationships, just as much as when you're looking for a new one. I've found two main areas to focus on with relationships that make the biggest difference.

The first is what we've already discussed: taking a look at what we learned from our parents about relationships, the experiences we've had in prior relationships, and how our past is affecting our current relationship.

The second way to use tapping is for the lighter stuff, the day-to-day frustration with a partner, the disagreements, and so forth. If you have an extremely open and loving relationship, you can even tap together. But I've found that, more often than not, it's more effective for each person to do that tapping individually and then come back to the issue after having released some or all of the charge around it.

One word of caution. When your partner is angry at you, it's rarely a good idea to suggest, "Why don't you tap on that?" This can often make things worse! People want their emotions and feelings to be acknowledged first, not just pushed away as if they're wrong or don't mean anything. So the first step always needs to be just that. Then, once your partner feels heard, you can consider tapping together to fully release the charge.

In the same vein, your job is not to "fix" your partner, and tapping isn't a tool to do that with. Work on your own stuff first. If your partner angers easily, don't think of ways you can change that. Rather, think about how you *react* to that anger. Are you open and loving? Or do you react back? Then use EFT on yourself to change the pattern. You'll be pleasantly surprised with what happens!

Exercise: Relationship Baggage

Instead of a tree, we're going to look at all the baggage we're carrying around when it comes to a relationship. (Feel free to do a relationship tapping tree as well, if you'd like!)

1. **Baggage around past relationship history.** Make a list of the significant relationships you've had up till now—even if some of these weren't long and involved love relationships. Include any that might have some residual effect, including flings, one-night stands, rebound make-outs, and office-party mistakes. (Even if the residual effect is simply embarrassment!)

2. **Find your reasons.** What do you believe were the reasons for this relationship ending? What matters here is the way *you* remember it—not the way your best friend or sister tells it.

3. **Conclusions.** As far as you can remember, what were the conclusions you came up with about why that relationship ended? Some ideas might be:

- I wasn't attractive/smart/sexy/thin/rich enough.

- He/she couldn't handle that I had kids.

- I was too needy/clingy/jealous.

- I was too insecure.

- There is something wrong with me.

4. **Rate it.** Take one of your statements and rate it on the 0-to-10 scale according to how true it feels when you say it. Write down the number.

- When have you felt that way before?

- What happened back then—what did you hear and see that brought you to that conclusion?

5. **Make the movie.** Use the Movie Technique (page 67) to tap on any incident that is connected to those beliefs, collapsing all the aspects from that event. Once you've run through the movie, go back and say the setup statement again and rate it. You'll probably notice your number has changed quite a bit.

6. **Keep going.** As new memories come up, tap on them in the same way until they, too, have been collapsed.

Go back to Step 3 and reexamine the reasons you gave for why the relationship ended. Most likely, you'll be able to put new eyes on it— seeing and feeling it differently.

Note: Tapping doesn't take away the facts of what happened—like if someone cheated on you—but it does sever the trauma (baggage) associated with those facts. You retain the learning from the event without having to keep the uncomfortable feelings associated with it.

CHAPTER 10

MAKING MONEY AND ACHIEVING YOUR DREAMS

Keep away from people who try to belittle your ambitions.
Small people always do that, but the really great make
you feel that you, too, can become great.

MARK TWAIN

By most stretches of the imagination, what I was attempting to do was impossible.

Fortunately, *I* didn't know that . . .

I had been studying EFT for several years, using it with clients, friends, family, and anybody else willing to give it a try. I was amazed by the results I was seeing in the people around me—and my personal results with it. I was even more astounded by what I was reading in Gary Craig's *EFT Insights* newsletter, which documented people from around the world achieving miraculous results on a huge variety of issues. (*EFT Insights* is now published by EFT Universe.) I said to myself, "There needs to be a documentary that shows EFT in action—and I'm going to make it!"

This statement might make sense coming from a documentary filmmaker or perhaps from a full-time EFT expert. But not from someone who was at the time buying, fixing up, and selling houses. Someone who had no experience whatsoever in filmmaking, limited financial resources (I was living in a 500-square-foot apartment), and no team or support staff to implement the idea.

What I did have was vision. I knew that this information had to get out into the world, that I was passionate about it, and that nothing was going to stop me. What I didn't know was everything that would have to happen in order to make my dream a reality. Ignorance can indeed be bliss!

Just two weeks after having the idea, I had maxed out my credit cards, gotten a bank credit line, and dug under the couch for any spare change to buy $40,000 worth of camera and audio equipment, lights, computers, and everything else I was told I'd need to make a movie. I had also enlisted the help of my younger sister, Jessica. Recruitment went something like this:

Me: Hey, Jess, you know that tapping thing? What do you think about making a movie about it? I don't know how we'll do it, but it should make for a good adventure.

Jessica: Well, I know nothing about making movies, but I do love tapping. Sure, why not!

And my best friend, Nick Polizzi . . .

Me: Hey, Nick, you went to graphic design school, so you're sort of artistic. You know that tapping thing we've done a couple of times? Want to make a movie about it, and can you film and edit everything?

Nick Polizzi: Ummm . . . I've never filmed a documentary before, but I'm sure I could figure it out. Why not?

There were more conversations to follow, but that's how it started. We had an idea, and we went for it. When I share this story on radio interviews or onstage, I love being able to say that the end product, *The Tapping Solution*, is a moving, heartfelt, well-produced documentary that has sold tens of thousands of copies and has changed lives around the world.

The reason I love to say this is that if you hear about three young people setting out to make a documentary film with a limited budget and no filmmaking experience, you might expect that the end product would look like a home movie. However, with a lot of luck and hard work—not to mention the magic of EFT itself—we were able to put something together that we are extremely proud of.

So how were we able to do this? And more important, how can you apply the same principles to follow your own passions, achieve a big goal, and make a difference in the world while being financially, emotionally, and spiritually rewarded? Why, tapping of course!

My Beliefs Prior to Making *The Tapping Solution*

The film is truly a product of EFT. I used tapping so consistently in the years before the project that you might say EFT made it possible in the first place.

As soon as I discovered EFT, I quickly recognized that I had a story around money and success that didn't serve me. (I saw this with the help of an amazing expert, Carol Look, who would later become my close friend.) For the previous eight years, I had been an entrepreneur, having lasted only three months at a corporate job after college before I quit. And while I loved the freedom of being an entrepreneur, my financial situation was boom or bust. I'd have some great years and then some terrible years. I'd be passionate about something for a period of time and then lose enthusiasm. There was no focus, no sustained passion for what I was doing—and the results showed.

Right around the same time I started making the film, "boom" had turned into serious "bust." My brother, father, and I had been in the business of buying, fixing up, and selling residential houses for several years. There was some fulfillment in the projects—I loved watching a dilapidated house get fixed up and having happy new owners move in—but it didn't feed my deeper passion. Just as I started making the film, the real estate market took a nosedive.

During this time, we were holding on to more than 30 residential properties that had not only declined in value but simply wouldn't sell. When the dust settled and we were able to sell or rent what we had, we found ourselves almost $1 million in debt! And this wasn't just corporate debt that we could write off and run away from; this was personal debt that all three of us were responsible for.

Without the resources and tools we had, most people would have crumbled at this point. Certainly, it was a big decision to continue making the film. A million dollars in debt and chasing a crazy dream! But I said to myself, "I need to figure out why this is happening and find a way to turn it around, all while focusing on my vision for this film." With a certain amount of introspection, the answer to why I was in this situation became clear.

The emotions, events, and beliefs I had developed around money, career, and finances were not supporting me. If you're not happy with your financial or career situation, they're not supporting *you*, either. I could have blamed the economy. I could have been resentful at the unscrupulous companies that ran up the real-estate market and created the mortgage mess, leaving the little guys like us holding the bag. Instead, I took personal responsibility and asked myself, "What do I really believe about money? Why am I in this situation?"

Let's take a look at what my tapping tree around money looked like back then. We'll break it down so you can identify what *your* tree might look like.

Remember, this isn't just about a simple exercise or pretty drawing. This tree actually controls your financial situation. If you want to change your finances, you have to change your emotional reactions, your wounds around money, and the underlying belief system that supports and feeds it all. Otherwise, anything new you try will be controlled by the old negative experiences, emotions, and beliefs, and you'll run the same patterns again and again.

Nick's Financial Tapping Tree

The Leaves (Side Effects)

Boom or bust

Not enough money

Lack of passion in career

Too many bills

Small apartment

Little free time

The Branches (Emotions)

Stressed out

Anxious

Fearful

Dispirited

Bored

The Trunk (Events)

The story from fifth grade

The last time I was wealthy

The Captain Kangaroo story

My boom-or-bust cycle

The Roots (Beliefs)

I don't want to stand out.

Rich people aren't good.

It'll be too much work if I'm wealthy.

I can't make money doing something I love.

I don't want to be criticized.

It's not spiritual to make money.

With these "programs" operating, at both a conscious and unconscious level, it was no surprise that I found myself in that situation. The roots I was working with—my beliefs about money and career—were disempowering. They were feeding the stories I told about my circumstances, which in turn fed my emotions, which in turn fed the side effects and the final outcome. All too often, we focus on only the leaves—the side effects or symptoms—even though that's not where the root of the problem lies.

Remember, this is my tree *before* I tapped on all these issues. If you look at this tree, can you imagine me deciding to throw caution to the wind, take out $40,000 on credit lines and credit cards, motivate and inspire my sister and best friend enough to join me in this crazy mission, and—most important—have it turn out to be a success?

Of course not! It just wouldn't have happened. I would have sat there twiddling my thumbs, coming up with all the reasons why it couldn't work, staying negative, anxious, and unfulfilled. If you're stuck about anything around your career, money, or finances, then you must take a look at your own tree and see what's underneath your current situation. It's not about the next big idea, get-rich-quick scheme, or huge opportunity. Those are a dime a dozen. What are *not* a dime a dozen are healthy financial tapping trees— people who can actually take those big ideas, dreams, and opportunities and make them happen.

At the end of this chapter, you'll have a chance to fill out your own tree to really see what's going on for you. But for now, let's continue the story of how we made the film so you can see how to make similar success happen for yourself.

Clearing the Limiting Beliefs

With all the tapping I did in the years before we made *The Tapping Solution*, I opened myself up to new opportunities and new possibilities for change. I let go of the old stories and adopted new, more empowering beliefs that gave me the confidence to move in a positive direction.

If I had remained afraid to stand out, there's no way I could have put this film out into the world.

If I had still believed rich people were bad, there's no way I could have accepted massive financial rewards for the work I was doing.

If I had kept worrying that being successful would mean too much extra work, I would have found a way to sabotage my success.

These beliefs *had* to change in order for my situation to change. To try to change it in spite of those beliefs would have been futile. Yet, that's what most of us have been engaged in throughout our lives! Sound familiar?

Beyond the tapping I did before making the film, I had to keep tapping throughout the process. I tapped on the financial pressure I felt, from the real-estate debt and from the movie. I tapped and tapped, and kept moving forward— eventually producing a successful film and getting out of debt completely!

Of course, even after all this tapping around my financial situation, I am not "done." Life continually presents new and better challenges. Overcoming those challenges is how we grow, find joy, and experience fulfillment. The great thing about EFT is that it helps you move toward challenges that are frankly a lot more fun than the ones most of us encounter. Today, my challenges are not about paying the electric bill; they're about feeling confident speaking in front of 10,000 people. And using EFT on that is an enjoyable experience!

For me, speaking to bigger and bigger audiences is the next step—the current challenge that I use EFT to work through. Adopting a next-step mentality can serve you immensely as you progress toward making your dreams come true.

The Next Step and the Next Step and the Next Step

I remember speaking in front of a small audience at "Passion into Profits," an event that focused on—you guessed it—turning your personal passions into profitable ventures. I told my story about making the film, emphasizing how I used EFT to face every new challenge, every new frustration, and every new setback that previously would have left me feeling powerless and stuck. I also focused my talk on worrying about only "the next step," whatever was directly in front of me. The task that needed to be accomplished in order to move the project forward. When I had the idea to make the movie, my first question was, "Who can I get to join and support me in this vision?" Once that was answered, the next question was, "What kind of equipment do we need to film a movie?" Each time, I took the necessary actions to answer the next-step question, and I continued to move the project forward.

I guess I wasn't clear enough on the importance of this in my speech at "Passion into Profits," because sure enough, the first question from the audience completely ignored the next-step philosophy!

A lady came to the mike and said, "I see that you've been able to create a physical DVD. I want to do the same thing with a physical CD. Can you tell me how you were able to get that created? I've never made a CD before. I don't know how to get it created—which vendors to use, etc."

I replied, "Sure, I'm happy to help. So you have all the content ready for the CD, and now you just need someone to create it?"

"No, I'm working on the script for the CD now . . . I haven't finished that yet, but I'm worried about how to actually get the CD made."

Can you guess what my reply was? *That's not the next step!* The next step is to work on the script. The next step after that is to record the CD. The next step after *that* is to do the artwork for the CD. Finding vendors won't be the next step for a while!

She felt stuck because she had jumped too far down the line in her vision, focusing on something that was simply not important at the time. I see this happen again and again. It's important to be aware of the end goal, the grand theme, the big vision. But once that is clear to you, then you just have to take the next step in front of you.

What's amazing about using EFT with this strategy is that it works perfectly on addressing just that: the next step. The next obstacle. What's in front of you right now!

Even though I'm overwhelmed by all the things I have to do with this project . . .
Even though I'm not sure what to do next . . .
Even though I don't feel confident that I can figure out how to get this done . . .
Even though I'm out of my league and don't know what I'm doing . . .

The lady who asked me that question could have even tapped on *Even though I don't know how to make the CD and I'm overwhelmed . . .* She would soon have recognized that everything was okay and that all she needed to do was focus on the next step.

Tapping diminishes the noise we experience around success and finances, and strengthens the mental, emotional, and even physical responses we have to life's challenges. These days, goals, visions, and dreams tend to be complicated by the speed of modern life—the speed of e-mail communications, the constant interruptions. As we discussed in Chapter 3, the feeling of being overwhelmed can be so extreme it can paralyze you. Tapping is an important and simple tool to quiet that noise and move you to a place of peace. From there, you'll have the resources to make the best decisions and take the next step.

The Cure for Procrastination

Even though I don't want to write anymore . . .
Even though I'm tired of writing this book and just want to watch TV . . .

Even though I want to put this off until tomorrow, I deeply and completely accept myself.

Tap, tap, tap . . . *I don't want to write anymore* . . . tap, tap, tap . . . *I want to watch TV* . . .

That was me, five minutes ago. Yup, that's some real-time tapping in action! I hit a lull in writing and just didn't want to sit here anymore. So I said to myself, let me tap for five minutes and see how I feel. I did, and here I am . . . *not* procrastinating!

Sometimes EFT is as simple as that: slotting a few minutes into your day. Tapping when you feel stuck, frustrated, or lazy. Of course, EFT is amazing for the huge challenges in our lives, but it works just as well for the little stuff. The thing is, it's the little stuff that turns into big stuff.

Procrastination is a little daily thing—but it's a big *life* thing. It kills dreams, stops million-dollar ideas, and keeps people stuck for years.

If your procrastination is really bad—as in you never get anything done, always put things off, and are miserable about it—then it's likely there are some deep underlying beliefs or traumas creating this pattern. But more often than not, moving through daily procrastination is as simple as doing a little tapping, getting the energy flowing again, and then moving forward.

Here's what I love about using EFT for procrastination: it doesn't necessarily make you do more work! What I mean is, it brings you to a place of peace and quiets the noise. From that place, you can determine what the right thing is for you in that moment. There are times when I've tapped on procrastinating on a project, and the end result *wasn't* that I started working on the project again. Instead, I realized I really needed some fresh air. So I went for a walk, cleared my head, and gladly went back to work at a later time.

There are other times when I've tapped on procrastination and have realized that I don't want to do the project at all! In those cases, I've made a decision to cancel the project or to take it in another direction. Using EFT in this manner brings clarity, focus, and awareness. It almost seems to bring more of your brain online. When that happens, we make better decisions. When we follow our intuition, we get better results all around.

TAPPING SCRIPT: Procrastination

(The tapping points chart can be found on page 21.)

Here's some tapping to do when you're stuck in a pattern of procrastination.

Karate Chop: Even though I don't want to _____, I deeply and completely accept myself.

Karate Chop: Even though I'm feeling really stuck and just don't want to _____, I choose to relax now.

Karate Chop: Even though I don't want to _____, and I want to do something else instead, I deeply love and accept myself.

Eyebrow: I just don't want to do this . . .
Side of Eye: I want to do something else . . .
Under Eye: I feel so stuck . . .
Under Nose: I'm procrastinating like usual . . .
Chin: I wonder why I don't want to do this . . .
Collarbone: I wonder what might be going on . . .
Under Arm: I just don't want to do this . . .
Top of Head: I'd really rather be doing something else . . .

Eyebrow: This feeling of being stuck . . .
Side of Eye: This feeling of being really stuck . . .
Under Eye: I want to procrastinate . . .
Under Nose: I'd rather do anything except this . . .
Chin: I wonder why I don't want to do this . . .
Collarbone: Should I even do this . . .
Under Arm: Why am I doing this . . .
Top of Head: Why am I doing what I'm doing?

And once you feel lighter about the issue, tap in some positive statements:

Eyebrow: I choose to be clear on what I want to do . . .
Side of Eye: I choose to relax my body . . .
Under Eye: I choose to relax my mind . . .
Under Nose: And get clarity on this issue . . .
Chin: It's safe to move forward . . .
Collarbone: I'm ready to move forward . . .
Under Arm: And to let go of whatever might be in my way . . .
Top of Head: Letting go of whatever is in my way and getting clarity now.

Take a deep breath . . . and let it go.

For an extended tapping session on this topic,
visit www.thetappingsolution.com/tap9.

Keep going, round after round, being as specific with your feelings as possible and noticing anything that comes up, until you feel complete and you're ready to move on to the perfect next step.

When Magic Happens . . .

During our Tapping World Summit, an annual online event that has been attended for free by more than half a million people in the past several years, I am always bombarded with amazing stories of change and transformation.

Last year, one really stuck out because it happened in real time. Alyssa, a young mother of two, had been out of a job for several months and was frustrated by her prospects. She had been on many interviews, but she knew the job market was tough, competition was fierce, and she was unlikely to find anything. She felt she was either over- or underqualified for whatever position she was applying for. Nothing seemed to fit just right. With this "knowledge" in mind, she found herself anxious at every interview and constantly frustrated. The result? No new job.

It just so happened that on a Sunday evening, she was listening to one of our summit presentations. The presentation was explaining much of what has been discussed in this chapter—how our emotions, past experiences, and limiting beliefs keep us stuck and running the same patterns again and again with the same results. Alyssa recognized the beliefs she was holding on to:

The job market is tough.
Competition is fierce.
I'm unlikely to find anything.
I'm either overqualified or underqualified.

She saw how these beliefs brought up anxiety, stress, and other negative emotions.

Once Alyssa recognized the patterns she was running, she tapped on them and found herself in a completely different place. As if by magic, she felt hopeful—she was excited . . . she knew the right job was out there for her.

The next morning, she went in for one of her previously scheduled job interviews. She e-mailed me later that day and let me know what had happened. She told me about the tapping the night before, the profound shift she had felt, and how amazingly well the job interview had gone. In fact, the interviewer told her that the position she had originally applied for had been filled, but there was a higher paying position available that she was a great fit for, and they would let her know the next day. Sure enough, the next day, Alyssa reported that she had gotten the job!

If we break this down logically, it's obvious why Alyssa got the job as a result of doing the tapping. Picture the two Alyssas—before tapping and after tapping. Before tapping, she would have gone into the interview anxious and stressed, and the people interviewing her would have noticed. She would have been running these negative thoughts through her head, and not only would they have affected her answers, her mood, and how she presented herself, but at the deepest levels, they would have affected the interviewers themselves!

After tapping, Alyssa was calm, confident, and relaxed. She believed in herself, in her abilities, and in the possibility of finally finding the perfect job. Who wouldn't want to hire such a star?

Oops . . . How to Make Money

Oh, my—I'm so sorry. This is supposed to be the chapter about making money, about getting out of debt, about becoming a millionaire! And I've spent our time going on and on about some tree, about limiting beliefs, about the next step and procrastination. You're here because you want to make more money!

Well . . . I've said it before, and I'll say it again—until it sinks in and becomes part of who you are. You *must* address the limiting beliefs, past events, and habitual emotions first. The rest of the stuff will fall into place. I've seen it happen again and again. I've experienced it firsthand and can testify to the results. Today, I spend my days doing what I love, with the people I love, and making a massive difference in the world. It's not because I found some get-rich-quick scheme; it's not because I inherited a lot of money or because I was hired by the right person. *It's because I cleared the limiting beliefs that were holding me back.* From there, everything else fell into place.

It can for you, too! But you've got to do the work . . . you've got to be meticulous in digging deep and finding what beliefs you hold, identifying the events that still have an emotional charge, and changing the emotions that keep you running the same patterns again and again.

Let's do that now, as we identify what your financial tapping tree looks like.

Exercise: What Does Your Tree Look Like?

You can draw your own tree or print out the blank copy at
www.thetappingsolution.com/tree

Fill out your own tree to get a visual representation of your financial situation. Sometimes it's painful when you see it all on paper—you see the reality of what you think and feel and how you act. But in this case that can be a good thing! Having a visual representation of your financial beliefs—all the ideas you've been consciously and unconsciously carrying around—will help you recognize the reality of your situation and will give you the concrete steps you need to change it.

The Leaves (Side Effects)

The leaves represent your current financial situation. Be honest about where you are. If you're in debt, that's an effect, so write that in. If your salary is not enough to pay the bills, write that in. If you don't have a job, or you make a good living but always seem to struggle to pay the bills, write that in. Include everything that represents your current financial situation.

The Branches (Emotions)

How do you feel about your financial situation? Are you angry? Are you sad? Are you frustrated? Do you get annoyed by the whole thing? Are you embarrassed by it? Ashamed? How does money make you feel? How does sharing your message or passion with the world make you feel?

The Trunk (Events)

What has happened in your life around money, finances, your career, that was negative? Do you remember your first job? Do you know what your parents' financial situations were as they were growing up? Can you remember any specific negative childhood experiences around money? Was money talked about at the dinner table or around the house?

The Roots (Limiting Beliefs)

This is where the real action is. What do you believe about money? What do you believe about following your passion? What do you believe about your career? Say out loud, "Money is _____" and fill in the blank, again and again.

Here are some of the most common limiting beliefs we hold about money. Which ones are true for you?

- Money is hard to come by.

- There isn't enough money for everyone; if I make a lot of money, I'm taking somebody else's piece of the pie.

- You have to work hard for your money.

- It takes an immense amount of knowledge and skill to make a lot of money.

- I don't deserve to make more than I do now.

- Money doesn't come easily.

- You can't have both time and money.

- We have always had to scrimp and save for everything we have.

- Having money isn't spiritual.

- Money is the root of all evil.

- Rich people are_____ [fill in the blank with your favorite negative judgment!].

- Money doesn't buy happiness.

- Money doesn't grow on trees (except tapping trees!).

- I am from a poor, working-class background.

- Money always seems to slip through my fingers.

- You have to rip people off to have money.

- I am unlucky and never make money.

- Things always go wrong for me.

- I can't afford it.

Bonus Exercise: Breaking Down Your Dreams, Goals, and Aspirations

Throughout the book, I've included one exercise per chapter. But so many people tell me their number one concern in life is money, that I've added a second exercise here. If you're really committed to changing your financial situation and making all your dreams, goals, and aspirations come true, do both exercises!

All too often, our dreams, goals, and aspirations consist of little more than a list like this:

- Make $1 million
- Get my book published
- Travel the world
- Support my favorite charity
- Etc.

It's certainly a great start to write down your goals. That said, if you don't dig deeper to find out what limiting factors are keeping you from achieving them, they're unlikely to happen as quickly and completely as you hope. You may have read plenty about how to strengthen the goal-setting process: add emotional value and visuals, expand on the feelings you'll have when you achieve the goal, include a time line, review your list often, and so forth.

And all those ideas are great, but if you're not in full alignment with your goals, you're basically wasting your time. The alignment I'm talking about isn't just a surface, conscious alignment; you need to be aligned at all levels. You need to address your *what if*s and your *yes, but*s. You need to look at the emotional and psychological limiting factors that you are choosing. When you do that, you get out of your own way. Only then can you avoid those patterns of self-sabotage that are all too familiar.

Here's a tapping exercise to help. Remember, the more issues you address on all the aspects, all the layers of your goals and dreams, the better your results will be. Perhaps commit to doing one goal or issue a day for 30 days, and see what happens.

Step 1: Write Down Your Goal, Dream, or Aspiration

You can make this a specific goal ("I want to earn $1 million a year"), a more general goal ("I want peace in my relationship with my mom"), or a vision ("I'd like to create dramatic social change").

Here and throughout this process, don't worry about getting the wording right; whatever language pops up in your head is right. But make sure to write it down.

Step 2: Write Down Your Immediate Gut Response to Your Goal

How do you *feel* when you read your goal? Are you 100 percent in alignment with it? How does your body respond to reading it? For example, you might write, "I feel uncomfortable when I read this. I'm excited; I'm anxious . . ." Be specific and give every feeling a 0-to-10 rating. For example, if you're feeling anxious as you read the goal, write "I'm feeling anxious, and the intensity is an 8."

You can write down more than one emotion or feeling. Do you feel tension in your stomach? Write that down. Are you slightly nauseous? Write them all down, along with the levels of intensity from 0 to 10.

Step 3: What Would Other People Say about Your Goal?

Friends, family members, society, co-workers—whoever pops into your head first, write down what they might say if you told them about your goal.

So if you think about sharing your goal with your mom and you picture her saying, "That's a silly idea!" write that down. Add how you *feel* about her thoughts; be specific and give your feelings a number.

Step 4: What Do *You* Believe about the Goal?

For example, "Part of me thinks this is impossible . . . I've never been able to do this before . . . who am I to achieve this?" Note the feelings this brings up. Be specific as you write them down and assign them a number.

Step 5: Tap Out All This Resistance, and Tap in Positive Feelings!

Systematically go through each item that brought up an issue, and tap on it until you bring the feelings around it down to 0. Keep noting anything else that comes up through the process. You may not be able to do this in one session, so take your time with it.

When you have tapped through all the issues (and make sure to keep digging for more hidden ones), you will have cleared the way for your goal to become a reality.

TAPPING SCRIPT: Dreams, Goals, and Aspirations

(The tapping points chart can be found on page 21.)

Let's go through one example of what executing Step 5 of this exercise might look like, once you've finished Steps 1 through 4 and are ready to tap. Feel free to tap along.

Step 1: Write Down the Goal
EXAMPLE: *I want to earn $250,000 a year.*

Step 2: How Do You Feel?
EXAMPLE: "Looking at this, I get a little nervous. There's a sinking feeling in the pit of my stomach and pressure around making this work. When I close my eyes, I feel this sinking feeling at a 7. When I ask myself what this feeling is, it's anxiety. I'm going to do some tapping on this now."

Karate Chop: Even though I have this sinking feeling in the pit of my stomach, I deeply and completely accept myself.
Karate Chop: Even though I have this sinking feeling about making $250,000, I choose to relax now.
Karate Chop: Even though I feel uncomfortable in my body when I look at this goal, I deeply and completely accept myself.

Eyebrow: This sinking feeling . . .
Side of Eye: I'm feeling a little nervous . . .
Under Eye: This sinking feeling . . .
Under Nose: In the pit of my stomach . . .
Chin: I feel pressure around making this work . . .
Collarbone: I feel this anxiety in my stomach . . .
Under Arm: All this anxiety . . .
Top of Head: All this sinking feeling.

Keep on tapping on whatever comes up until you find some relief. Then move on to the positive:

Eyebrow: I choose to relax now . . .
Side of Eye: And release this sinking feeling . . .
Under Eye: I let it all go . . .
Under Nose: From the pit of my stomach . . .
Chin: All this anxiety . . .
Collarbone: Releases now . . .
Under Arm: All this fear about making $250,000 a year . . .
Top of the Head: Releases now.

Step 3: What Would Other People Say about Your Goal?
EXAMPLE: "If I told my friends I wanted to make $250,000 a year, half of them would laugh at me, and the other half would tell me I was being greedy. When I think about telling my friends, I just feel small and not confident at all. This feeling is at an 8."

Karate Chop: Even though I don't feel confident telling my friends about my goal, I deeply and completely accept myself.
Karate Chop: Even though I don't want my friends to know my goal, I deeply and completely accept myself.
Karate Chop: Even though I know they'll judge me if I tell them my goal, I deeply and completely accept myself.

Eyebrow: I don't want to tell my friends . . .
Side of Eye: When I think about telling them, it makes me feel small . . .
Under Eye: This feeling of being small . . .
Under Nose: I'm worried that they'll judge me . . .
Chin: I'm worried that they won't like me . . .
Collarbone: I'm worried about what my friends will think . . .
Under Arm: If I tell them my goal . . .
Top of Head: Or if I achieve my goal!

Now, the positive:

Eyebrow: I release this feeling of being small . . .
Side of Eye: I choose to feel big!
Under Eye: I'm confident in my goal . . .
Under Nose: And I release any anxiety about it . . .
Chin: I'm confident in what I want for myself . . .
Collarbone: And I'm confident that the right people will support me . . .
Under Arm: Feeling strong and confident . . .
Top of Head: Feeling strong and confident!

You get the idea! Continue on to tap out Step 4, your own beliefs about your goal. Then rinse and repeat as necessary!

The key to this process is to get specific about your issues and your feelings and to be *systematic* about the tapping—go through all the different aspects of the issue that arise, one by one.

If you're thorough in this process, it's unlikely you can tap through everything listed in one sitting. So take your time with it and perhaps just focus on one section per day. It's better to be thorough, even if it takes a few days or weeks, than to rush through it and risk missing some of the deeper beliefs that might be influencing you.

CHAPTER 11

ELIMINATING PHOBIAS AND FEARS

*According to most studies, people's number one fear is public speaking.
Number two is death. Death is number two. Does that sound right?
This means to the average person, if you go to a funeral,
you're better off in the casket than doing the eulogy.*

JERRY SEINFELD

Lindsey was terrified of clowns.

I know, it sounds pretty funny. I can hear you snickering: "Clowns? Really? This is a serious problem? She was scared of *clowns*?"

But the reality is, clowns *terrified* her. While it might seem amusing to those of us who don't share that fear—and while she was aware that it wasn't rational—she was frightened nonetheless.

Lindsey is a fun, bright, happy 24-year-old and one of the team members at our company, The Tapping Solution. When she was five years old, she had walked in the room while her parents watching the Stephen King miniseries *It*, which features a murderous clown. While she has no recollection of the incident—her parents told her what happened and why they feel this is where her fear of clowns started. Clearly something made an impression on her.

I had known about her fear but didn't understand how serious it was. Then I heard from another team member that Lindsey had seen a picture of a clown and had started crying. I realized at that moment that this was a full-blown phobia that was affecting her life.

This fear perfectly illustrates an underlying element of all fears and phobias: the conditioned response. It's not a logical fear, and it serves no purpose. But once the pattern has been programmed into the system, the conscious mind cannot override it.

While the clown phobia seems especially amusing, the pattern is the same whether the fear is about public speaking, enclosed spaces, heights, needles, germs and dis-ease, dentists, or snakes. The phobia usually starts with a negative experience. After that, the patterns of fear keep running again and again, each time the person encounters that scenario.

You might argue that the fear of snakes is real—snakes can be dangerous—whereas the fear of clowns is not real because clowns aren't dangerous. Yes, humans have a natural, smart, genetic tendency to be wary of potentially dangerous snakes; that's very different from a phobia. I don't have a snake phobia, but I would be scared if a venomous cobra were in my office right now. That's a natural and rational response.

What makes a phobia different is that it is not rational. The fear is present even if there is a nondangerous snake in an enclosed cage across the room. Likewise, most of us would be a little nervous about speaking in front of 5,000 people; even speakers who have done it hundreds of times might feel a little agitation or excitement. A phobia, on the other hand, would keep us from putting ourselves in that situation in the first place!

You might remember that the original tapping breakthrough happened when Roger Callahan was working with Mary on her water phobia. Her fear disappeared instantly after tapping. It worked then and continues to work very effectively with fears and phobias of all varieties.

Using EFT to Clear Out Fears and Phobias

In just about an hour of tapping, we turned around Lindsey's phobia. I'm sharing the process with you here, because it's similar, no matter what fear you're working with.

Even talking about clowns made Lindsey anxious and fearful. So we began the tapping with the very simple and broad statement *Even though I have this fear of clowns, I choose to relax now.* Go slowly with fears and phobias; there's no reason to suffer through the process. We did several rounds of *Even though I have this fear of clowns . . .* and then tapped through the points, repeating "this fear of clowns . . . this anxiety . . . this stress in my body . . . " We continued until she found herself calm and relaxed.

Now I was able to ask her when the fear had started. She shared with me what she had heard from her parents—the experience of seeing the movie *It* as a child and being terrified. She didn't have a conscious memory of this experience and didn't feel anxiety when she talked about what her parents had told her. But just to be sure, we did some tapping on it. We proceeded to tap on *Even though I saw this scary movie when I was a kid, I deeply and completely accept myself.* Again, we weren't able to measure a level on it, because she wasn't emotional about it, but I felt it would be smart to do a couple of rounds just in case.

At this point, I could see that Lindsey was relaxed, so I took the next step. Confronting fears and phobias is all about baby steps. (You may remember the concept of "baby steps" from the movie *What About Bob?* with Bill Murray—what we're doing is not that different!) So I went on to ask Lindsey, "If I were to show you a picture of a clown right now, how would you feel?" Notice I didn't say, "I'm *going* to show you a picture of a clown" or "Think of a scary clown." I wanted to continue to ease her into the process.

"I'd be a little scared," she replied. "I'm feeling a little anxious right now." So we went on to tap on that—*Even though I'm feeling a little scared . . .* and so forth—until she found herself calm again.

"Lindsey, I'm going to send you a picture of a clown via e-mail," I went on. "How does that feel? Are you okay with that?"

"Yes," she said. "That's fine."

We were doing this session over Skype video, so right away I sent her a drawing of a cartoon clown. She opened it up, and I asked her, "How do you feel when you see that?"

"A little anxious," she replied. So we tapped on that until her anxiety went down.

From there, we went on to look at a photograph of a real clown. This is where it gets interesting. When she saw the picture of the real clown, she said, "I hate the red nose. That really freaks me out." This was an aspect of her phobia. With phobias, you want to be especially careful to look for all the different aspects of the issue—and to clear them all in order to have full relief. An aspect will always be specific. If Lindsey is specifically scared by the red nose, just tapping on *Even though I have this fear of clowns . . .* might not clear the fear. So we had to be more specific, tapping on *Even though this red nose really freaks me out. . . .*

We continued to tap on more and more pictures of clowns. Finally, I sent her a picture of the clown from the movie *It*. I warned her beforehand, and we tapped on her anxiety about even seeing it. Then, when the anxiety number was down, she looked at it, and we tapped. After several rounds, she was able to look at the clown image and say, "I don't like the clown. He's creepy, but I can look at him and my body feels fine." When I looked at the creepy *It* clown, I felt the same way! She no longer had a phobia of clowns. She didn't like looking at creepy clowns— but neither do most of the rest of us! Our work was a success.

Identifying with Fears and Phobias

One interesting thing to note about the session with Lindsey is that something that came up toward the end, as the phobia was clearing. She got visibly upset and said, "I don't know who I will be without this fear." Again, I know it seems amusing because her fear was about clowns, but it is so indicative of the patterns we all run—no matter the challenge, fear, or phobia. Being afraid of clowns was part of who Lindsey *was*. At some level, she defined herself that way: "I am afraid of clowns." She had grown up afraid of clowns, all her friends knew she was afraid of clowns, and she took actions to make sure she didn't face clowns in her life. This fear was part of the fabric of her life, her identity. Who would she be without it?

We tapped on *Even though I don't know who I'll be without this fear of clowns . . .* and *Even though I'm used to being afraid of clowns, I don't know how to act without this fear, I deeply and completely accept myself.* And so forth. These statements began opening up her mind and body to a new possibility, and she then started shaping a new identity without this limiting fear.

She can continue to tap on positive statements of her new identity, such as *I am someone who is free of phobias; I now find clowns funny; I choose to be courageous, fun, and bold, even around clowns!* and so forth. This serves to reinforce the new identity that she's already partially stepped into, and it is likely to give her even greater confidence. Without reinforcing the change by tapping in more positive statements, she might not be scared of clowns, but not have any positive emotions around them, either. Tapping further can make any encounter she has with them fun!

It's Not about Being Brave or Not

Kris Carr is a brave woman.

She's spent the past 10 years battling a rare cancer, documenting her journey in the film *Crazy Sexy Cancer* and being a guiding light to millions through her film and *New York Times* best-selling books. In other words, she is no stranger to overcoming obstacles and living a life of freedom, high energy, and joy.

So as we walked together up a mountain near her home in Woodstock, New York, I was surprised by something she shared with me. She was saying that at the top of the mountain there's a steel tower you can climb and see in all directions for miles. I said, "Great, let's go up!" to which she replied, "Oh, no, I'm not going up there! I'm scared of heights."

She instantly knew she'd said that to the wrong guy. If an issue is tappable, I'm going to get you tapping! And what's more obviously tappable than a fear of heights?

I promised her the experience would be painless; she wouldn't have to do anything she didn't want to do. So we began tapping right then and there, starting with the anxiety she was feeling at the thought of tapping. Just like talking about clowns made Lindsey anxious, the possibility of having to face any heights made Kris anxious. Her body and mind started imagining negative future scenarios and creating fear around them, even though they weren't real and hadn't happened yet.

. . . .

Tapping Tip: Future Fears

How often does your mind play tricks on you, creating fear, anxiety, feelings of being overwhelmed, and stress over things that have yet to happen—and might not happen at all? Use EFT in those moments to clear negative future visions.

. . . .

Kris and I spent the rest of the climb up the mountain tapping on the anxiety she was feeling. By the time we got to the top, she felt calm. I took a look at the tower. It was perfect, because it had multiple sets of steps at various levels. She could take her time, moving up the levels slowly, tapping each step of the way.

We started at the bottom of the platform, tapping on the anxiety she was feeling. We went back and forth between the global statement *Even though I have this fear of heights . . .* and specific statements about her body state, both emotional and physical.

For example we tapped on

Even though I feel all this anxiety . . .
Even though I feel like I can't take a deep breath . . .
Even though I have this knot in my stomach . . .
Even though my body feels shaky . . .
Even though I'm scared of falling . . .

We systematically worked through the different aspects that were coming up in her mind and body. Slowly, we started climbing. We went step by step, only moving when she felt comfortable and safe. Up we went, tapping and climbing together the whole way. Her loving husband, Brian, was there with us, shaking the platform as we climbed to make sure she *really* overcame her phobia. (Not a recommended strategy when someone wants to get over a phobia, by the way, and Kris certainly let Brian know how she felt about his contribution!)

When we got to the top, Kris's reward for having overcome her lifelong fear of heights was a majestic autumn view for miles in every direction. An appropriate metaphor for the reward we get when we finally let go of those lifelong fears, phobias, and limiting beliefs: we can then see a beautiful, clear view of our lives and the world.

Professional Profile: David Feinstein, Ph.D.

David Feinstein, Ph.D., has seen it all when it comes to alternative therapies. After his appointment to the department of psychiatry at Johns Hopkins Medical School in 1970, the department chair called Dr. Feinstein into his office and gave him an interesting and life-changing assignment. "I keep hearing about these new therapies coming from the West Coast," he told David. "Are they just more California fluff or developments worth knowing about? Go find out."

More than 200 new brands of therapy were popping up, and Dr. Feinstein spent the next seven months investigating 46 of them. He would study their literature, conduct extensive interviews with their users, and even directly experience them in weekend workshops or other participatory formats. Some of these therapies included Transactional Analysis, Bioenergetics, Gestalt, breathwork, sensitivity training, Rolfing, Reevaluation Counseling, LSD-assisted psychotherapy, and (likely one of Dr. Feinstein's more memorable experiences!) a nude encounter group. Perhaps most important, not only did he meet the people using the technique, but he also followed up with them months later to see how they were doing.

In the majority of therapies he explored, people seemed to have a positive initial experience—as in feeling good during a weekend workshop. But during the follow-up interview, the participants often shared that they had gone back to their old ways and hadn't seen any real change. Fortunately, Dr. Feinstein persisted in his quest to find a tool that made a definitive and measurable difference in people's lives. Eventually he stumbled across the tapping therapies and EFT.

During his first experience with EFT, in a class with fellow psychology professionals, Dr. Feinstein recalls, with amazement:

> A woman suffering from longstanding, severe claustrophobia had been preselected to be the subject. She was shown where and how to tap on a series of points on her skin while remembering frightening incidents involving enclosed spaces. To my amazement, she almost immediately reported that the scenes she was imagining were causing her less distress. Within 20 minutes, her claustrophobia seemed to have disappeared. This self-reported improvement was stunning enough. But when asked to step into a closet, close the door, and remain there as long as she felt comfortable, she stayed so long that finally she was beckoned to come out. She emerged jubilant and triumphant, astonished that she'd stayed calm in a situation that would have put her into uncontrollable panic half an hour earlier.

"I'd never seen any therapy work that quickly," Dr. Feinstein told me. "The speed was remarkable."

Having built his career around traditional clinical approaches, when he became convinced of the power of EFT and started teaching classes on it, he would often start with a disclaimer.

"I can't fully express how surprised I am to find myself standing here," he would say, "telling you that the key to successful treatment, even with extremely tough cases, can be a mechanical, superficial, ridiculously speedy physical technique that doesn't require a sustained therapeutic relationship, the acquisition of deep insight, or even a serious commitment to personal transformation. Yet, strange as it looks to be tapping on your skin, it works!"

Since that initial experience and following further research, he's worked tirelessly to document and validate this powerful tool. He's written more than eighty professional articles and eight books about energy medicine, and he has served as a clinical psychologist on the faculties of the Johns Hopkins School of Medicine, Antioch College, and the California School of Professional Psychology.

Having had the pleasure to interview and speak with Dr. Feinstein on multiple occasions, it amuses me to see that even today, part of him is still surprised by the speed and effectiveness of EFT. His clinical, traditionally trained mind seems to have trouble fully accepting something so quick, effective, and easy to use. And I can't blame him—my nonclinical, alternatively trained mind struggles with it as well!

Two Fears Handled in One Hour

Meggan is a dynamic writer, lecturer, and coach to thousands of women around the world.

She was scheduled to speak at an important conference and reached out to me for some help. Meggan had often taken the stage before, with extremely positive feedback from her audiences. But up until that point, she always read her speeches from behind a podium. She never felt fully comfortable with the experience, either. For the upcoming event, she wouldn't have a podium. She was also planning on speaking without a set script. The prospect terrified her, so she reached out to me, having heard how effective EFT could be when it came to public speaking phobias.

When we began our session, I asked her to visualize being onstage, without the podium or her written speech, and to tell me what she experienced. Particularly, I wanted to know what she felt in her body. I find that focusing on physical sensations is a great way to get started addressing fears, because it helps us connect more fully to the feelings and determine what's really going on.

She shared with me that she felt a constriction in her chest and throat when she thought about the event; not a surprising location for a fear of public speaking. I asked her to give the constriction a number, and she said it was a 7 on a 0-to-10 scale. We began tapping with some very simple statements:

Even though I have this constriction in my chest and throat, I deeply and completely accept myself.
Even though something feels stuck in my throat, I deeply and completely accept myself.
Even though I have this anxiety in my chest and throat, I choose to relax now.

We kept tapping through various statements and the points, until she could no longer feel the constriction in her chest and throat. I then had her go back to the image of herself speaking up onstage at the event. What did she feel? What did she see? She shared that she felt better and saw the speech going well, but only once she got started. "I think getting started is going to be tough," she said.

We'd cleared out the stuck energy in her chest and throat, and now the next aspect of her phobia had arisen. So we tapped on the issue of getting started until it cleared and she felt confident enough to continue.

I continued to ask her to visualize the event and to look for anything that didn't feel right. I even added to the potential pressure, on purpose, in order to make sure everything was clear. For example, I had her visualize the audience not smiling when she first came out, to see if that would bring up any anxiety. Audiences are generally very receptive and welcoming to the speakers, but I wanted to push her buttons a little bit, to make sure we handled all the different aspects of her phobia.

This process continued, with more tapping, digging deeper and deeper, until she could no longer find any anxiety, stress, or worry about the speech. Instead, she reported, "I'm actually excited for this and starting to think about what I want to discuss. I could never go there before because I was too terrified of the whole experience!"

I've mentioned it several times but it bears repeating because it's so crucial. *The way to get lasting results with fears or phobias is to dig deep and address all the aspects of the issue.* This is a time when it's good to look for what's wrong, to identify problems, to push within yourself and see how it feels!

Meggan was delighted with how she felt, and we were about to sign off from the call when she shared with me that she was excited to use EFT on her other fear: flying. She was going to have to fly to the event, after all! The fear of public speaking had taken only 30 minutes to address, so I offered to continue helping her with the fear of flying right then, and she agreed.

She shared with me that 15 years earlier, she and her sister had flown together on a small airplane, and the flight was the worst experience of her life. From the start, the turbulence was unlike any she had ever experienced, with the small plane dropping several feet at once, again and again.

She had been sure she was going to die. The pilot didn't say a word to reassure the passengers, and the muted cries and screams of the people around her made everything worse. They finally landed safely, but to Meggan's mind and body, the trauma of the experience never left. She had worked on healing and had made progress, but at the deepest level, the trauma was still there—affecting her life in all sorts of ways.

This wasn't just a fear of flying that we were working on together, it was a deep-seated fear about life—about safety, about who she was in the world, and about not having to be on alert at all times. That one experience had taught Meggan that she needed to be vigilant, that the world was inherently unsafe, and that her body wasn't safe, either.

Ask Yourself . . . Fears and Phobias

What fears or phobias do you have, and how might they be affecting other parts of your life?

What beliefs do you have about yourself and the world because of these fears?

I used the "movie technique" with Meggan, asking her to recount to me what happened, while tapping at the same time. I could tell from Meggan's body language and tone that just talking about the issue brought her some anxiety, so I was careful to move slowly. I told her that if she ever felt the emotional intensity was too high, or if she didn't feel safe, we could back away from the experience. This is one of the great things about working with people on video Skype or in person rather than by telephone: the visual cues give you invaluable information.

Meggan recounted the story of the plane flight from start to finish. I focused on helping her feel safe, guiding her with questions that brought her deeper into the experience when needed and pulled her further out when things seemed to get too intense. She told me what had happened, step by step, and tapped the whole time. Her first recounting of it was very emotional, but I could see her calming down as she tapped. I then had her tell me the story again, and again, and again, until there was no emotional intensity to any element of it.

In the end, when she thought of the traumatic flight, she broke down in tears of joy because she was no longer experiencing the fear and pain that just 30 minutes earlier was paralyzing to her.

I'll let an e-mail that I received from Meggan the next day give you a fuller idea of the results she experienced:

I've been sleeping like a teen since our call. If it weren't for my toddler, I might still be in bed. It's not fatigue; it feels more like make-up sleep. The part of me that was terrorized into hypervigilance during that flight 15 years ago, to stay awake, to keep watch, to be ever on the lookout for my safety finally took a bow and stepped down. Not trusting life takes a lot of energy (smile). I have this visceral knowing that when the make-up sleep has run its course, I'm going to have crazy amazing energy.

I'm so fascinated, and semiperplexed, at the session's effectiveness. I keep trying to conjure the fear I once had for flying and also the naked, exposed feeling I had about speaking without a script in public, and I just can't access it. It's not there. I remember who I am, or who I was before these fears made a home for themselves within me. I don't get how tapping works, and I don't need to—it just does.

Tapping accessed the actual wound and just lifted it. Poof. Tapping returned to me the actual feeling of calm and safety in my body that the trauma of that flight has been blocking ever since. Like a magician pulling the white tablecloth out from under a dining set, tapping revealed that my trust in the world, in my life, has always been there—as my ground of being—and that the fear was simply obscuring its permanent presence within me.

I'm a convert. A smacked-on-the-forehead, true-believer convert. My gratitude is endless.

. . . .

Tapping Tip: Addressing the Fear of Flying

If you or someone you know is scared of flying, here's how you can use EFT to help:

1. **Practice beforehand.** Tap before you're going to fly, trying to re-create the flying experience in your mind. Envision yourself going to the airport, checking in, waiting for the plane, boarding the plane, sitting down, hearing the engines turn on, feeling the plane start to move, feeling the plane take off, being in flight, feeling the plane descend, and feeling the plane land.

As you go through each element of the flight, notice which ones get to you. Where is the anxiety? Where is the fear? Is it when the engines turn on? Is it when you're flying and there's turbulence? Tap on each of these elements.

The most effective thing you can do if you're not actually flying is to do your best to relive the memory in your mind and body. The same thing goes for all fears and phobias. The real test, of course, is when you're actually confronted with the situation! But in the meantime, you'd be surprised how effective it can be to simply relive the memory.

2. **Tap during the flight.** I'm always delighted when I see people tapping on a plane (more often than you'd think!). It's a great way to bring down anxiety, fear, and stress. I've even tapped myself during really bad turbulence that pushed my own comfort zone. Don't be worried about other people noticing; they rarely do. Most of the time they're concerned with their own issues. If they do notice, you can easily share this powerful tool with them.

. . . .

Exercise: Overcoming a Fear or Phobia

Overcoming a fear or phobia can be a massive personal victory, leading to even greater success in other areas of our lives, such as relationships, finances, and even personal health. And the reason is that these fears and phobias inherently signal to the rest of our consciousness that we don't have full control over our lives. If Lindsay isn't able to control how she reacts to clowns, can she control the rest of her life and her emotional responses?

If Kris is limited by not being able to climb to the top of the mountain and go up the tower, how else might she be limited? If Meggan has to worry about anxiety and panic taking over at any point, can she really feel safe?

Knowing we have the power and resources to control these fears—rational or irrational—strengthens what we can create and accomplish in all aspects of our lives.

So pick a fear or phobia right now and tap through it yourself. It doesn't have to be a massive phobia or a lifelong fear. If you can't find anything (I know you can, but if you really can't . . .), then help someone you know overcome their fears. Here are some common fears and phobias. See if you relate to any of them:

- Animals
- Bridges/Tunnels
- Bugs/Spiders
- Death
- The Dentist
  (or Other Medical Fears)
- Elevators
- Enclosed Spaces
- Flying
- Heights
- Needles
- Physical Pain
- Public Speaking
- Riding in Cars
- Selling/Cold Calls
- Social Phobias/Anxiety
- Water

CHAPTER 12

CLEARING OTHER LIFE CHALLENGES

As we've seen in this book, tapping is a vital tool for overcoming many common challenges we face around our body, weight loss, money, and relationships. But it can also be applied to a host of more specific issues. In this chapter, I'll highlight some of these so you can determine how to use it for yourself and your loved ones. Remember, though, just because you don't see an issue covered here, that doesn't mean EFT would not work to clear it. Whatever your concern, EFT can likely help in some way.

Insomnia and Creating Deep, Restful Sleep

As you briefly saw in Chapter 6, many people report that one of the beneficial side effects of using EFT is that they find they are sleeping better than ever before. This makes sense, of course, because as we tame the stress of our day, sleep naturally improves.

Time and time again I've seen deeper sleep be a positive "side effect" to tapping on stress and other issues. As you might remember from a few of the testimonials in this book, people often report that they experience deeper sleep than they've ever had before, without tapping directly on sleep issues. Notice if your sleep improves as you bring down the stress and other issues in your life.

Most of us have trouble sleeping from time to time, so when you find yourself restless and unable to sleep, try a few tapping rounds. It can be as simple as saying, *Even though I'm having trouble going to sleep . . .* and tapping through those statements. Also, if you find that you're stressed out about a particular issue or problem, tapping directly on that stress can help you sleep. For example:

Even though I can't stop thinking about what happened at work today . . .
Even though I'm stressed out, overwhelmed, and can't sleep . . .
Even though my mind is racing and won't stop thinking . . .
Even though I can't go to sleep . . .

For those suffering from mild or severe insomnia, it might take some more work to break the existing patterns. The first place to start is the stress in your life—look at what's making you anxious, what's literally keeping you awake. If, after having addressed that, you're still having trouble, your issue might be sleeping itself. What I mean by that is that you've probably built up a lot of anxiety, stress, and frustration *about* going to sleep. If you've had years of trouble sleeping, you're likely carrying a buildup of anxiety that will resurface anytime you try to go to sleep. Your sleep patterns themselves might be what's stressing you out.

Just identify the patterns and then tap on them one by one. You'll likely have to do it several nights in a row—maybe even several weeks in a row—but it's well worth the investment. Deep, restful sleep isn't only vital to the health of our bodies and minds, it's also a wonderful part of life.

Here are some of the concerns, in the form of a tapping tree, that might keep you up at night. See which apply to you, and tap on them, or any combination of them.

The Leaves (Side Effects)

Lack of sleep, interrupted sleep, snoring, not waking up refreshed, nightmares.

The Branches (Emotions)

Stress about sleeping itself: What if I don't get enough sleep? Stress about something the next day: The big presentation, big meeting, extra responsibilities, or just going to work. Anxiety, feelings of being overwhelmed, frustration, fear, sadness, and more.

The Trunk (Events)

Has anything happened to you related to sleep—for example, the time when you were woken up in the middle of the night because of a fire, or the time when you were seven years old and fell out of your bed? It's likely there aren't many events related to sleep (as compared to other issues), but if you have some, put them here.

The Roots (Limiting Beliefs)

I can't sleep, I've never been a good sleeper, I have nightmares, I wake up every hour, I'm always tired, I am an insomniac.

Tap through the items in your tapping tree to create deep, restful sleep.

Addictions: Smoking, Alcohol, and Drugs

Let me start by making an obvious statement: Addictions are complicated.

They are rarely a quick fix, so it's not like we're going to tap on a few acupressure points and a lifelong alcohol problem will suddenly go away. That being said, EFT is a fantastic tool to handle the two main challenges of overcoming addictions: the physical craving for the substance and the underlying emotional causes of the addiction.

The Physical Craving

In the same way that EFT works with food cravings, it can handle cravings for cigarettes, alcohol, and other drugs amazingly well. Several years ago, right after I had hosted a screening of the movie *The Tapping Solution* for a small audience, I was given the chance to lead someone through this process.

The movie had been very well-received, and after the screening, audience members were excited to experience EFT for themselves. The movie runs about an hour and a half, and we were 30 minutes into the post-screening discussion when a gentleman in the front raised his hand, "I'm sorry, but I've been in here for more than two hours. I'm desperate for a cigarette, can we tap on it?"

We spent no more than five minutes tapping *Even though I'm craving a cigarette . . .* and brought his craving down from an 8 to a 0. He was astonished to discover he didn't want or need to smoke, and he stayed for the rest of the discussion. He shared how excited he was because he was enjoying the discussion and had been mad at himself when he had the craving, since it would take him away from the group.

The key with cravings for anything is that you actually have to *do* the tapping for it to work. And that's where addressing the underlying emotional causes, the "roots" of your cravings, is so important.

The Underlying Emotional Issues

Dennis, a retired man from Florida, was one of hundreds of people who applied to attend our four-day event in Connecticut. His application stated that he was looking to quit smoking. He'd tried everything and was finally ready to do whatever it took to quit. I was excited to have him. I knew that if we had him tapping all weekend, he could easily handle his cravings. That meant he wouldn't smoke for several days. If we handled the underlying emotional challenges, too, he would be well on his way to quitting by the time the event was over.

During the first day of the event, everything seemed to go as planned. Tapping away, he didn't smoke any cigarettes—and didn't crave them, either. During the second day, things got a little more interesting. In the EFT session, Dennis shared with Steve Munn, the practitioner working with him, that he had felt like an outcast for the past 20 years. He smoked and most other people didn't, so he often felt guilty and ashamed. Steve tapped with him on releasing this guilt and shame. Such negative emotions don't help us quit; they actually keep us beating ourselves up and being stuck.

Once they cleared the negative emotions, Dennis had a surprise announcement.

"I've been ashamed and embarrassed about smoking my whole life," he said. "I'm going to keep smoking for now and enjoy it!"

You can imagine my mixed feelings when I heard this. Here I am, filming a documentary about the power of EFT and figuring that the "stop smoking" case will be a slam-dunk. And now he says EFT has helped him to *keep* smoking? Is that really what happened—and can I show this in the film?

I did indeed show it, because I felt it was important to be balanced and not hide anything that happened. And I felt, and still do, that there were some important lessons to learn there.

Lesson 1: Taking Positive Steps Forward

While it might seem like Dennis went backward—he came to us to quit smoking and left *wanting* to smoke—I believe the opposite is the case. In releasing his resistance, guilt, and anger at himself, Dennis took a positive step toward quitting somewhere down the line.

Sure, he might have guilted himself into stopping; he might have been so angry at himself that he stopped for a while. But if he didn't address the underlying negative emotions, it would all likely come back. And if it didn't come back as a smoking addiction, it would pop up somewhere else—as a food addiction or another compulsive behavior. That's why we so often see weight gain in people who stop smoking; they replace their habit of smoking—its comfort and emotional relief—with eating.

We're not trying to "stop" the smoking, the drinking, or the drug use. By focusing purely on the effect, the habit, we can tame the cravings, but we're unlikely to have long-term success. What we're trying to heal is the underlying patterns *causing* these things to happen. Only then can we create deep, lasting, and healthy change.

The reality is that drugs, alcohol, cigarettes, and other addictive habits *work*. They do the job they're supposed to do: they numb pain, distract attention from problems, provide physical and emotional relief. Only when we address what's causing the underlying pain and emotional turmoil can the habits change for good.

Lesson 2: You Have to **Want** *to Change*

We had ten people attend our four-day event for the filming of *The Tapping Solution*. Out of those ten, seven got really astounding results, and three got what I would call average results. The three certainly had breakthroughs—aha moments. I'm sure it was a positive experience for them. But measured on outward criteria, such as "Did he or didn't he stop smoking?" those three people didn't get 100 percent of the results they were looking for.

When we went over the event later and analyzed what worked, what didn't, and how to present it in the film, we found out something that astonished me but makes total sense.

We had had hundreds applicants for the event, and one of the criteria we looked at is how thoroughly people had filled out the application form and how committed they seemed to be to change. While EFT can address resistance to change, as we saw in Chapter 4, we wanted people to start with a level of energy and enthusiasm that would drive the process forward, at the very least.

In our research after the event, we discovered that the applications of all three people who hadn't gotten optimal results had been filled out by someone else! In Dennis's example, his wife really wanted him to quit smoking and had filled out his application. Sure, Dennis himself had shown up, so part of him wanted to change. But the drive clearly didn't come from him.

The lesson is this: *you've* got to want to change. If you don't think you do, go back to Chapter 4 to identify what resistance you might be harboring. If you've been procrastinating about doing what it takes to change or you keep sabotaging yourself, you may not be in alignment with the change you claim to want. The information in Chapter 4 can help shift that.

By the same token, if you have loved ones whom you want to change, know that they must do it for themselves. You can open a door for others, but you can't push them through it. So focus on opening doors. Share this book with them; share *The Tapping Solution* film; share any other resources you can think of. Then shower them with love, support, and understanding. That's the biggest gift you can give.

Expediting Addiction Recovery

David Rourke, an EFT practitioner who has been attending Narcotics Anonymous for 25 years, has dedicated his career to working with addicts—people who have serious issues with alcohol, heroin, and other intensely mind-altering substances. Over and over, he's introduced addicts to tapping and has seen how important it is for promoting recovery.

True recovery from serious addiction can take years. It's complex and typically involves multiple stages—from the contemplation phase, where addicts are finally acknowledging they have a problem but still need the drug to cope, to the preparation stage, and later, to sobriety.

What David has seen repeatedly is how EFT helps addicts move through that process. Sticking with recovery is a major accomplishment—around 90 percent of addicts relapse within 24 hours of completing a 28-day recovery program. With addicts, David explains, true recovery is about the *whys*—the underlying emotional issues behind addiction that we discussed earlier. And as we learned in Chapter 6 with Jessica's cold and Jodi's fibromyalgia, tapping on the symptoms—in an addicts' case, the habit of drinking or doing drugs—isn't enough. An addict who started using heroin after his son died would need to tap around his grief, in addition to his heroin use.

By getting at the core issue and releasing the emotional energy that may be contributing to the substance abuse, addicts are often better able and more willing to stick with the recovery process.

At the preparation stage, when addicts are actively planning to quit, there's another equally important factor that comes into play. Addicts need a strategy, what David calls the *how*. With addicts, he explains, "If you're going to take something away, you better have something to replace it." Tapping can be that replacement. So when a recovering alcoholic has friends over for dinner, he or she can substitute the activity of tapping for the activity of drinking wine. Not necessarily publicly tapping, but privately in the bathroom or kitchen—taking a break to tap if the cravings increase.

The calming effect of EFT can also help recovering addicts stop obsessing about wanting to use. Instead of relapsing, they can tap on what they're feeling and reconnect with their own inner strength. "We all have all the answers for ourselves," David says. "EFT helps us access those answers."

Sports Performance: The Secret Tool the Pros Use

Professional athletes at the highest levels of competition use EFT not only to improve their sports performance but also to change their lives. That includes a major league baseball team—one that has won the World Series in the past ten years. (That's as specific as I can get without breaking confidentiality agreements.) There are PGA golfers using EFT to cut strokes off their game, to calm their nerves and steady their hands. And there are NFL players who have used EFT to get back on the field after an injury faster than the competition.

Athletes are using it, with great results. So why aren't they talking about it? The reasons are obvious. First of all, professional sports is so competitive that a slight advantage can make all the difference; the edge EFT can give a player or a team might be worth millions of dollars, not to mention massive recognition and prestige. If you had that kind of advantage, you wouldn't share it with your competition, either!

On top of that, tapping looks strange to someone who doesn't know what it is. It often involves addressing underlying emotional issues that macho athletes don't want to admit they have. When Alex Rodriguez, star of the New York Yankees, was seeing a therapist, the press and public were all over him, ridiculing him. Can you imagine what the press would say if a star athlete announced he was tapping?

While I understand why athletes are reluctant to admit that they're using EFT, it's frustrating as well. The public has a lot of respect and admiration for athletes, and if they saw athletes using this strange tapping technique, they'd likely try it too! Celebrities and athletes can truly lead the way in making this technique mainstream—thereby changing millions of lives and, as you'll see in Chapter 13, the world at large.

Getting Back on the Field

The thing about baseball is that every mistake, every misstep, is logged, tracked, and analyzed. One off day, with a couple of errors, goes in the record books forever.

It's hardly surprising that major league baseball players have to manage their fair share of anxiety. That's where EFT expert Stacey Vornbrock comes in. She works with professional athletes, using tapping to help improve their game.

One pro ball player Stacey worked with had become so overwhelmed by anxiety that he'd developed a set of specific rituals that had to be done in a precise order before each game, in the hopes that they would act as a magic formula to calm his nerves. But it had gotten to the point where he was always the last one on the field. Even worse, his rituals weren't doing the job. His anxiety continued to grow and grow, and his performance was suffering.

He came to Stacey, and they tapped on the core issues causing his performance anxiety. Very quickly, he was able to relax, and after years of obsessing about his pregame rituals, he was able to stop using them. What's more, he was no longer the last player out of the clubhouse.

It was great progress, but there was more tapping to do to get his performance numbers back to where he wanted them. After working through his emotional angst, it was time to address past injuries, another common obstacle to peak performance in professional athletes.

There was one past injury in particular that was holding him back—restricting his range of movement, agility, and confidence. Stacey led him through tapping rounds, using her injury recovery protocols to release the emotional energy his muscles had stored since that injury first happened. It worked! His body returned to its preinjury form, and he was once again able to make aggressive plays and dives. His performance numbers quickly improved, boosting his confidence, energy, and motivation to play to the very best of his ability.

Recovering from Past Injuries

Stacey has seen again and again how damaging past physical trauma can be to athletes, who are expected to perform at the top of their game day in and day out. One professional golfer had suffered a brutal physical assault many years earlier and came to her seeking new ways to improve his game. She soon realized that the physical beating he had endured—the unfortunate result of a wrong-place-wrong-time moment—had gotten locked in his body. He was a natural athlete, but since the assault, he'd been unable to trust that his body would do what he needed it to.

They tapped on releasing the original event and reconnecting with his body's innate athletic abilities. Before long, he was able to release the negative emotional energy that had been inside him all that time and allow his body to hit the shots it naturally knew how to execute. Not only did his game improve, but the emotional freedom he recovered gave him the energy to pursue even more opportunities in his career—and his life.

Professional athletes are an extreme example of the performance issues anyone can experience. Whether it's anxiety over your tennis game or lingering discomfort from that old knee injury, you can rest assured that what works for professionals is equally effective for casual-but-committed athletes. While tapping can't necessarily replace good conditioning, it can have amazingly positive effects on your mind and body—helping your body heal and freeing you from the emotions that can prevent you from performing at your full potential.

Unlike conventional therapies, tapping also helps athletes at any level reconnect with their bodies. Athletes who work with trainers and take frequent lessons, Stacey explains, can go into information overload.

"The more they get into their left brains," she says, "the worse they play, because there's too much going on."

EFT can help you use your *subconscious* to improve your performance by quieting the mental noise that tends to get in the way. Rather than trying to consciously *think* your way to a better swing, you can let your brain absorb the information, give your body time to practice the movement, and use tapping to release your anxiety and clear the way for your body to incorporate those instructions on its own. Just think about commanding all the muscles in your body to throw a base-ball or swing a golf club. It's an impossible feat to do with the conscious mind. It ties in with the "bodymind" concept we discussed in Chapter 6. The subcon-scious provides the instructions, and the body follows. For top athletes, it's often a critical advantage to have a tool that integrates the "bodymind" and lets their bodies *feel* their way to enhanced performance.

Working with Children and Teenagers

EFT has proven to be enormously effective with children of all ages, from tod-dlers to teenagers. Depending on the age, the approach can be different. So if you're leading your child, or any young person, through tapping, here are a few tips.

As the adult, you need to enter *their* world. Our natural temptation is to want to bring kids into our adult world, but the more you can use *their* language, and try to get your head into *their* reality, the better. So if you're tapping on your teen-ager's anxiety over failing a test, keep in mind that his or her top concern may not be the event's effect on college prospects, but instead what friends and/or teach-ers will think. Anxiety about looking "uncool" or being the "class loser" can be a huge deal. Make whatever emotions the teen shares the focus of the tapping, not your own concern that low grades could sabotage a future education.

One of the great things about EFT is that it doesn't have to be serious. You can clear fears, anxiety, and all kinds of other emotions using humor and playfulness. It works with adults and is even more important with kids. For example, you may want to pretend you're a monkey or make funny sounds at each tapping point— whatever it takes for the child to be engaged and feel safe.

You may need to break some of the rules with kids, and that's fine. With younger children especially, there may be times when you do things differently, like skipping the setup, or the karate-chop statement. Just go with the flow and see what works. For very small children who can't tap by themselves, you can tap on them gently.

Preteens, teens, and even younger kids can get overly focused on extremes; everything is either perfect or a total disaster. Let them express those emotions in their own way, and tap on those extreme scenarios. Avoid trying to rationalize with them, which can make them feel misunderstood and unwilling to try tapping.

Quieting Fears

Sam's favorite position in his favorite sport had suddenly become his biggest nightmare. At nine years old, he was ready to surrender his spot as the softball's team star pitcher.

Without warning, Sam had developed an extreme fear of pitching—he worried he'd be hit by the ball, break his leg, or even die. His anxiety had gotten so acute that he could no longer walk to the pitcher's mound.

Sam's mom took him to see Brad Yates, a well-known EFT practitioner. They began by talking about what Sam had been feeling about pitching. Brad then introduced tapping, making sure to use simple, easy language, something like, "Look, we're going to do this process. There's energy in your body. There's stuff that's going through your body that makes you feel uncomfortable, and we're going to tap on certain points to calm your body down. That's going to help you let go of that uncomfortable feeling. It's going to help the fear go away."

Looking a little shy at first, the boy agreed to follow along. They spent about an hour together. At the end, Brad had Sam shut his eyes, imagine pitching, and share what that felt like. "I'm excited," Sam said, smiling. At his next game, he reportedly pitched well and loved every minute of it.

Calming Preteen Angst

It was supposed to be Emily's first year of middle school.

The problem was, she'd developed so much social anxiety that she'd begun refusing to go to school and was also having trouble sleeping.

Then one night, her parents read her Brad Yates's children's book about EFT, *The Wizard's Wish.* Emily fell asleep quickly and easily. It was such a surprising and welcome change that her parents took her to see Brad, hoping he could help her clear some anxiety with EFT.

At first Emily resisted the idea of tapping. But eventually she let Brad lead her through several rounds. Noticing some improvement in her anxiety levels, Brad decided to "test-drive" the results by taking her to school.

As they neared the school, Emily refused to get out of the car. They went through more tapping rounds together. Soon, Brad asked her how she was feeling about going to school, and she said, "I'm okay with it." After that one session, Emily was able to return to school, and she now has special permission from her teachers to leave class to use tapping when her anxiety level begins to rise.

When Brad shared this story with me, I had to laugh, because it struck a personal chord for me. I have a distinct memory—and it's a story my whole family still tells—of being reluctant to go to school. I was in second grade, and we had just moved to the United States from my native country, Argentina. One day my great-aunt Nellie was driving me to school. She got out of the car and closed the door, at which point I locked all the doors and stayed in the car! This was before power locks, so it was easy for me to keep the lock pressed down as she tried to get back inside.

Eventually I relented, got out of the car, and went into school. But I wasn't happy! I sure could have used EFT back then, working out my anxiety, fear, and overall stress about such a big change.

Giving Teenagers an Emotional Outlet

Maggie, a client of mine, shared a beautiful story about how she used EFT with her 16-year-old daughter. One element made me jump up and down with excitement. She told me that her daughter had come to her asking for help with some problems she was having at school. Her daughter knew about tapping, and they'd used it before with great results. While Maggie and her daughter have a close relationship, like most teenagers, she wasn't comfortable telling her mom all the details of the challenges she was facing. And those of us who can remember being teenagers understand why.

Brilliantly, Maggie thought to tell her daughter that if there was anything she didn't want to talk about, she could just give what was happening a title—as in a movie title—or just share the emotion without the specifics. This is a tool I often use with clients when I notice they seem hesitant to share details about a particular situation; it's usually because they're ashamed of what they did or their role in the problem. But I had never thought about how powerful this would be when working with teenagers. A parent can help a child, work on tapping together, provide encouragement, and alleviate emotional burdens without pressing for details.

As any parent knows, this is huge! Once they had tapped for a while on the initial issues, Maggie's daughter became more comfortable and ended up sharing what was going on. By letting go of her desire to know every detail, Maggie gave her daughter the space she needed to discuss, and tap on, what was really happening.

Surrogate Tapping: Toddlers, Pets, and More

There's been a lot of interest recently in the topic of "surrogate tapping," which is basically tapping your own body on behalf of someone else. There are lots of benefits to it, including that it enables you to tap on toddlers, pets, and other groups who can't tap for themselves. All these groups (and many more) have been shown to respond very well to surrogate tapping.

Before you do any surrogate tapping, however, it's critical to check in with yourself. It's important to clear the issues and emotions around *why* you feel compelled to tap on someone other than yourself. It's a lot easier to decide what's "wrong" with another person than to look at your own behavior. Often another person's behavior *seems* like a problem to us because it makes us feel unpleasant emotions like fear, anger, or jealousy.

For example, doing surrogate tapping on your toddler to "always listen to Mommy" probably won't work if you're doing it because his behavior scares you. In that case, you need to tap on your fear, on why his perfectly normal—and, yes, erratic—toddler behavior makes you focus on every worst-case scenario you can imagine. EFT is not a tool for making people do what you want; it's about clearing emotional energy. So make sure any surrogate tapping you do is coming from as emotionally pure a place as possible. And if you suspect that might not be the case, then you can do tapping on *Even though I'm trying to change them and want to fix them . . . !*

One of the most popular audios we've shared with our community over the past several years is a guided tapping meditation on surrogate tapping, created by my sister, Jessica. The stories people have shared regarding their experience with this simple audio have been incredible. You can listen to it for free at www.thetappingsolution.com/surrogate.

Better Eyesight

We've known it, heard it, been told it for years—your eyesight deteriorates as you age. It's a fact of life, right?

Okay, but what if that's only true *sometimes?* What if poor or worsening eyesight were connected, in some degree, to your *emotions?*

After hearing from clients that their eyesight was improving by doing tapping, Carol Look did an experiment exploring that exact question. She led 120 volunteers through eight weeks of daily tapping exercises. Each week, they focused on a different emotion—releasing anger one week, processing fear the next, and so on. Through this work, she was able to help people literally see themselves and their lives more clearly. After following this tapping protocol, approximately 40 percent of study participants reported a noticeable improvement in several of the major eyesight categories—including the ability to see brightness, color perception, eye fatigue, nearsightedness, and farsightedness. Participants reported the biggest improvements after tapping to release anger, with the next-highest improvements after they'd tapped on anxiety.[1]

You can see the full results of the study and learn more about Carol's program at www.thetappingsolution.com/eyesight.

Managing Allergies

Some call allergies a "phobia of the immune system." And given how well tapping works with fears and phobias, it's no surprise that the practice has been linked to dramatic improvements across multiple allergy categories, from wheat to chemicals, pollen, and more. The most common protocol is to have the allergen, the thing you're allergic to, in front of you while you tap on your allergy. By focusing on your immune system's reaction to this substance—and any emotions you may have around that substance or around your allergy itself—you can simply tap on anything and everything that comes up.

Sandi Radomski has had great success helping allergy sufferers with tapping and other innovative tools. You can learn more about her work at www.thetappingsolution.com/allergies.

Increasing Creativity and Improving Performance

We already saw how EFT can alleviate performance anxiety in sports, but that's just the beginning. Tapping is also enormously effective for other performance issues, including musical and dance performance, writer's block, public speaking, meeting business and sales goals . . . the list could span a football field! By clearing the negative emotional drivers behind blocked creativity and stunted performance, tapping gives you direct access to your natural talents. Once those talents can engage without interference from long-held fears and worries, you'll be amazed by how well you can play, write, create, dance, sing, speak, sell, and do whatever it is you were born to do! You'll be able to perform at your highest level more easily and more frequently and have more fun doing it.

Exercise: Find Something Fun to Clear

We've covered lots of big topics in this book, from relationships to money, food to stress relief. Let's take a minute to lighten the mood and have some fun! Tapping can help you make all kinds of positive changes, including letting you overcome weird, unusual stressors or obstacles that may have become part of your life over the years.

One woman I met had been unable to take vitamins or green "superfood" powder for 20 years. It was something she knew was good for her health, but she was blocked around it. She'd open the bottle and immediately feel nauseated. That was it—the end of the line, as far as she could go.

I decided to focus on her aversion for a few minutes, to see if we could clear it. First I opened the container of green powder she had in her kitchen. She withdrew, fighting nausea as usual. She explained that her dad used to make her take all kinds of vitamins and minerals growing up, and they had always grossed her out. Even now as an adult, she'd never been able to get over it.

We began tapping, using her memories as our guide, saying phrases like, *Even though my dad used to make me take vitamins . . . even though I hated it. . . .* Sure enough, after just a few rounds of tapping, she was able to drink the green powder! Another one-minute-wonder result!

Take a moment to think about your life and any little habits, aversions, or patterns you'd like to break or overcome. Try to figure out how they started. Was there an emotional trigger? A memory or association that helps to explain how and why that habit, aversion, or pattern started? Tap on what you uncover. You'll be amazed at the little things you can clear out of your life with tapping!

CHAPTER 13

A NEW VISION FOR HUMANITY

Never doubt that a small group of thoughtful, committed citizens can change the world. Indeed, it is the only thing that ever has.

Margaret Mead

Now that you've seen the impact EFT can have on your own life, I want to share some of the amazing work people are doing around the world. The exciting truth is, tapping is proving to be a powerful healing tool for a variety of issues around the globe, with particular effectiveness on trauma. Though I'll spare you talk of world peace, I will say that tapping is healing populations that historically haven't responded well to other, more conventional therapies. It's also demonstrating tremendous potential to help advance growth in struggling economies, make overburdened health-care systems run better (and at lower cost!), and reintegrate disenfranchised populations into war-torn societies.

As you'll see, the potential of EFT to improve our world is nearly limitless.

PTSD: The Invisible Epidemic?

Post-traumatic stress disorder, or PTSD, is often associated with war veterans. The unfortunate reality, though, is that PTSD affects all kinds of people around the world—including the many millions of survivors of natural disasters, war, torture, dis-ease, rape, and so much more. The scarring aftereffects of trauma don't discriminate by race, age, or gender. Symptoms can be as acute in a young child who lived through a tsunami as they are in a soldier returning from Iraq.

The National Institute of Mental Health (NIMH) defines PTSD as "an anxiety disorder that some people get after seeing or living through a dangerous event."

When you're in danger, it's natural to feel afraid. This fear triggers many split-second changes in the body to prepare to defend against the danger or to avoid it. As we discussed early on, this fight-or-flight response is a healthy reaction meant to protect a person from harm. But in persons with PTSD, the reaction is changed or damaged. They may feel stressed or frightened even when they're no longer in danger.[1]

Looking at that definition, it's easy to see how PTSD could be described as the "invisible" global epidemic. At any given moment, all over the world, people are struggling to recover from trauma, unable to feel safe long after they and their loved ones are out of danger. With the spread of EFT, I'm happy to report, we may finally have a way to bring trauma victims back to a normal life; to calm their fears and anxiety; to lessen their physical pain; to end their depression, insomnia, nightmares, and paranoia; and to give them hope for the future and restore their ability to live active, productive lives.

Healing the Wounds of Genocide in Rwanda

Just talking to Lori Leyden about her work in Rwanda, you can't help but be overwhelmed by the healing power of EFT. That such a simple practice can promote healing on every conceivable level—physical, emotional, mental, and spiritual—in a nation as deeply scarred as Rwanda, makes you pause long enough to imagine the profound change tapping could effect around the globe.

In 2007, Lori, a psychotherapist, Ph.D., and stress-management expert, got a call asking if she would give permission to have her first book, *The Stress Management Handbook,* translated into Kinyarwanda, the language of Rwanda.

Well aware of the 1994 genocide that led to the murder of 800,000 Rwandans in 100 days, Lori was eager to get involved.

"My heart opened. I knew this was a life changing moment so I asked what else could I do to help and was invited to Rwanda to do trauma healing work with orphan and widow genocide survivors," she recalls.

During her first trip to Rwanda in 2007, Lori worked with a group of 100 orphan heads of household. These are young people, now in their 20s who were 6 to 10 years old at the time of the genocide, and they were left to care for two to six other children with no visible means of support and no hope for the future.

On their first day together Lori asked the group what healing they wanted for themselves and their fellow orphans. Their list began with healing for the wound of rape, hopelessness for the future, poverty, memories of their families being murdered, and the despair of being an orphan left to care for other children.

Momentarily awed by the work ahead, Lori says, "I remember saying to myself, *Oh my gosh. Is EFT really powerful enough to deal with such intense trauma?* and my heart said, Okay, we're going in."

So she went ahead with a tapping protocol for their first request—healing for the wound of rape. After completing just three rounds of tapping, their SUDS level went from 10 to 2 and their relief was visible and palpable. "For the first time, these young adults survivors were experiencing a sense of peace and safety in their bodies and minds that they had never felt before," she says.

Since 2008 Lori has been part of a volunteer team that works regularly with 500 orphan genocide survivors attending a residential high school orphanage in a very remote area at the top of a mountain in one of the districts hardest hit by the genocide. While their work at the orphanage was extremely successful—reducing trauma outbreaks at the school by 90 percent in just one year—Lori came to realize that trauma healing wasn't enough. Once these young people graduate, they are traumatized again with a hopeless about their future, because they have no opportunities to go to college, learn a skill, or start a business that would lift them out of the cycle of poverty they live in.

Lori explained to me how she decided to expand the scope of her work into a program she calls Project LIGHT: "The burdens that these traumatized widows and orphans live with are so heavy—murder, torture, mutilation, HIV, homelessness, poverty. . . . It's estimated that 90% of the people in Rwanda witnessed some brutality of the genocide, so you've got an entire country living with some level of post-traumatic stress disorder. . . . each time I return from Rwanda I am more inspired by these young people. Their resilience, compassion, commitment, and ability to forgive open my heart to a true knowing that world healing is possible."

So in May 2011, with support from *The Tapping Solution,* Lori developed a new form of humanitarian aid based on tapping. It is the world's first international youth healing, heart-centered leadership and entrepreneurship program—and it is achieving profound results. "We use tapping as the basis for all elements of our program from physical and emotional healing to problem-solving, creativity, productivity, focus, concentration, conflict resolution, and team building as well as personal and spiritual growth," says Lori.

Project LIGHT uses a train-the-trainer model to create ambassadors who can then teach tapping techniques to thousands of others in their communities.

Mattieu, Yvette, Desire, and Fidel are some of the first Project LIGHT ambassadors who have transformed their own despair and grief into love, compassion, and joy for themselves and others. In addition to teaching tapping in their communities, they have also been elected and appointed as leaders in local government positions. Now, just as important, they are finding their way out of poverty by developing self-sustaining microfinance businesses.

While Lori's stories of healing through EFT come by the dozens, it's a Project LIGHT ambassador named Chantal who first comes to her mind. Aged eight at the time of the genocide, Chantal's entire family was murdered. She received a machete chop to her neck that almost severed her head, and then she awoke on a pile of dead bodies next to her uncle. She crawled to the nearby woods, where she saw the murderers finish off anyone who was still alive, including her only remaining family member.

After that day, Chantal lived on the streets or with abusive strangers, while she continued to suffer tremendous pain from her emotional and physical wounds. The list of post-traumatic stress symptoms she experienced ran the gamut— "anxiety, fear of the future, hopelessness, depression, sleeplessness, pain. I could go on and on," Lori says.

When Lori met Chantal in 2009, she was homeless once again. Each night, she would sneak into a construction site to sleep in a small shed. There was very little Lori could do for her then but two years later when Project LIGHT was launched, she knew Chantal would be a perfect ambassador candidate. Miraculously, Lori was able to find her and bring her into the first Project LIGHT residential training program. Within days of learning tapping, Chantal's outlook shifted. "She had hope enough to begin to see that she could change her life. Her physical pain abated and her emotional symptoms were reduced by thirty-six percent in the first week," Lori explains.

Now 26 years old, Chantal "has become an amazing inspiration," Lori beams. "As a result of the Project LIGHT program, Chantal has opened her own village grocery store where customers of all ages come not only to buy a piece of bread or a cupful of sugar but also to seek her wise counsel and learn tapping—plus she's been appointed by her village elders to the National Women's Leadership Committee.

Hearing Lori's stories convinced me more than ever of how effectively EFT can heal our world—no matter the challenges. If Chantal can heal her terrible wounds, why can't anyone, anywhere do the same?

Given its groundbreaking success, Lori's currently seeking funding to expand Project LIGHT. "I've had interest from Kenya, India, and South Africa," she says. "I hope that through Project LIGHT, tapping can gain greater legitimacy and fuel the movement to bring this leading-edge healing modality to those who need it most around the world so our next generation of young people can heal, work, and lead us into a peaceful future."

To learn more, visit ProjectLightRwanda.com.

Breaking Down Global Barriers

Thinking back on my discussion with Lori, it's impossible not to be awed by both the results Project LIGHT is achieving in Rwanda and the intensity of the work they're doing. Lori views tapping as a kind of gateway into other healing practices, like meditation, prayer, singing, and other energetic work. She and I talked about how tapping is such an effective way to help people open up and to give them the focus they need to meditate, or even pray, on a deeper level. That flexibility is just one of the many reasons that tapping is working so well in so many parts of the world. It can accommodate any number of different cultures, belief systems, religions, and other rituals and practices.

An example of EFT's cultural and religious adaptability is the Israel Trauma Care Center, located in Safed, Israel. In so many ways, the ITCC is several worlds, generations, and cultural divides away from Rwanda. Opened in 2006 after northern Israel was subjected to more than 500 terrorist rocket launches, the center teaches EFT to Safed residents suffering from a broad range of PTSD symptoms—from sleeplessness to panic attacks to intense fear of loud noises. The center's success using tapping with local residents has, in fact, been recognized by Safed's mayor.

Recovering from the Devastation of Natural Disaster

At the moment the Pangandaran earthquake hit Indonesia in 2006 Tedi was a seven-year-old boy playing, running, and laughing with his friend on the beach. When the ground began to shake beneath them, the two boys and a neighborhood sheep dashed into the closest house. Moments later, the house and its new occupants were swept away by a tsunami and transported into the jungle. When the water level finally receded hours later, Tedi found himself trapped inside the wrecked house, terrified and alone, his friend and the sheep both dead. Two full days passed before Tedi was rescued; by then, he was physically depleted and emotionally and mentally devastated.

Barely able to sleep and wetting himself uncontrollably, Tedi's PTSD was sabotaging his young life. Determined to restore the boy's spirit, Deepak Mostert, the founder of TREST (Trauma Relief & Emotional Support Techniques) Aid, began teaching Tedi to use EFT. After just one session, Tedi's trauma symptoms dissipated. Several years and much tapping later, Tedi is once again the strong, courageous young boy he was. He is quickly becoming a leader in his own right, attending all the EFT sessions Deepak leads in his hometown.

For Deepak, whose TREST Aid organization has been helping survivors overcome PTSD in disaster areas since 2006, Tedi's progress is but more proof that tapping is the fastest, most effective treatment for trauma survivors.

A former policeman and a psychotherapist by training, Deepak set his sights on helping trauma victims in early adulthood. His interest in trauma developed after he suffered PTSD from being trapped in a burning building at age 22 and then in a burning car at age 31. When an earthquake hit Java, Indonesia, in 2006, killing nearly 6,000 and leaving 1.2 million homeless, Deepak jumped at the chance to help a local nongovernmental organization, or NGO, establish a program for schoolchildren there. Children whose bodies had survived but whose spirits, minds, and hearts seemed irreparably broken.

Upon arriving at that first disaster area, Deepak was faced with a sea of somber young faces that seemed unlikely to respond to traditional counseling—which would be too slow for such a large and deeply scarred group. Resolved to have the greatest possible impact, Deepak began experimenting with EFT, which, he soon discovered, could alleviate trauma symptoms in hundreds, and soon thousands, of young victims in a matter of hours or days. Working with groups of 100 children at a time, Deepak helped them rediscover their smiles and be freed from headaches, backaches, acute anxiety, fear, hopelessness, helplessness, and grief.

As word of Deepak's astounding success spread, he and his team began training still larger groups, including government health workers, psychologists, students, youth organizations, and teachers, who then used their skills as EFT trainers to help other affected communities.

Deepak founded TREST Aid during that first visit to an earthquake zone in 2006; it is the first humanitarian aid organization in the world to implement energy therapies like EFT for psychological disaster management. Thanks to the organization's ongoing dedication, he and his team have trained 15,898 new EFT instructors. During just that first project in Java, they and their trainers used tapping to help heal 377,214 trauma-stricken students in three short weeks.

The impact of the TREST Aid program, Deepak admits, has "exceeded all my expectations." Tapping, he explains, addresses the psychological symptoms through the body, which is an important and powerful resource for PTSD sufferers.

"Psychologically, a trauma process is a down-spiraling vortex," he says. That vortex often involves physical memories like the smell of fire or the feeling of water filling your lungs. Because tapping lets survivors access their emotions and their physical energy simultaneously, it can free them from trauma much faster than talk therapy. "For most trauma survivors, it is not safe to feel the body. By learning to reconnect with our body [through EFT], we learn to ground ourselves in the experience. It is like acquiring an anchor. With it, your boat is no longer drifting into this down-spiraling vortex."

Since its inception, TREST Aid has run relief programs in seven disaster areas, impacting more than one million survivors in Indonesia alone. Through his work, Deepak has discovered that the post-disaster rebuilding phase—which typically occurs months or years after the actual disaster, when survivors return to their villages and begin reestablishing their lives—can unleash acute PTSD symptoms at an almost epidemic level. To alleviate the tremendous stress of this period, TREST Aid returns to disaster areas repeatedly, in order to continue training local populations in EFT.

From the outset, that training has proven uncommonly successful. "For every 1,000 survivors that have undergone the training," Deepak says, "as few as two or three of them will require follow-up trauma relief support." Spending about three hours per school at three schools per day, a TREST Aid team of four volunteers can train between 1,200 and 1,500 students and between 60 and 120 teachers in a single day. With sufficient resources, that number can increase significantly, with four TREST Aid volunteers reaching as many as 250,000 survivors in a month.

"Trauma," Deepak believes, "is a major block to human evolution." Determined to increase his impact, he has developed a three-level training program that he hopes to implement in disaster areas around the globe. His goal is to start a training institute for government and community organizations around the world that would provide EFT training for dealing with trauma in the field of disaster management. To learn more, visit TRESTAid.com

Healing Hearts, Minds, Bodies—and Economies

Hearing Deepak Mostert discuss his disaster recovery work in Indonesia, I was intrigued by his observation that the most acute PTSD symptoms arise months or years after the event. By that time, of course, most relief-aid programs have ended, and for the first time since the disaster, local populations must leave the temporary camps they've been living in and return to their former hometowns (or elsewhere) to resume "normal" life.

It's entirely understandable that people would be consumed by fear, anxiety, grief, and other latent PTSD symptoms during this recovery phase. Imagine, for example, returning to your former home after a war or natural disaster and being constantly reminded of the loved ones you lost.

As poignant as the situation is on a personal level, this rebuilding phase is equally critical on a broader economic level. The fact is, recovering from natural disaster requires enormous investment. The financial burden on governments to rebuild entire villages—and infrastructure like roads and utility networks—can be crippling. The cold, hard truth is, governments desperately need the local population to return to their lives as productive, working citizens. The more effective the local population can be during this stage, the faster the local economy can begin to function on its own, without governmental relief.

If the people returning to their former homes are emotionally and physically disabled by PTSD, however, they'll be incapable of running farms, opening stores, driving taxis—doing whatever it is they do to support themselves and, in turn, the local economy.

When you consider that a four- or five-person TREST Aid volunteer team can enter those areas, and in 30 days use EFT to treat hundreds of thousands of PTSD sufferers, you begin to see how critical a role EFT can play in reestablishing entire economies and societies. Without real emotional support for local residents, the rebuilding phase can quickly dissolve into mass chaos, putting economies that are already under duress into crisis. With EFT providing deep and lasting emotional recovery, the rebuilding phase can progress. This allows broken communities to start anew and spurs the commerce necessary to any functioning economy.

As Lori Leyden of Project LIGHT asserts, without the healing provided by EFT, people are unable to reengage in society, return to work, reopen businesses, go to school, or live healthy, productive lives. With the kind of emotional healing tapping offers, however, humans become amazingly resilient—capable of overcoming even the most horrific and catastrophic of events.

The Oaxaca Project: Accelerating Healing and Improving Quality of Life

Deborah Miller's work with EFT is as soulful and inspiring as it is heart-wrenching. An EFT practitioner and Ph.D. in cell and molecular biology, Deborah volunteers her time and talents to the children's cancer ward at Hospital General Aurelio Valdivieso in Oaxaca, Mexico. Known as the Oaxaca Project, Deborah's work has exposed dozens of young cancer patients—as well as their families and the attending hospital staff—to the tremendous emotional, mental, physical, and clinical benefits of EFT.

Head oncologist Dr. Armando Quero Hernández, who has worked at the hospital for 15 years, has witnessed enormous transformations from Deborah's tapping work.

"As a result of EFT, I started to see changes: the families less tense, and the kids more dynamic, more comfortable," he says. Often, Deborah adds, ill children become so anxious about their disease and so weary of the pain and hospital visits that they inevitably endure, that they become depressed and despondent. One little girl, Dr. Hernández recalls, had lost so much hope that she began refusing her medication and wouldn't cooperate with any form of treatment. The situation became so dire, in fact, that the girl's mother considered taking her very young daughter home to die. After using EFT with Deborah, however, the girl began to relax, smile, and laugh and soon agreed to continue the medications and treatment her body required to survive.

Even for terminal cases, Dr. Hernández says, EFT "plays a very important role," lowering suffering and providing the children and their parents with peace of mind. So often, Deborah elaborates, tapping takes the entire cancer ward from a place of "misery to hope and peace." Many young cancer victims become afraid of needles, hospitals, and even the color white (hospitals and everything associated with them have a tendency to be white). Through EFT, they're able to release these fears—and feel happier, more energetic, and even physically stronger. The patient's parents benefit as well, using EFT to cope with the tremendous emotional, mental, and financial strain they must endure.

The positive implications of EFT on an individual level can quickly benefit institutions as well.

"EFT results in a more tranquil emotional state and hematological recovery, which, in itself, has implications at the clinical level," Dr. Hernández asserts. Take Diego, an adolescent whose cancer unexpectedly relapsed, causing his health to spiral downward at an alarmingly fast pace. After using EFT with Deborah, his emotional state—as well as his immune and hematological response—improved dramatically. As a result of his faster recovery, Diego required less attention from hospital nurses and staff, who could then tend to other patients in need.

Having seen any number of similar scenarios play out, Dr. Hernández asserts that, in addition to providing these ill children with a greatly improved quality of life, EFT has the potential to provide considerable advantages to hospitals like his. By improving patients' emotional states, EFT appears to facilitate immune function. When used on an ongoing basis, EFT may help decrease infections, reduce complications, and even lower the amount of medication patients need. As a result, less laboratory work and fewer nurses are required to treat a given patient. This provides substantial savings to the hospital, and may enable a facility like the Hospital General Aurelio Valdivieso to help an even greater number of young cancer victims at a lower cost.

In addition to helping patients and their families, EFT is proving to be an important tool for the nurses and medical staff. Dr. Hernández reports that, thanks to tapping, "the environment becomes more positive." EFT also improves "how the doctors confront problems, and . . . it helps the staff give [more of their] attention to the child with cancer," he adds.

For Deborah, whose upbeat, caring demeanor seems never to waiver, the Oaxaca Project is, first and foremost, a chance to bring joy and laughter into these children's lives.

"You fall in love with these children," she says, smiling. "They're beautiful. They're powerful. They're brave. They're living with this incredible disease and doing their best to get beyond it. Giving them tools and seeing them flower right in front of you creates a beautiful sensation." Often, she admits, she's so consumed in play and laughter with the children that she forgets she's in a cancer ward. The

Oaxaca Project, she explains, "isn't about illness. . . . What its true purpose is, is to create wellness." To learn more, visit OaxacaProject.com.

Advancing Modern Medicine

One of the exciting things about the Oaxaca Project is how Deborah integrates EFT into the conventional medical model. She uses EFT not to interfere with the treatments doctors are providing to the children, but to lessen the anxiety that patients feel about their dis-ease and the surgery and other treatments they need. As Dr. Hernández pointed out, her work has also affected the doctors and hospital staff—giving them a new tool to use in their own lives, as well as the lives of their patients.

Dr. Patricia Carrington, an EFT practitioner who contributed to *The Tapping Solution* movie, has researched some of the EFT work being done here in the United States with nurses, medical personnel, and patients. However small the scale, the results still speak for themselves. From decreasing the need for medication, to lessening pain and anxiety in patients, to giving hospital workers an outlet for stress, tapping is improving the care patients receive—and at a lower overall cost than conventional medicine alone. As Dr. Carrington asserts on her website, "I can envision a day when EFT is an accepted procedure in hospitals and a part of standard preoperative protocol. This seems to be a vision worth holding for all of us."[2]

Dimming the Nightmares of Warfare

Given how tapping is helping trauma sufferers from Rwanda to Mexico, you may not be surprised to hear that there's also impressive EFT work being done with war veterans here in the United States.

Depression, anxiety, sleeplessness, nightmares, alcoholism, drug abuse, violent behavior, suicidal tendencies, paranoia—this is the short list of PTSD symptoms regularly suffered by veterans of war. It's a level of trauma that hasn't been effectively treated with conventional therapies, which is why Gary Craig, founder of EFT, and Dawson Church, Ph.D., and founder of the Soul Medicine Institute, initiated the Stress Project. The Stress Project teaches veterans to use EFT to tap their way through enormously painful, often gruesome, chronically haunting war memories.

To test the theory that tapping can, in fact, "do this job," Craig and Church gathered five severely traumatized veterans from Vietnam and Iraq and spent five days using EFT to work through their PTSD.

That initial group of five has since ballooned to more than 3,000 veterans. The remarkable outcomes produced by the Stress Project have even swayed committed skeptics like David Gruder, Ph.D., a clinical and organizational psychologist from San Diego, California. Now describing himself as "very, very enthusiastic" about EFT, Gruder's dramatic change of opinion is "because of one thing, and one thing only," he explains. "It's called *results*."

And while the numbers are impressive—a 25 percent decrease in cortisol after one hour of tapping; a 63 percent drop in standard PTSD symptoms (after six sessions); a greater than 50 percent decrease in anxiety and depression after EFT—it's the personal stories of these haunted vets that are most convincing.

Take Art Fritog, for example, a Vietnam war veteran whose PTSD had gotten so out of control that he would fly into violent rages and threaten to kill his wife of 33 years and their children. After just three days in the Stress Project, Art could discuss his feelings calmly with his wife, holding her hand tenderly, often smiling and laughing. It was, she explained gratefully, "the first real conversation we've had in five years." Commenting on his own post-EFT state of mind, Art added, "I can't emphasize enough how important it is to know that you can actually feel like a real person again and not be afraid."

There's also Andy Hodnick, who began the Stress Project with a debilitating stutter; battling severe paranoia; antisocial, violent behavior; and nightmares from his tour of duty in Iraq. After using EFT, Andy shared his memories without stuttering or getting agitated. His paranoia also subsided to the point where he could eat in restaurants, which he'd been avoiding for some time.

Last but not least is Carlin Sloan, an Iraq vet who, prior to the Stress Project, used alcohol like many addicts use street drugs—drinking until he was so blitzed that he'd pass out, then reaching for the bottle the second he awoke. It was the only way he knew to quiet the memory of watching a child be blown up and having a crowd of women run at him soon thereafter, yelling that the child's death was his fault. Crippled by guilt, haunted by his memory, and trying desperately to cope with searing pain in his jaw and neck, Carlin repeatedly threatened to reenlist; he was consumed by his PTSD and unable to return to civilian life.

Just days after using EFT, Carlin slept through the night without alcohol, the tremor in his hands disappeared, and he reported waking up "feeling good."

Months later, Carlin had stopped drinking entirely, and no longer felt guilt or experienced pain in his jaw or neck. Perhaps most important, though, his demeanor had changed dramatically.

"I'm happy," he reported. "Before I did the EFT thing, for me to say 'I'm happy'—that would just have been weird. And I say it probably like ten times a day now." To learn more, visit StressProject.org.

Lowering the Burden on Health-Care Systems

As with the patients in the Oaxaca Project, one of the broader benefits of EFT for veterans is that it's providing fast relief for symptoms that would otherwise require long-term medication and psychotherapy. As a result, of course, health insurance companies are spared the burden of supporting costly, ineffective treatments over months and even years.

With that idea in mind, imagine what could happen if tapping were an accepted health-care practice. It's easy to see how health insurance companies, hospitals, and doctors could provide better treatment at a substantially lower cost if they integrated EFT with medication and conventional treatment. The hugely positive impact those cost savings could have on the health-care system could pave the way for substantial improvements, including coverage for a larger percentage of the population, better care for the sick and elderly, and more.

Dare to Imagine a New World

EFT can treat, and actually heal, populations that otherwise would remain emotionally, physically, and mentally debilitated by trauma. When you think of that, it's easy to imagine how tapping could turn into a worldwide movement for change!

Exercise: Can You Help?

The organizations discussed in this chapter—Project LIGHT, TREST Aid, the Stress Project, and the Oaxaca Project—need all the support they can get to continue their amazing trauma healing work. I hope you'll take a moment to check out their websites and make whatever donation or contribution you can. Like most nonprofits, their most pressing need is financial support, but they also need people to spread the word. So consider sharing these websites (and this book) with your friends and family via e-mail, Facebook, Twitter, or other forms of communication. And thank you.

Project LIGHT

ProjectLightRwanda.com
Using EFT and real-world skills training to help an entire generation of genocide survivors recover from PTSD and create a new life (and country) for themselves.

TREST Aid

TRESTAid.com
Teaching EFT to earthquake victims of all ages in Indonesia to resolve their PTSD and help them start anew.

The Oaxaca Project

OaxacaProject.com
Working with young cancer victims in Oaxaca to promote healing and instill peace of mind using EFT.

The Stress Project

StressProject.org
Using EFT to help veterans resolve the PTSD of war in Vietnam and Iraq.

CHAPTER 14

A NEW VISION
FOR YOU

You're braver than you believe and stronger
than you seem and smarter than you think.

CHRISTOPHER ROBIN (IN THE MOVIE *WINNIE THE POOH*)

For the vast majority of my life, I navigated the world believing things just happened. I had no awareness of why—no sense of the root causes of my behavior and what I could do about them. If I was angry at someone, it was because they had done something to deserve it. If I felt hurt, it was a justified feeling, because someone had "made" me feel that way. If I acted a certain way, it was a "personality trait."

I acted, reacted, made decisions, experienced negative emotions and outcomes, and believed that that was just the way things were. If you're familiar with this kind of existence—whether now or in the past—you know it's not a fun one. Not believing that we are in control of our own destiny is one of the more painful ways to live.

Fortunately, I got to the point where I slowly started taking responsibility for my life. I gained awareness that I had been shaped by my past experiences. I saw that while negative experiences in my life were not my *fault,* they were indeed my *responsibility.*

In those first couple of years of personal awareness, I knew I wanted to change, wanted to act differently, wanted to make better decisions—but I didn't know *how.* I didn't know how to break the patterns that had been running my life for so long. How could I stop doing what I had been doing all my life? How could I stop reacting in ways I didn't want to react? How could I finally make decisions that empowered me? How could I let go, forgive, heal, and move forward in all areas of my life?

Fortunately, when the question and desire are strong enough, an answer appears. For me, it appeared in the form of this strange tapping technique! As I've shared with you throughout the book, I was startled when I first experienced the power of EFT. And I continue to be astonished every single day with the magic it creates in my life and the lives of those around me.

I hope that the preceding pages have educated you, inspired you, and most important, actually helped you achieve the changes you most desire. If you've read the book through once without doing a lot of the tapping, that's okay. But I do urge you to go back to the tapping scripts and look further into the resources online that can help you truly experience EFT.

This book is by no means a comprehensive guide to all things tapping-related. It pained me to be able to share only so much with you—but I can't burden you with a 3,000-page tome! The story of any given client I've worked with could fill a book by itself. I can only hope that this small taste of the power of EFT has excited you and inspired you to learn more—and continue this journey in your own life.

In this book we've covered a wide variety of topics—from physical pain and illness to childhood traumas, from relationships to making money, losing weight, and more. As you continue in your journey, you might want to zero in on one topic or specific outcome at a time in order to be able to focus on it and easily quantify your results.

The Challenges with EFT

If there's one thing that I've found most challenging in spreading the message of this powerful tool, it's that it's so new and such a break from our existing paradigms, that we don't have any cultural reinforcement to remind us to actually do it.

When we turn on the TV, we get cues to eat terrible food, drink alcohol, take pharmaceutical drugs, and buy a car. (A gecko helpfully instructs us where to buy insurance for said car.) But yet to appear on the tube, unfortunately, is a commercial that reminds you to take the time to slow down, forgive, heal, and love. I've often stated publicly that the greatest thing that could happen for the personal-development/alternative-health industry would be for someone to figure out how to make $1 billion helping people heal—thus being able to run a commercial during the Super Bowl right next to one for pharmaceutical drugs. An ad that offers a *different* possibility for change.

Until that happens, it's up to you to do your best to remind yourself to tap, to hang out in those places online where others are tapping, and to gather friends who tap. The more you use EFT and establish positive personal reinforcement for the difference it's making in your life, the easier it will be to remember to use it.

Sharing Tapping with Friends and Family

It's likely that after having positive experiences in this book and reading about the success of others, you've already thought of a person or two (or ten!) who might benefit from using EFT. One of the primary reasons why I originally made the documentary film *The Tapping Solution* was because I wanted people to have a tool they could use to *passively* share EFT with others.

The key word there is *passively.* And I'm sharing this with you from my own personal experience of discovering the delicate balance between enthusiasm, wanting to help, and being overbearing and obnoxious. I've found, after a lot of trial and error, that the best way to promote tapping is to share your personal experiences and how it helped you, or to pass along the movie or this book and gently suggest that people give it a try. It's not your job to convince anyone to try the process, and if people sense from you that you're coming to fix them, they'll resist. If, however, your friends and loved ones sense that you are coming with an open heart, simply trying to be supportive, then they're likely to listen to what you have to say. Going Deeper . . . and Helping People Yourself

As I shared above, this book is just a start, a jumping-off point, on this journey of self-healing. If you want to go deeper—and I highly encourage you to—please explore all the other resources we have available online, many of which have been mentioned throughout this book. You can start by visiting www.thetappingsolution.com.

I also often get asked about how to become an EFT coach or get trained to teach tapping to others. The ability to connect with people who need help—and to guide them through the journey of healing and growth—continues to be one of the most rewarding experiences of my life. I cannot recommend it more highly. We've listed resources for that path at www.thetappingsolution.com/training.

A New Beginning

At its deepest level, the process of EFT is one of healing, releasing, and learning from past traumas and negative experiences. This is like peeling away layer after layer of an onion. The anger we feel is released, only to find sadness underneath. The sadness gives way to understanding. The understanding leads to awareness and joy. The awareness and joy usher in peace and love. Layer by layer, we peel away the past—often doing some crying along the way—and what's left is the real self. The beauty of who and what we are at our core, the understanding and forgiveness of our past, and the possibilities for our future.

It is possible to move through this world full with happiness, joy, and peace. It is possible to be a shining light, a beacon of hope and healing. I could never have imagined that one of the paths to this level of joy, peace, and abundance would involve tapping points on the body. But then again, the most amazing things in life have a level of mystery that few of us can comprehend.

There is one thing I do know from personal experience. It goes beyond the incredible science and research that is coming out validating the power of this technique, beyond the millions of people using it, beyond the jaw-dropping results that humanitarian organizations around the world are having with it. Past all that lies my own truth. What I know for myself and what I hope you know or are starting to know: *EFT works.*

I've seen it. I've experienced it. I've had it transform my life in astounding, deep, and beautiful ways. I continue to be awed and inspired about what is possible for you, for me, and for humanity.

I can't wait to meet you somewhere on the road of life and hear *your* personal experience. I can't wait for you to tell me how EFT helped you heal, how your pain went away from tapping, how you finally broke through the blocks to abundance you'd been living with for decades, how you finally forgave those who hurt you, how you finally created the life of your dreams.

I wait eagerly to hear your stories. Please share your experiences and results with me by e-mailing stories@thetappingsolution.com. Until then . . . remember to keep tapping!

P. S.

You're still here? Fantastic! This is a little bonus section for those of you who stepped up and finished the book. First off, congratulations are in order. Unless of course you jumped to the last pages to see how the book ends—but since this isn't a novel, that's unlikely.

If you've made it this far, I know this much about you: you're committed to change, to a better life, to improving yourself and the world. It's my hope that what you've learned in the preceding pages can help make that a reality.

If you're really ready, if you want change to happen faster than you've ever experienced—if you are ready to finally live the life you've dreamed of, then I've got a little something extra for you.

I've created a short course designed to take what you've learned in this book and bump it up it to the next level, and you'll find it at www.thetappingsolution .com/mygift. This course is 100 percent free and is my gift to you for reading the book and making this commitment to yourself and the world.

Just don't tell anyone else about this link or what's in the back of the book, okay? They have to earn it! You did!

P. P. S.

Thank you. :)

(I write with smiley faces all the time in my e-mails. How else can I properly convey my feelings? My editor thought it wouldn't be wise to scatter them throughout the text, and I understand. Fortunately, I snuck this last one in without anyone noticing.)

One more, just for you: :).

RESOURCES

If you're looking to take your tapping experience to the next level, we have a variety of resources on virtually every subject covered in this book:

A Monumental Discovery: Get more information on the exciting new science and research behind tapping at www.thetappingsolution.com/research.

Quick Start: Experience Tapping Now: Watch a short video that takes you through the tapping at www.thetappingsolution.com/tappingvideo.

Relieving Anxiety, Feelings of Being Overwhelmed, and Stress: Want to get a real grip on your daily stress? Get a free daily stress relief meditation (normally sold for $19.95 and free to all purchasers of this book) at www.thetappingsolution.com/stress.

Overcoming Your Resistance to Change: Learn more about overcoming specific barriers to change at www.thetappingsolution.com/change.

Tapping through Your Past: Do you feel like traumas from the past are holding you back and keeping you stuck? Finally break through at www.thetappingsolution.com/thepast

Healing the Body: Tapping has proven incredibly effective at supporting the bodies healing process. Learn more at www.thetappingsolution.com/heal.

Releasing Physical Pain: Our "Pain Relief World Summit," an online event attended by more than 100,000 people could be just what you need to overcome physical pain. Get a free preview at www.thetappingsolution.com/painrelief.

Losing Weight and Letting Go of Fear, Guilt, and Shame around Food: Download a free tapping meditation designed to help you lose weight (normally sold for $19.95 and free to all purchasers of this book) at www.thetappingsolution.com/weightloss.

Creating Love and Healthy Relationships: Manifest the love you desire or improve your existing relationship at www.thetappingsolution.com/love.

Making Money and Achieving Your Dreams: Download a free tapping meditation to relieve financial stress and anxiety and create a more abundant life (normally sold for $19.95 and free to all purchasers of this book) at www.thetappingsolution.com/money.

Eliminating Phobias and Fears: From fear of flying to fear of public speaking, eliminate your specific challenge at www.thetappingsolution.com /overcomingfears.

ENDNOTES

Chapter 1

1. J. Fang et al. "The Salient Characteristics of the Central Effects of Acupuncture Needling: Limbic-Paralimbic-Neocortical Network Modulation." *Human Brain Mapping* 30, no. 4 (April 2009): 1196–1206; K.K. Hui et al. "Acupuncture Modulates the Limbic System and Subcortical Gray Structures of the Human Brain: Evidence from fMRI Studies in Normal Subjects." *Human Brain Mapping* 9, no. 1 (2000): 13–25.

Chapter 6

1. R.L. Nahin et al. "Costs of Complementary and Alternative Medicine (CAM) and Frequency of Visits to CAM Practitioners." *National Health Statistics Reports,* no. 18. (July 2009), http://nccam.nih.gov/sites/nccam.nih.gov/files/nhsrn18.pdf.

2. "The Human Brain," The Franklin Institute: Resources for Science Learning, http://www.fi.edu/learn/brain/stress.html.

3. "Stress," eHealthMD, http://ehealthmd.com/content/what-stress.

4. "Not Effective and Not Safe: The FDA Must Regulate Dangerous Antimicrobials in Everyday Products," Natural Resources Defense Council, April 2010, http://www.nrdc.org/health/files/antimicrobials.pdf.

Chapter 12

1. "The Results of Carol Look's Eyesight Experiment," Carol Look: Attracting Abundance, http://www.attractingabundance.com/eft/carol-looks-eyesight-experiment.

Chapter 13

1. "What Is Post-Traumatic Stress Disorder, or PTSD?" National Institute of Mental Health, http://www.nimh.nih.gov/health/publications/post-traumatic-stress-disorder-ptsd/what-is-post-traumatic-stress-disorder-or-ptsd.shtml.

2. "Dr. Pat Carrington's 'EFT at Work in a Hospital' Series," EFT: Founding Masters, http://www.eftmastersworldwide.com/content/eft-at-work-in-a-hospital.

INDEX

ACKNOWLEDGMENTS

I know it's cliché to say, "I owe the creation of this book to so many people" . . . but I do! I'm so grateful for all the love and support from my amazing family. My wonderful wife, Brenna, you were so supportive and helpful while writing this book; you are my biggest cheerleader. You keep me healthy, happy, and inspired to make a difference in the world. I love you! To my incredible siblings and business partners, Alex and Jessica. Jessica, thank you for having the courage and faith to start this crazy journey with me. You are such a star, and it's a joy to be able to work with you every day. To Alex, none of the amazing success we've experienced would have been possible without you. You are a genius businessman and I can't wait to see what we come up with next! To the best mom and dad anyone could ever wish for, thanks for making me who I am, and loving and supporting me every step of the way. Karen, Malakai, Lucas, little ones to come, my first reader, and dear aunt Penny, the Taylors, especially my reading buddy Alison, and the rest of the gang around the world—love you all.

To my dear friend Kris Carr, I'm so grateful for all your help every step of the way, starting with an introduction to Patty Gift all the way to the publishing of this book. My life is infinitely richer because you're in it. To the aforementioned Patty Gift, my brilliant editor and friend. I'll keep writing books just to have an opportunity to chat with you. To Louise Hay, the visionary and leader behind the transformation of hundreds of thousands around the world, it is an honor and a privilege to be published by you and to count you as a friend. To the rest of the gang at Hay House: Reid Tracy, one of the most compassionate and brilliant businessmen I have ever met, thank you for your faith and support. Nancy Levin, thanks for putting me onstage and helping me shine. To Laura Gray, Sally Mason, Gail Gonzales, Christy Salinas, Margarete Nielsen, and everyone else at Hay House, thank you!

I'm eternally grateful to Cheryl Richardson, for not only believing in us from the beginning and giving us an interview for *The Tapping Solution* film, but for her wise guidance, counsel, and support in writing this book. You were so, so helpful—thank you!

To one of the most compassionate and loving (and smart!) doctors I have ever met, Mark Hyman. Thanks for the amazing foreword and for sending me your toughest cases!

To Nick Polizzi, the brilliant director and editor of *The Tapping Solution,* who took this leap of faith with me way back . . . I am grateful every day for your brilliance in making the film happen in the first place and your lifelong friendship and support. To Kevin Gianni, for your support and friendship, and for being a part of this rollercoaster ride of the last 15 years. Now it's getting fun and I can't wait to read your bestselling book.

To my friends in the tapping and personal-development community: Carol Look, Lindsey Kenny, Dawson Church, David Feinstein, Dr. Joe Mercola, Arielle Ford, Marci Shimoff, Jack Canfield, Joe Vitale, Rachel Goldstein, Brad Yates, Dr. Erin Shannon, Lori Leyden, Stacey Vornbrock—thanks for your incredible contributions to the world and to this book.

There are so many people who helped make this book happen: Wyndham Wood, Autumn Millhouse, Mary Ayers, Kelly Notaras, Michelle Polizzi, and Stephanie Marohn—thank you!

To the Tapping Solution Team, Heather, Lindsey, Joel, Kris, Tara, April, Jessie, Shalane, Lisa, Jason, and Cassy, and by the time this book comes out, probably another ten amazing team members—thank you for helping me change the world. ('Cause that's what we're doing!)

To all the people who have opened their hearts to my coaching and have contributed their experiences to this book, I've been transformed in helping you change! To the hundreds of thousands of people on my e-mail list: though I know very few of you personally, I am touched by your support and your commitment to yourself and to the world.

And lastly, to the foundation upon which my work stands, the incredible innovations and breakthroughs made by Roger Callahan, Gary Craig, and Pat Carrington. Without you, none of this would be possible!

ABOUT THE AUTHOR

Nick Ortner is the creator and executive producer of the hit documentary film *The Tapping Solution*. He has also produced the annual worldwide online event, the Tapping World Summit, which has been attended by more than 500,000 people. Ortner is a dynamic speaker, presenting breakthrough live tapping sessions around the world. He lives in Connecticut. Follow Nick on Twitter @nortner and see him on Facebook at www.facebook.com/tappingsolution.

Hay House Titles of Related Interest

We hope you enjoyed this Hay House book. If you'd like to receive our
online catalog featuring additional information on Hay House books and products,
or if you'd like to find out more about the Hay Foundation, please contact:

Hay House, Inc., P.O. Box 5100, Carlsbad, CA 92018-5100
(760) 431-7695 or (800) 654-5126
(760) 431-6948 (fax) or (800) 650-5115 (fax)
www.hayhouse.com® • **www.hayfoundation.org**

Published and distributed in Australia by:
Hay House Australia Pty. Ltd., 18/36 Ralph St., Alexandria NSW 2015 •
Phone: 612-9669-4299 • *Fax:* 612-9669-4144 • www.hayhouse.com.au

Published and distributed in the United Kingdom by:
Hay House UK, Ltd., 292B Kensal Rd., London W10 5BE •
Phone: 44-20-8962-1230 • *Fax:* 44-20-8962-1239 • www.hayhouse.co.uk

Published and distributed in the Republic of South Africa by:
Hay House SA (Pty), Ltd., P.O. Box 990, Witkoppen 2068 •
Phone/Fax: 27-11-467-8904 • www.hayhouse.co.za

Published in India by: Hay House Publishers India,
Muskaan Complex, Plot No. 3, B-2, Vasant Kunj, New Delhi 110 070 •
Phone: 91-11-4176-1620 • *Fax:* 91-11-4176-1630 • www.hayhouse.co.in

Distributed in Canada by:
Raincoast, 9050 Shaughnessy St., Vancouver, B.C. V6P 6E5 •
Phone: (604) 323-7100 • *Fax:* (604) 323-2600 • www.raincoast.com

@ @ @

Take Your Soul on a Vacation

Visit **www.HealYourLife.com®** to regroup, recharge, and reconnect
with your own magnificence. Featuring blogs, mind-body-spirit news,
and life-changing wisdom from Louise Hay and friends.

Free e-newsletters from Hay House, the Ultimate Resource for Inspiration

Be the first to know about Hay House's dollar deals, free downloads, special offers, affirmation cards, giveaways, contests, and more!

 Get exclusive excerpts from our latest releases and videos from *Hay House Present Moments*.

 Enjoy uplifting personal stories, how-to articles, and healing advice, along with videos and empowering quotes, within *Heal Your Life*.

 Have an inspirational story to tell and a passion for writing? Sharpen your writing skills with insider tips from *Your Writing Life*.

Sign Up Now!

Get inspired, educate yourself, get a complimentary gift, and share the wisdom!

http://www.hayhouse.com/newsletters.php

Visit www.hayhouse.com to sign up today!

  HealYourLife.com

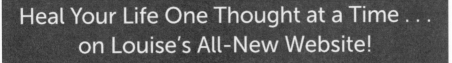
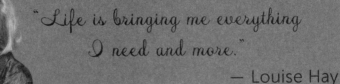

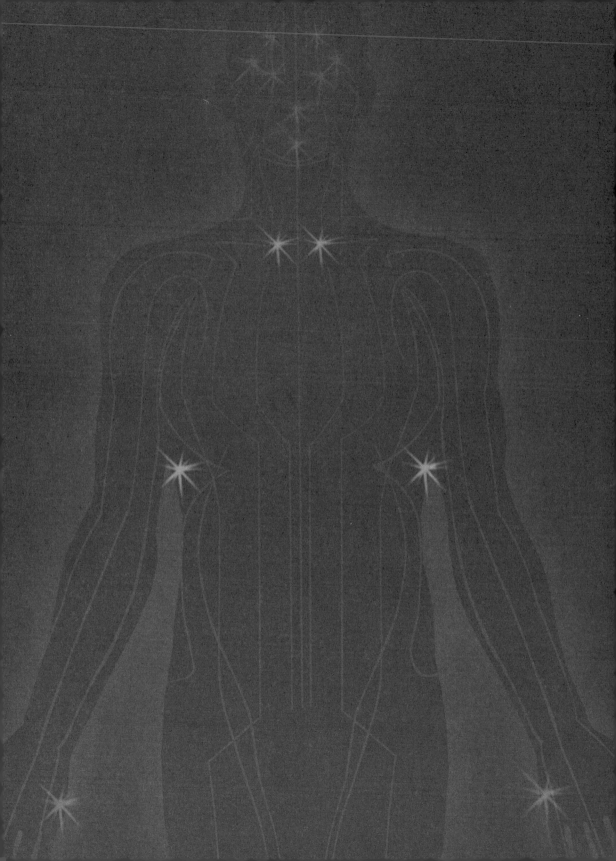